the *Lonely Road* Home

the Lonely Road
Home

*The Struggle of our Veterans
to Return Home After Combat*

*To Ann and John.
Thank you for your
friendship and service
to our country.*

Zane Del Chambers

Zane Del Chambers

TATE PUBLISHING
AND ENTERPRISES, LLC

Published by Tate Publishing & Enterprises, LLC
127 E. Trade Center Terrace | Mustang, Oklahoma 73064 USA
1.888.361.9473 | www.tatepublishing.com

Tate Publishing is committed to excellence in the publishing industry. The company reflects the philosophy established by the founders, based on Psalm 68:11,
"The Lord gave the word and great was the company of those who published it."

Book design copyright © 2015 by Tate Publishing, LLC. All rights reserved.
Cover design by Joseph Emnace
Interior design by Angelo Moralde

Published in the United States of America

ISBN: 978-1-68118-449-4
1. Psychology / Psychopathology / Post-Traumatic Stress Disorder (PTSD)
2. Biography & Autobiography / Military
15.03.27

Dedicated to my Lord and also to my beautiful, loving, and wise wife, and beautiful, talented children, who have stood by me through all the trials of these years.

Lastly, dedicated to all veterans of the United States military of all branches who have served and to those who are still serving sacrificially and honorably.

Contents

Preface

Former US Army General and Secretary of State Colin Powell once said, "Experts often possess more data than judgment."[1] His words capture so well the difference between knowledge and wisdom. In America, however, we certainly love our experts. We look to them for advice on all manner of things. Unfortunately, as I have found in life, the experts can often be wrong.

I state this up front to explain that I do not consider myself an expert. The greater my education about the world and the greater my experience in life, the greater is my impression that I don't know very much at all. Nonetheless, by virtue of my fifty-three years, my very active and adventurous life of travel, my leadership of literally thousands of people, my eclectic military career, my extensive research on the topic of PTSD, and my time teaching in the classroom at West Point, I can honestly say that I know a little more than the average person. I don't see myself as smarter or better though. Rather, I see myself as someone who is simply further along the road of life than others, someone who has experienced more.

It is by my gaining of greater experience, wisdom, and knowledge that I hope to enlighten my readers about two subjects: a glimpse of what life is like for America's troops, especially those who are deploying, and what it is like to live with PTSD. So, although I am not an expert, having lived through these experiences and being further along the road, I hope to help others who may be struggling, who may need to understand what they are going through, and, perhaps, who may need some encouragement.

Moreover, I have a breadth of eclectic experiences in the military, so I hope that my observations and explanations can open up this world to people who want to know more about what life is like for our troops and what sacrifices they make every day on behalf of their fellow Americans.

I enlisted in the army in 1979 as a communications specialist and served for three years, earning my way to the first rung in the noncommissioned ranks, so I understand what life is like for our enlisted troops. I also served a couple of years in the Georgia Army National Guard in a scout platoon, and then in a mortar platoon. So, by virtue of this experience, I also understand about some of the problems that face our reserve and National Guard troops when they are activated to serve in a combat zone. Lastly, I have served as an officer for twenty years in the army, primarily in human resources. But my jobs have allowed me to work with marines, seamen/petty officers (navy and Coast Guard), and airmen (Air Force). Furthermore, my eclectic experiences while serving as an officer and my four years as a government civilian working with the army have allowed me to work with logistics soldiers, infantry, aviation, field artillery, air defense artillery, rangers, and Special Forces.

It is by virtue of the breadth of my eclectic military experiences that I can understand the life of the common troop and the more privileged military leader. Moreover, these eclectic experiences have put me in touch with so many wonderful troops from all walks of life, from every corner of our nation, developing in me the tremendous love and respect that I have for all who serve in uniform, regardless of rank, service, or branch.

Moreover, as to my experience with PTSD, I have grappled with this malady for over nine years now, beginning in early 2005, during my combat tour in Iraq. It has been over nine years since I returned from my deployment to Iraq, and four of those years were the most difficult, chaotic, heartbreaking, and confusing years of my life. They were years full of grief, fear, confusion, darkness, despair, turmoil, and the resulting trouble from living a dysfunctional life, driven by my dysfunctional mind and emotions. I was truly not myself during those years. I was certainly in control of my mental faculties, and I still had an incisive, tirelessly curious, precisely calculating, and intellectually sharp mind, but my perspective on life and the way I processed information and situations were decidedly warped and negative. When I think back on those years from the perspective of a clear mind and peaceful heart, I simply cannot understand some of the things I did. It is like looking at another man's life.

This book is my hope to ease the struggle for others who may not even understand what they are going through or for the loved ones of those struggling with PTSD who want to understand. I have read the unending stories of emotional, psychological, and legal problems for returning troops of all services, cultural backgrounds, educational levels, experience/age levels, genders, and regions of the country or territories and islands under the protection of the US government and military. I have also read with particular interest about the mental health issues and the out-of-control suicide rate. After surviving this journey through the "valley of the shadow of death," I am deeply concerned about my fellow troops who are returning; therefore, I feel compelled to write this book in hopes that I can offer, sooner rather than later, some comfort, direction, or understanding to my fellow soldiers who have suffered since returning to the States, whether it was one deployment or any number of multiple deployments that broke your spirit.

For years now, various media and military sources have been reporting about the alarming epidemic of suicides among our troops. The rate is almost as high as one suicide per hour per day every day. While I find these statistics horrifying, I must also admit that I came close to being one of those statistics.

Writing my story is part of a catharsis in order to find healing of my heart and mind, but the greater part of the healing in telling my story is my belief that my suffering from Post-traumatic stress disorder (PTSD) is not in vain if I can help ease the struggle of others.

That said, PTSD is a very real physical, emotional, and spiritual malady that is affecting, perhaps, hundreds of thousands of our soldiers returning from the Iraq and Afghanistan wars.

Perhaps, the best way to understand it is through the words of Dr. Jonathan Shay. Dr. Shay, a clinical psychiatrist, treated, perhaps, thousands of Vietnam veterans and gained incredible insight through his experiences with the veterans. He wrote about those experiences in two books, *Achilles in Vietnam* (New York, Scribner 1994) and *Odysseus in America* (New York, Scribner 2002). One of the greatest contributions he made in these books was his brilliant insight in diagnosing PTSD as a "moral injury."

His concept of moral injury makes perfect sense and explains both the contributing factors for developing PTSD and the emotions and thoughts that PTSD sufferers experience. The moral injury, as he explains, is a violation of all that is right. That violation may come as a result of witnessing, being a victim of, or participating in a horrific act that overwhelms your mind and emotions, and that which goes far beyond the boundaries of acceptable human behavior and into the realm of cruelty or evil.

During my research, I found some sources indicating that the moral injury could also come from being pushed continuously beyond your normal limits, day after day, until you break down physically and mentally/emotionally.

With the moral injury comes a shattering of the sufferer's worldview, the construct of all our values, experiences, and beliefs, which helps us to understand and interpret the world as well as make sense of it. When an egregious violation, which goes beyond the experience or well beyond the rules of acceptable human behavior, occurs, a moral and emotional crisis occurs. The worldview is shattered, leaving the sufferer with the feeling that nothing makes sense anymore.

When I first started writing about my PTSD experiences shortly after returning from Iraq (in late 2005), this need to make sense of the chaos of my life was my primary motivator, so, at least, partly, I write out of the necessity to make sense of what seems insensible. I want to try to find order in the chaos of my emotions and memories. I write to find order in life and to hopefully rediscover the meaning of my life and, perhaps, some sense of peace. And lastly, I write as a beggar, hoping to find bread and show other beggars the way to the metaphorical bread.

Introduction

In this book, I hope to capture and convey some of the daily experiences of the American troop as well as those of our troops deploying into combat in our most recent wars in Iraq and Afghanistan. Moreover, I hope to shed light on the homecoming trials of our soldiers, such as PTSD, and on the challenges of the Vietnam veterans during that war's decade ('60s) and afterward. We owe a tremendous debt of gratitude to the Vietnam veterans for their selfless sacrifices on behalf of all Americans, sacrifices that were paid in blood, sweat, and tears during a time in when their fellow American citizens did not fully support the troops.

And it is because of the Vietnam veterans that we know much more about the psychological impact of combat tours on our current generation of troops and about the affliction that we call post-traumatic stress disorder (PTSD). Armed with this knowledge, mental health providers serving veterans of the current wars should be providing much better treatment than the Vietnam veterans received when they returned home, but from the suicide statistics of our current era veterans, it seems likely that some are not even getting the treatment they need. Regardless of the generation though, the road home for our returning warriors is fraught with peril and much suffering and is often a lonely road to travel.

Wounded Warrior Project, a veteran's service charity, has a profound and succinct motto that gets this lonely struggle: "The greatest casualty is being forgotten." This, of course, refers to the tendency of society and communities to forget about the troops after they've returned from war, and the consequence is that for months and years after, the veterans will struggle with physical and mental/emotional wounds long after the public has forgotten the war. The issue of veterans being forgotten is not unique to American society. British writer Rudyard Kipling's poem, "Tommy," from his poetry collection, *Barrack-Room Ballads*, published in 1892, captures this tendency of society—perhaps, all societies—to forget the returning warrior, although the subject is a British soldier, suggesting that the problem of the forgotten or neglected veteran is a universal problem. The last three stanzas of that poem are as follows:

> Yes, makin' mock o' uniforms that guard you while
>   you sleep
> Is cheaper than them uniforms, an' they're starvation
>   cheap;
> An' hustlin' drunken soldiers when they're goin' large a bit
> Is five times better business than paradin' in full kit.
>
> Then it's Tommy this, an' Tommy that, an' "Tommy, 'ow's
>   yer soul?"
> But it's "Thin red line of 'eroes" when the drums begin
>   to roll,
> The drums begin to roll, my boys, the drums begin to roll,
> O it's "Thin red line of 'eroes" when the drums begin
>   to roll.
>
> We aren't no thin red 'eroes, nor we aren't no blackguards
>   too,
> But single men in barricks, most remarkable like you;
> An' if sometimes our conduck isn't all your fancy paints,
> Why, single men in barricks don't grow into plaster saints;
>
> While it's Tommy this, an' Tommy that, an' "Tommy, fall
>   be'ind,"
> But it's "Please to walk in front, sir," when there's trouble
>   in the wind,
> There's trouble in the wind, my boys, there's trouble in the
>   wind,

O it's "Please to walk in front, sir," when there's trouble in
the wind.

You talk o' better food for us, an' schools, an' fires, an' all:
We'll wait for extry rations if you treat us rational.
Don't mess about the cook-room slops, but prove it to
our face
The Widow's Uniform is not the soldier-man's disgrace.

For it's Tommy this, an' Tommy that, an' "Chuck him out,
the brute!"
But it's "Saviour of 'is country" when the guns begin
to shoot;
An' it's Tommy this, an' Tommy that, an' anything you
please;
An' Tommy ain't a bloomin' fool—you bet that Tommy
sees![1]

In America, the Vietnam veterans were our forgotten soldiers
during that era. Thankfully, the current generation of Americans
is very supportive of and appreciative of the troops, and, perhaps,
some of this appreciation is spilling over to touch the Vietnam
veterans, giving them the recognition that is way overdue. On
the web site goodmenproject.com, author, speaker, and human
rights advocate Raymond Bechard penned an excellent tribute to
the Vietnam veterans entitled "Why Vietnam Vets are America's
Greatest Generation." Bechard writes:

> The lack of respect and gratitude we gave our returning
> Vietnam Vets 40 years ago seems even more deplorable
> when compared to how deeply we embrace those return-
> ing from Iraq, Afghanistan, and all other places of military
> service around the world today.
>
> Were they heroes? Yes. Did they sacrifice their lives for
> others? Yes—over 58,000 of them. Did they serve with
> honor, bravery, and courage under impossible circum-
> stances? Yes. Did war change, even destroy their lives,
> their families, their careers, and the dreams back home.

Absolutely! And all this can be said of our soldiers for the past 236 years. But Vietnam Vets are a different kind of hero than the rest. In many ways they are heroes above the rest....

The Vietnam War was a mess. It was initiated by and fought for reasons only the most cynical Washington politicians could understand or justify. It divided America unlike any issue since the Civil War...Yet, despite all the wretched inevitability and with everything telling them not to go, those young men went and fought. Unlike all our other wars, the American men who sacrificed themselves in Vietnam carried the added burden of fighting and dying in war without faith. Our national heart was not in it. We didn't believe in the fight. We were never willing to win, only to throw young, expendable bodies at an enemy who eluded us...The Vietnam Veteran is our greatest hero because he fought two enemies: the North Vietnamese and us. Even though we blamed him for something that was our fault...he carried on because of something greater; some need to help where and when no one else was willing to. He served because he was noble. He sacrificed because of the friends next to him in the trenches. He did his duty because his nation—a nation he so badly wanted to believe in—told him to...he struggled every day to wade past all the obstacles and do the right thing. In the face of disease, death, and defeat, he somehow put aside the petty selfishness of the world—along with his own doubts—and fought the good fight.[2]

Bechard perfectly captures the heroic sacrifice and lack of recognition that the Vietnam War troops received. Of course, the title of his article is a takeoff on Tom Brokaw's bestselling book *The Greatest Generation* released in 2001, which was about the World War II generation of men and women who rose Phoenix-like from the ashes of the Great Depression to build possibly history's greatest military-industrial juggernaut, which defeated the seemingly undefeatable German Army.

Most certainly, our military men and women in that war achieved incredible feats. I would never take away the glory and due recognition of any of our veterans from whatever generation. The WWII vets certainly deserve credit for their great accomplishments, the sacrifices they made, the hard times they endured, and the ways they dramatically changed our nation and world. These veterans received tremendous recognition, respect, and honor upon their return home. Moreover, they received much adulation in the communities from which they came as well as in the various media for what they did, although it did, unfortunately, take us almost sixty years, April 29, 2004, to plan, build, and dedicate a proper monument on the mall in Washington, D.C. in honor of their great accomplishments.

In contrast, our Vietnam veterans came home to a hard, and sometimes even cruel, reception. In his 2002 book about the Vietnam veteran's homecoming, *Odysseus in America*, Jonathan Shay writes:

> By 1970, when the bulk of the Vietnam veterans had already returned from the war, the situation for them was worse than it had been for their fathers, in terms of a supportive community in which to digest their experiences, because of the intense struggle over the wisdom and legitimacy of the war itself and how it was being conducted. So most veterans had to face their nightmares, their storms of fear and rage, their visitations by the dead, their lacerating guilt alone.[3]

In that era, although the Vietnam War was not widely supported, there were a few on the fringe who decided to express their opposition to the war by mistreating our returning heroes. In their zeal to oppose war, they apparently could not separate in their minds and their dogma the political powers running the war from the brave, humble troop going to that war in an honorable act of sacrificial service. These extremists were unable to distinguish between the rightful political targets of protest and the humble troops who had little influence on the conduct, morality, or motivation for that war. Unfortunately, without that critical community support when they were fighting the war and when they returned home from that war to heal from the horrors they faced, many of them faced a very lonely struggle trying to completely return home, emotionally and spiritually.

Also, among the factors mentioned by Bechard, this was a different kind of war. Unlike past wars, there was no front line, which had an enormous psychological impact since you often never knew where the enemy was or when he might hit you. Not only did the enemy use constantly changing, hit-and-run guerilla tactics, but he also recruited from the common folk in South Vietnam, well behind the "front lines." So, those that tried to kill you at night might be the common peasants tilling the fields quietly as your patrols passed the next day.

Plus, there was a barbaric, evil cruelty to the tactics of the enemy, using such tactics as pungi sticks, sharpened wood or bamboo sticks placed in shallow, concealed pits designed to inflict cruel and painful leg injuries, and even, perhaps, ugly infections since the tips of the sticks were often coated with feces or other filth to immediately introduce deadly bacteria into the fresh wounds. Additionally, many times, seemingly senseless tactics were employed by clueless leaders who might order a brutal, bloody assault on a piece of enemy-held territory, only to abandon that position the next day and then return to refight another bloody battle to reclaim the ground that they had just relinquished. To the common troop on the ground, I imagine that it made no sense.

Also, the morality of the war was so conflicted. National civilian leaders of the military did not seem to have clear objectives other than a nebulous mission to fight the communists (the so-called Cold War) and keep another "domino" from falling to the communist offensive. And the American public was so conflicted about the war that Vietnam vets received little moral support, challenging these heroes' sense that they were fighting for the higher ideals of freedom on behalf of their countrymen.

It is because of the lack of recognition and poor reception of the Vietnam warriors that, I believe, we must get it right for the current generation of warriors returning from Iraq and Afghanistan, especially given their hardships of multiple deployments, which is having an impact on their families as well.

In the Hawaiian newspaper, the *Star-Advertiser*, a November 11, 2010 article perfectly captures the plight of these returning warriors.

> Nine years of war—the longest sustained combat in American history—has brought with it a weariness with Iraq and Afghanistan for the public at home and a raft of problems for an all-volunteer force that keeps going back, including depression, suicides, and marital breakups.[4]

The American troops of all services have made and continued to make tremendous sacrifices every day for their fellow countrymen and women. The full weight and difficulty of those sacrifices may never be fully understood by their fellow Americans, even those who honor and celebrate our brave men and women in uniform. But that sacrifice is most certainly worth celebrating and honoring in any way possible, which most communities throughout the land do on key holidays like the Fourth of July, Veteran's Day, or Memorial Day.

But we can never forget that many veterans continue to sacrifice and suffer numerous long years after they have left the battlefield and left the service. The source of their suffering may be from multiple wounds and physical ailments as a result of enemy action or the incredible hardships of military life, training, and combat on the human body, making many soldiers' bodies break down long before their nonmilitary peers of the same age.

Many also suffer the debilitating wounds of post-traumatic stress disorder (PTSD) and traumatic brain injury (TBI), both of which have emotional, psychological, and physical manifestations that damage the veteran's body and rob him or her of much quality of life, the ability to fully participate in life, in relationships with loved ones, etc.

In an article from the Associated Press published May 20, 2011 in *The Boston Globe*, Lieutenant General Eric B. Schoomaker, the army surgeon general, succinctly explained the magnitude of stress that soldiers endure in combat: "There are few stresses on the human psyche as extreme as the exposure to combat."[5]

Moreover, due to the extreme pressure of combat, it should not be surprising that many troops will succumb sooner or later to post-traumatic stress disorder or other mental health problems. We are even seeing a tragic suicide epidemic among our returning warriors from the current wars. In a Department of Veterans Affairs mental health services report entitled "Suicide Data Report, 2012," Janet Kemp and Robert Bossarte explain the tragic statistics of veteran suicides: "If this prevalence estimate is assumed to be constant across all U.S. states, an estimated 22 Veterans will have died from suicide each day in the calendar year 2010."[6]

Seeing such statistics should motivate all of us to make sure that these veterans are not forgotten and that they get the therapy and other services that they need before they reach the point of believing that their life is over and that they are helpless in the face of these powerful emotions and psychosomatic health issues. It is my prayer and hope for this book that I can, at least, enlighten a few people so that they can understand the plight of many of our veterans and, perhaps, know that they can reach out to help or, at the very least, be a little more understanding when returning warriors act in unusual or risky ways in response to their inner turmoil.

As we observe the plight of our returning veterans, we should keep uppermost in our minds the words of John Bradford (1510–1555) when he was awaiting his own execution in the Tower of

London at the hands of "Bloody" Mary I (Tudor, 1516–1558). As Bradford watched the other "criminals" being led off to execution, he remarked, "There but for the grace of God goes John Bradford." The altered, popularized version, which most people quote, is: "There, but for the grace of God, go I."[7] This is a fitting reminder that the challenges of our neighbor could easily be our own, given the right circumstances. So, if we can help our fellow man or woman who has fallen on hard times, then we certainly should, especially those brave US troops who have served our country so honorably and sacrificially on land, air, and sea.

Preparation and Departure

"Doth God exact day-labour, light denied?"
I fondly ask. But Patience, to prevent
That murmur, soon replies, "God doth not need
Either man's work or his own gifts; who best
Bear his mild yoke, they serve him best. His state
Is kingly. Thousands at his bidding speed
And post o'er land and ocean without rest:
They also serve who only stand and wait.

—John Milton, excerpt from
"When I Consider How My Light Is Spent."[1]

If you hate waiting, then the military is not the life for you. Most veterans will remember the old joke about having to "hurry up and wait." In most military procedures or events, there is the inevitable frenetic, manic storm of activities to get there, get on line, get in position, get in formation, assemble at the starting point, etc. Then, after you breathlessly make it to your designated spot—adrenaline still pumping and with your equipment, vehicles, and weapons ready for action—you are ironically and instantly put on hold with a long, dreary wait or pause before you can even take the next step or start the event (like a convoy out to a training area).

There's actually a good reason why the military does this. In military duty or operations, timing is everything. Unfortunately, the military is comprised of inherently flawed human beings, and a huge group of such flawed creatures tends to magnify the innate individual flaws of the discrete members. So, all military leaders with a few years' experience know the tendency for flaw in human beings, especially a huge group of them (even if they have had some military discipline instilled in them from initial entry training). Human beings—in this case, military men and women—make mistakes, miscalculate, and inevitably end up being later than they should have been. To get around this, most good military leaders—commissioned, warrant, or noncommissioned—always build in lots of time to compensate for the unavoidable human errors and to still be perfectly on time.

Our preparation for deployment was no different. There was a months-long period of tremendously frenetic activity with everything being due yesterday and everything having dire urgency. And at the end of that chaotic, manic period, immediately before deployment, there was the inevitable period of waiting and almost complete cessation of activity, like the calm in the eye of a hurricane, as we all went on block leave spending time with our families for a couple of weeks (within a month of our deployment date) or just metaphorically marching in place while anxiously waiting out the final days, hours, and minutes before we would step onto that airplane to fly to Kuwait for final training and prep, followed shortly by our deployment into Iraq for our combat mission.

Preparing for the Unknown

But even with all of our preparation and all of the informational briefings about the mission, all of the individual research we did as we looked online for stories explaining what it was like and talking to people who had been there, even with all that knowledge, we still did not fully comprehend what the deployment experience would be like. It's just one of those things in life, the full weight and scope of which you cannot imagine until you have been through the reality of it. There are certain experiences that are beyond understanding until you have actually experienced them: true love, bringing a child into this world, being a parent, international travel, the glorious and sensual pleasure between a man and a woman in love and committed to each other, etc. War is certainly one of those experiences, and most of us who were deploying, even with our military training and our deployment exercises designed to replicate the situations and conditions of our deployed environment, just did not understand what we were about to go through.

Moreover, it could be difficult for the common troop or civilian to understand war from our culture's portrayal of war. Most of my images of war were from the sanitized versions on television that I encountered while I was growing up in the '60s and '70s. There was a plethora of television shows about the military and war as I grew up from the ridiculously silly *Hogan's Heroes* (1965–71) to the comical but a little more serious *M*A*S*H* (1972–1983) to the more serious *Combat* (1962–67). But regardless of what show you watched, the portrayals of war were, for the most part, sanitized and unrealistic, nowhere near the more realistic modern productions that have revealed as much as is possible the ugly, bloody violence of war such as *Band of Brothers* (2001) or movies like *Saving Private Ryan* (1998) or *The Hurt Locker* (2009).

Nonetheless, it was from the more sanitized versions of war that we formed our impressions of war while I was growing up, and it was those clean, bloodless images that we replicated in our childhood war games where war was always heroic and the morality was always clear and simple. Right, wrong, good, and bad were easy to discern. Nobody really got hurt, unless they deserved it, and those who deserved it accepted their fate with dignity once shot by an imaginary bullet, nobly but melodramatically crumpling to the ground, acceding to the clear, simple moral order of the universe.

I imagine some of us were naïve about the moral simplicity of war, of course, but we came by our impressions honestly from some of the above-mentioned war movies and military-themed serial shows on television during the '60s and '70s. In the compressed, euphemized, and ameliorated images from these various television shows and movies, we saw war glorified with the hero always charging the enemy recklessly in a grand moment of self-sacrifice and brazen courage, for which he would be duly rewarded with many medals or for which he would be long remembered and toasted over drinks on holidays if he gave his life for his country. But these heroes on the movies or television and the images that they portrayed rarely captured the real ugly horror or brutality of war and the consequences afterward as we would discover in time.

War in the American media for a long time had been, for the most part, simplified and neatly sanitized for public consumption. The producers, directors, and writers probably assumed that the public really didn't want to see the gritty details. In recent years, however, Hollywood has increasingly tried to capture the realism and horror of war, with some productions coming very close such as the *Band of Brothers* series, which was based on Stephen Ambrose's book about E or Easy Company of the 506th Parachute Infantry Regiment, part of the vaunted 101st Airborne Division, during World War II.

For those who are unfamiliar with the story, the *Band of Brothers* book and movie cover the company's early training at Camp Toccoa, Georgia, then their deployment to England for completion of their combat preparations and on through their combat jumps and hedge-to-hedge and town-to-town fighting across Normandy in the early battles of D-Day and the Normandy Campaign. The story of the book and movie also cover their participation in the failed Operation Market Garden, which was implemented as an attempt to capture key river bridges over the "Maas (Meuse River) and two arms of the Rhine (the Waal and the Lower Rhine) as well as several smaller canals and tributaries,"[2] bringing the fight to the heart of Germany and hopefully to end the war by Christmas 1944. The mini-series, of course, covers this story but does so with very realistic scenes, with very little or none of the airbrushed reality of war movies back in the '60s, '70s, or earlier.

But even with the better-researched, well-directed, and superbly-acted productions like *Band of Brothers*, there will always be something missing, the long grievous suffering of the participants for many years afterward, long after the neat time-limited package of the video representations offered to the civilian public. So, even the best movies or television shows will always fall short of the brutal reality, the utter horror, the incredible suffering, and the devastating aftermath for participants and victims of war. But then, war, like those other experiences mentioned previously, is something that one cannot fully understand without experiencing it.

Until a person becomes part of war's ugly reality, the amazing spectacle of war, and even sometimes the perverse beauty of the magnitude of horror, it's easy to conceive of war in heroic terms in such an airbrushed, idyllic way. When something is too distant to be real, it can easily be romanticized. But when the real, harsh experience and memories of war pierce deep into your darkest memories and dreams and come to haunt or torture you day after day, night after night long after you have left the battlefield, the reality of it is so shockingly different from what you might have expected beforehand.

I had watched others go off to war in my youth, the Vietnam era, not fully understanding what was happening in that war and the tremendous risk to life and limb, the sacrifice on the altar of their country that these young men, and even women, undertook. As a mere child, I saw these people as larger than life so their experiences were incomprehensible. I truly could not grasp or interpret in my childlike naivety the historical events that, like a whirlpool in a fetid swamp, would suck these youth, the cream of the crop, the fruit of the best of America, into a halfhearted, politically and statistically driven war that was more or less a part of America's crusade against communism following the Second World War.

The Vietnam War was different, though, from the supposedly glorious past wars where objectives and victories were clear and understandable, military units and targets were usually not hidden or amorphous, the enemy's identity and location were clear, and the battle lines were clear and distinct. This war was a step down that path of modern combat into complete chaos where the enemy could be anywhere around you, could do unpredictable things, and was so idealistically or dogmatically driven that he would defy common sense and human decency.

This war was also another step down that path that the Korean War took us on where our national interests were not so clearly defined or delineated. There was a vague moral connection to the great fear of the communist hoards' supposedly inevitable world domination. We had no idea in the '50s, '60s, and '70s that communism would eventually choke on its own corruption. In those days, there was still a tremendous fear (whether real or imagined) that the communist nations would gradually conquer the world piece by piece until we (America) were left alone or until one of the string of mad men dictators of the large, nuclear-armed communist countries was crazy enough to plunge us all into a worldwide holocaust.

But with the Vietnam War, we had the progressive, educated, smart people running our war as H.R. McMaster reveals in his 1997 book, *Dereliction of Duty*.[3] Supposedly, these "experts" would reduce war to discrete steps, to scientific precision, and would win that war by using their charts and superior intellect. Their approach to this war was, to frame it in a word, hubris, excessive pride, believing that they could do what no one else had been able to do in thousands of years of human history (i.e. completely control the violence of war and make it subject to rationality).

Moreover, in these politicians' arrogance, they truly believed that they knew more about running a war than our experienced troops and military leaders, and, being thus self-deluded, they tried to micromanage the war from thousands of miles away, often interfering with commanders and combat operations on the ground with demoralizing, or even disastrous, results. The arrogance, erroneous beliefs, and misguided actions of these politicians during the Vietnam War were thoroughly exposed and explicated in *Dereliction of Duty*.

Despite the halfhearted commitment of the American political leaders and the American public, our troops did win most, if not all, of the tactical victories in that war—thanks to our troops' amazing professionalism, courage, dedication, and honor. Our nation owes a tremendous debt of gratitude to all of our veterans, our citizen-soldiers, for their sacrificial service throughout the history of our country, and especially to those who fought the Vietnam War.

In my estimation, these men and women who valiantly fought the Vietnam War displayed so much more courage and paid a higher price than veterans of other wars, since they fought without the critical public support that troops require to maintain their moral strength and courage, which, I believe, is absolutely indispensable for their moral, spiritual, and emotional healing after the cessation of the guns.

I believe this is still a festering wound for many Vietnam veterans. Being a soldier who has served in combat, I take very seriously the issue of public recognition and respect of the troops, and I am dismayed to have discovered over the years about the inadequate, underwhelming, or even hostile, reception that these Vietnam veterans received back then when they returned from the war as opposed to the proper reception and respect that our troops serving in the current wars receive.

But since I was a mere boy during the time of the Vietnam War, I had no idea about all the cultural winds and political machinations that were driving that war and the response to that war from some segments of society, nor did I have any idea what the experience was like for the young men who were going over-seas to fight this war. I only caught sporadic, episodic clips on television news about the ongoing war, and I knew from the report of some of my friends that their brothers, young men in our community, were going off to fight this war, whether by choice or by compulsion (the draft was still in operation at the time, although the majority who served in Vietnam were volunteers according to the organization Vietnam Helicopter Flight Crew Network as posted on their website: http://www.vhfcn.org/stat. html#weSTY).

The war did, however, became more personal to me when I was about nine or ten (1970 or 1971) when my best friend's brother was being sent to Vietnam. I remember one summer evening going over to my friend's house and meeting this brother who had just returned from his basic training and from the additional Advanced Individual Training (AIT), which would train him for the army career branch that he had chosen.

Looking back in hindsight, with the wisdom of many years, I can only imagine the whirlwind culture in which this young soldier was struggling to become a man and in which he was trying to make his mark. Knowing the history of the '60s and '70s, I can easily understand how the idealism of youth, the belief in higher, transcendent things could have quickly crashed head-on into the reality of a culture and society in chaos, quickly changing (some changes were certainly for the better, such as the Civil Rights Movement), but our culture in the '60s and '70s was increasingly pushing the boundaries of freedom and becoming more secular-ized as it tried to shake off the sometimes limiting but protective bonds of God and Christian faith.

It was primarily young men who were sent to Vietnam, although there were many women who went as well and served very honorably. In the Vietnam era, most army women were still serving in the Women's Army Corps (WAC), although I would not be surprised to find out that women served outside of this organization even back then. The WAC began operation in 1942 and was disbanded in 1978, at which time women were integrated and dispersed throughout the regular army branches to serve alongside the men (which many had already been doing but under the control of the WAC). But since the large majority of the services were comprised of men in those days, I only saw young men going off to war from my limited vantage point. In any case, since Vietnam was primarily an infantry war, a majority of the young men who served in that war probably served as infantrymen. My friend's brother was no exception.

Now, trained, ready, and looking very sharp in his army summer dress uniform (khakis), he was home from his training for one last fling before he would be shipped off to duty in Vietnam. The army in its decency was giving him this one last time to visit home and, perhaps, sow a few wild oats before he left for war. Perhaps, this would be the last time in a long time before he would be able to enjoy certain simple pleasures such as a home-cooked meal, an ice-cold American beer, and the intimate company of a girl from home—the trifecta for a young soldier. Perhaps, this would be the last time he would ever enjoy these things if he did not return alive, a tragic thought but a very real possibility.

Looking back now from the experience of many decades, I can guess that he was probably considering the thought that he might not ever return, since so many of our soldiers were dying in that war. It's a thought that every soldier or service member from any branch probably thinks of at some point when going off to war. I never suspected in my childish naivety that such heavy, profound thoughts might be going through the mind of this young, confident, lean, and heavily muscled warrior who seemed immortal, like a Greek god. I had no idea either of how great and heavy the weight of this first realization of one's mortality was until much later in life when I would be forced to consider the frailty of my own life during Desert Storm (although I ultimately did not deploy to that war) and when preparing for deployment to Iraq.

But at this point in my boyhood, this young man in his crisp uniform seemed like a giant, like one of the heroes of an ancient epic or a hero of the romanticized war movies or television shows that I saw often on the tube. He was lean and powerful, moving with the forcefulness of conviction and the confident, smooth, stride of a well-trained athlete. He was slightly bronzed, perhaps, from many days of army training outdoors in the hot Georgia sun of Fort Benning where infantry soldiers have been trained for many years. He exuded the promise, the potency, and the virility of youth. He towered above me.

Had I known more about human nature, which I would learn over many decades, and had I been more perceptive at the time, I might have seen the awkward, uncertain, and anxious desire to prove his masculinity while simultaneously exulting in the power and autonomy of his nascent manhood, barely covering the nagging doubts about his ability or his fear of possible failure. These are feelings and thoughts that I would experience as a young man many years later.

In any case, he had found the mother lode of masculinity, the quickest way to manhood, reputation, achievement, and societal privilege—becoming a soldier. Yet, this was a mixed blessing in the turbulent time of the late '60s when our culture was not as supportive of American troops.

Mistreatment of Vietnam Troops

It is tragic and very sad to think about the way these young men were treated by some segments of the public in those days. Unfortunately, the troops were not so highly regarded by some members of our society and were sometimes mistreated in embarrassing and demoralizing incidents in public.

Looking back on that Vietnam era and with my experience of many decades and my personal experience with both combat duty and with PTSD, I cannot imagine how those brave men and women went through that war only to return home to such an unpleasant reception. These men and women bore moral, spiritual, and emotional wounds, which they would bring home with them. While in Vietnam, they were probably sustained only by comforting thoughts of home and of returning to their hometowns where, hopefully, life would again make sense and be peaceful.

Tragically, they often had that comfort or relief snatched away from them by misguided people. These brave troops certainly did not deserve such treatment, even if the war was politically questionable. The troops were only performing their patriotic duty and had no control over the political machinations that drove this war, so educated, rational people should have recognized this fact.

There were certainly some who stepped out of line during that war, as has probably happened in every war throughout history—for example, the much-discussed (in military as well as academic institutions) and much-maligned Lieutenant William Calley of the infamous My Lai Massacre. I, like any good and moral military leader in their right mind, would never encourage or excuse any such atrocities. But I can also understand how, in the moral chaos of war, someone led by morally ambiguous orders, someone perhaps possessing an unsound mind, heart, or character, or someone who had experienced way too many human horrors, might easily find themselves perpetrating such actions in the fog, confusion, and moral relativity of war. Moreover, they probably would later be horrified by their own actions when looked at in the clear light of day, when later examined in the safety, security, sanity, and order of a stateside, civilian existence that seemed alien to them at that moment, worlds away, while they were still in the moral, spiritual, and emotional whirlwind of combat.

Dr. Shay in *Achilles in Vietnam*[4] offers a compelling explanation of such over-the-top behavior in war. He juxtaposes incidents that were reported to him by his Vietnam vets against the seemingly outrageous actions of Achilles in the *Iliad* after slaughtering the Trojan warrior, Hector. Achilles kills Hector in retribution for Hector's killing of Achilles's beloved Patroklus. Then, in a maniacal, vengeful frenzy, Achilles shockingly defiles the body of Hector by dragging it around behind his chariot in front of the walls of Troy. Dr. Shay describes Achilles's actions as the "warrior's rage" where intense grief leads to an out-of-mind rage (53–55)[5] or the state of "bezerkness" (77–99)[6] in which the soldier may enter a super aroused or adrenaline-driven state, pushed over the edge by an outrageous betrayal of "all that is right"—an egregious moral violation by the enemy, perhaps, by the death of a highly valued or respected soldier, the excessive cruelty of enemy tactics, a violation by leaders consistently not meeting their expected moral obligations, or possibly a violation by fellow soldiers committing atrocities or failing to fulfill their duty.

Knowing what we know now about the psychological state of soldiers in an extremely violent and chaotic combat environment, William Calley would seem to be as much of a victim as he was a perpetrator in the political, social, and moral chaos of the Vietnam War. But soldiers like him do not exemplify the vast majority of our troops who served honorably during that war. Most of our troops served their country very honorably in that war, serving selflessly and sacrificially, some even giving that "last full measure of devotion" that Lincoln spoke about at Gettysburg on November 19, 1863.

Many of those who were fortunate enough to return home with their lives suffered for many years or, perhaps, still suffer long after their initial sacrifice for their country. They then lived with the burden of severe wounds or with the horror of their combat experiences on a daily basis for decades with post-traumatic stress disorder. Many of these Vietnam veterans, like many veterans who had gone before them and those who had come after, suffered for decades after combat, paying a high price for their service that their fellow American citizens are, ironically, not even aware of, maybe even apathetic about or opposed to, but a debt which can certainly never be repaid.

But the extremist bullying by war protestors of that era are no better than the infamous Westboro baptist protestors of recent days who are known for picketing military funerals, supposedly at the guidance of God, heaping insult and injury upon the already broken, grieving hearts of the families of the fallen heroes. I don't know what god such people serve, but it is certainly not the God that I read about in my Bible, a God who loved the world so much that He would not withhold anything from the people of the earth whom He loved, not even sparing His own beloved Son, who was sent in a miraculous, gargantuan, and incomprehensible act of sacrificial love for the purpose of redeeming us back into fellowship with Him. No man or woman has ever loved so much as this man Jesus and His Father in heaven. I still do not understand why He would even want to bother with the human race with all of the evil and selfishness that I see on a daily basis as exemplified in these misguided war protestors from Westboro Baptist or the ones who abused the troops during the Vietnam era.

But a God-sized love like that is, perhaps, not within our capability to ever fully comprehend on our own power. Even when He hung on that cruel cross, He lovingly pleaded for mercy for His persecutors: "Then Jesus said, 'Father forgive them, for they know not what they do'" (Luke 23:34, NKJV). This was certainly not a man who would say such things as "God hates fags" or "God hates soldiers" as the Westboro baptist legalist god does. We are taught in 1 John 4:20 (NKJV) that it is impossible to love God while hating men: "If someone says, 'I love God,' and hates his brother, he is a liar; for he who does not love his brother whom he has seen, how can he love God whom he has not seen?" This, of course, leads me to believe that these people are not serving the one true God.

In any case, despite the misguided efforts of extremist and hypocritical protestors, our American troops over the past two-plus centuries have been undaunted in their devotion to duty, no less during the Vietnam era. The Vietnam troops served in the harshest of conditions and the greatest of danger—thousands of miles from home, for months on end in an alien and inhospitable land, with few creature comforts, serving dutifully, honorably, and sacrificially giving every single day whatever their country demanded of them, without hesitation, question, or challenge for the most part.

Then they often returned home to an ungrateful community that did not honor and could not understand their sacrifice, what they had gone through and what mental, physical, and emotional turmoil many of them continued to suffer every day, trying to hold the pieces of their shattered lives together, trying to make sense of life after the horror of combat, trying to find at least one person that they could talk to who could understand their agony, and trying to find some chemical or other relief that would put a Band-Aid over the gaping moral wound that they had sustained and which did not seem as if it would ever heal.

What greater sacrifice has any man or woman offered, save our Lord Jesus, that can compare with what these Vietnam veterans went through—the insults and mistreatment given to them by their ungrateful countrymen and the continuous suffering from their war experiences, while some hobbled emotionally, spiritually, and psychologically for the rest of their lives?

Boy Soldiers

But as a boy living in the '60s, looking at this young warrior, I had yet to understand all of these life lessons and issues that the years would reveal to me. At this moment of my childish innocence, I could only see the heroism and courage in this citizen-soldier—my friend's well-muscled, athletic, warrior brother, resplendent in his uniform—who was preparing to go into what I saw at the time as the glory of war but which time would tell was actually the anarchic moral storm of the Vietnam War.

Looking at him through the lens of my memory, I could see that, despite his untried, inexperienced masculinity, he exuberantly played the part of the hero-warrior, playing to his appreciative audience of hero-worshipping boys—me, my friend, and a few other boys about the same age—all of us dreaming of one day being such virile, powerful, confident, capable, and strong examples of American masculinity.

Our little troop, with this warrior-hero leading us, set off on a walk from my friend's house through the neighborhood in the soft, sweet, progressively dwindling twilight of a typical southern summer's evening in Georgia (in the last years of that tumultuous decade of the 1960s). There was just a hint of the evening's gradually cooling air and an occasional, tentative cooler breeze as the encroaching evening tried to seduce us into the lazy, fanciful daydreams that are common at the end of a good southern summer day. The crickets had already started up their evening serenade, and some cicadas could be heard singing their alien trill in trees on the distant edge of the neighborhood.

As we walked through the drowsy, quiet neighborhood, this young warrior talked about the exploits and daring deeds he expected to do once he got "over there." He even taught us some of the Jody calls, the singsong cadences that soldiers are taught with by their drill sergeants or drill instructors during instruction on marching. We naively repeated the chorus to his prompts, not fully understanding the words: "We gonna go to Vietnam to kill Charlie Chang" (words which a more modern audience might now find offensive). We echoed the words, dutifully imagining ourselves as young soldiers responding to our friend's brother as our drill sergeant. "We gonna go to Vietnam now, Little Liza Jane." Again, we echoed the line in unison.

I didn't fully comprehend the words that I was dutifully repeating and didn't even realize that the words might be offensive to some. War was an idealized adventure to me as a young boy. It was a fantasy with clear-cut moral lines of good and bad, heroes and villains. It was a movie scene. My simplified conceptualization of war wouldn't change very much until I reached young adulthood though. My first close encounter with war would come years later when I was a young lieutenant, fresh out of college and ROTC and then on active duty with a unit in Germany when Desert Storm broke out. I was eager and enthusiastic at the time, trying to make my mark in the world. In those days, my youthful, masculine zeal often rode roughshod over the truly important things in life simply because I didn't have enough experience about life to know what was really important and because, like all young men, I hungered for achievement, advancement, and recognition, things that I thought were the real treasures or the spoils of life.

Desert Wars

At the time, mid 1990's, as the situation was just beginning to heat up with Saddam Hussein's saber rattling and threats of invading Kuwait, I was in the midst of a three-week army course in nuclear-biological-chemical (NBC) warfare. Most nations around the world at the time had signed on many years earlier through the United Nations to the various international agreements banning use of these weapons (still remembering the horror of World War I and the atrocities perpetrated by both sides in the use of chemical weapons in the brutal trench warfare where there was nowhere to run when these evil weapons were dropped arbitrarily and sporadically among the troops on both sides; it was complete and utter moral anarchy, evil of the highest order). And in the modern era, most of these nations, at least, gave public lip service to the prohibition of these NBC weapons. Unfortunately, in the paranoid world of international diplomatic relations, many of these same nations, which repudiated NBC weapons publicly and may have signed the agreements, nonetheless still harbored and maintained such weapons just in case they were needed once again should their enemy in future conflicts step over that unthinkable line using these weapons of mass destruction (WMD).

We have seen recently that nations such as Syria have no moral compunction and no hesitation for using these horrific NBC weapons, even on their own people during civil war, even on innocent civilians. Moreover, other nations such as Iran and Iraq have shown a propensity to use such weapons in the past if they think they can gain a tactical or strategic advantage, or even crush a budding revolt among their own people. With so many nations possessing these weapons and showing willingness to use them, the American military forces have undergone preemptory training for several decades on how to respond to such attacks as well as how to operate in an environment where these weapons have been used.

So, here I was in this NBC school, "volun-told" to attend, so that I could be the resident expert for our unit on NBC warfare. As the trained and educated expert, I would be the go-to guy for subordinates and superiors whenever they needed information, briefings, inspections of NBC equipment rooms (suits, masks, and supplies), guidance on planned NBC training events, or even planning and leading of NBC training exercises. The three-week school covered every possible scenario in which we might encounter NBC weapons. We studied all of the most horrific and crafty weapons that man could devise in the areas of nuclear weaponry, germ warfare, and chemical assault. The course also covered the aftermath, the results, with historical films on the use of these weapons.

In my youthful enthusiasm, I approached this school with the usual dogged determination, which I put into all of my duties as a lieutenant, even the most mundane or menial tasks. The more mundane and distasteful things are usually tossed to the lowest ranking dog in an organization anyway, and, at the time, that was me. But I surmised that these tedious tasks were my required dues, payment that had to be rendered in order to reach higher positions later, and, in any case, they would add to my kitbag of skills to make me more adaptable to any job or situation in the future. So I accepted them willingly, although sometimes grudgingly, because I had faith in the army's commitment to advancing the best, whether they be the most intelligent, the most willing, the most capable, or the most diligent. At the time, I did not doubt my chances of success because life had not yet thrown me enough curveballs to make me question my abilities or my opportunity for success.

As I studied the material for this school and saw all the horrendous films of what chemical weapons would do to people and animals, I still did not fully comprehend the urgency or the importance of knowing these things and preparing for these scenarios. I didn't believe that there was even a ghost of a chance that these weapons would ever be used by any military force that we might face, so I took in all the information like mindless trivia that I was required to learn. I felt that all the material I studied, though consequentially horrific, was merely history, merely interesting knowledge to indulge curiosity. But toward the end of that school, an event would occur, which would drastically change my attitude toward this subject.

Shortly before I went to the school in the summer of 1990, Saddam Hussein had his armed forces massed in southern Iraq near the border with Kuwait. There was a lot of sabre-rattling" by Hussein, threats of the use of military force because he had accused the Kuwaitis of slant drilling to basically steal Iraqi oil by means of underground piping and drilling across the border into the underground oil resources in Iraq's Rumaila oil field. He had also begun making an argument that during the Anglo-Ottoman Convention of 1913 Great Britain had erroneously and arbitrarily established the sheikdom of Kuwait when that land should have been part of Iraq.

"The Iraqi government also argued that the Kuwaiti emir was a highly unpopular figure among the Kuwaiti populace. By overthrowing the emir, Iraq later claimed that it had granted Kuwaitis greater economic and political freedom."[7]

As one book on the subject notes, "Kuwait had been loosely under the authority of the Ottoman vilâyet of Basra, and although its ruling dynasty, the Al Sabah family, had concluded a protectorate agreement in 1899 that assigned responsibility for its foreign affairs to Britain, it did not make any attempt to secede from the Ottoman Empire. For this reason, its borders with the rest of Basra province were never clearly defined or mutually agreed upon. Furthermore, Iraq alleged that the British High Commissioner drew lines that deliberately constricted Iraq's access to the oceans so that any future Iraqi government would be in no position to threaten Britain's domination of the Persian Gulf.[8]

Of course, most observers believed that the real motivation for Iraq's hegemonic ambitions lay in their inability to pay off their war debt from the Iraq-Iran war (1980–88). Iraq had borrowed many billions of dollars from Kuwait to fund their fight against Iran, but they were unable to pay that debt off, primarily due to the low price of oil. As the low oil prices lingered on, making it less likely that Iraq could pay off their debts, they had asked Kuwait to forgive the debt, but Kuwaiti leaders refused. To make matters worse, one of the main reasons for the low price of oil in the oil glut of the 1980s (which made it difficult for Iraq to pay off the debt) was that Kuwait was producing way over their established quota, which was set by the oil cartel, the Organization of the Petroleum Exporting Countries (OPEC). So, as you can imagine, the Kuwaiti overproduction did not sit well with the Iraqis.

In any case, on August 2,1990, after querying the United States about a possible invasion and receiving a vague answer that they interpreted as concurrence, the Iraqis invaded Kuwait and subdued the outgunned and far smaller Kuwaiti armed forces in only a couple of days. Once the world got news of the invasion and occupation, it was universally condemned. But Saddam Hussein believed he was in the right and refused to budge. Of course, everyone knows the story of how the elder President George Bush cobbled together an international coalition, which amassed forces in Saudi Arabia over a period of several months. Then the allied forces, after months of preparatory bombing of Iraqi forces and hard military targets, attacked on January 16, 1991 and continued fighting on through February but were overwhelmingly successful in defeating the Iraqi forces and liberating Kuwait.

Although the whole military operation may seem rather small in scope to us now, compared to the long current wars of Iraq and Afghanistan, at that time in 1991, success in the fight against Iraq did not seem so certain. The American military, although well equipped and trained from the Reagan-era buildup, had not been really tested in a big fight since Vietnam. There had only been the smaller military "adventures" such as Grenada (1983) and Panama (December 1989).

Also, there were so many unknowns about the Iraqis. For instance, there was the fear of the impact of the wildly inaccurate Scud missiles. Although the Iraqis did not seem to be able to aim these missiles very accurately, they were still able to land them in populated areas, especially Israel, bringing terror and danger to various countries in the region and to our allied forces amassing in Saudi Arabia. Moreover, Hussein was known to possess large stores of chemical and biological weapons, and he had shown a willingness to use such weapons against the Iranians and Kurds during the 1980s. So, there was a real, tangible fear that this war could result in a bloodbath with high numbers of casualties and possibly horrific wounds from the chemical weapons if Hussein was crazy enough or foolish enough to use them.

Having just learned the horrifically destructive potential of Hussein's chemical weapons at my NBC school classes, I, like many other soldiers and Americans, was deeply concerned about whether this madman who did not seem at all rational might do anything and everything to avoid defeat. Also, since my unit was one of the ones chosen to deploy into Saudi Arabia for Desert Storm, I came to the startling realization that I could be one of those people that might be hit by Hussein's chemical weapons.

Preparing for Fatherhood

What had previously seemed like a distant threat was now becoming all too real. When all this sank in, I finally began thinking about the real possibility of my own mortality. In those days, as I thought through all of this, my first concern was for my wife. We were still newly married, just shy of five years, and I feared what would happen to her if I deployed and did not return.

Like me, she was still very inexperienced in life, and she had not yet become the strong, capable, and determined woman that she would eventually develop into years later, so I worried about what kind of life she would lead after my death. I thought of my responsibility to provide for her financially until she could get through the grief of my loss and get on with her life. I also started thinking about a subject that I had avoided before that point, the issue of having children in our marriage. Like many young newlywed adults, I wanted to enjoy life and the company of my sweet, beautiful wife for a few years before we added the responsibility of children. I also wanted, like many people, to reach a certain level of professional and financial success before adding children to the equation.

I didn't know then how wrong my perspective was about the issue of children. Like many people, I erroneously looked at them as a burden in which I would put out far more than I would get back, and so I thought that parenting would be a life of stoic sacrifice that might never pay off. Of course, this is a common misconception of people who have not actually been through the experience of parenting, but nothing could be further from the truth. Raising children is the most miraculous, natural, and wonderful experience in the world, as I would find out later. The moment of birth is an astonishing miracle that brought tears to my eyes as I watched each of my four children enter this world for the first time. Each newborn child is a miraculous combination of the substance of the woman's body and the man's body, joined together in love (hopefully), to produce an infinitely unique creature who is distinctly different from the father and mother yet bears profoundly reflective traits from both, which can be discovered over the life of the child as you try to raise them up in love, respect, wisdom, and courage.

Moreover, being infinitely unique, these children bring experiences and joys to their parents that would never be found in a childless life. But that is the way with most important things in life. The really valuable experiences that bring deep satisfaction and enjoyment take some investment of time, energy, and emotion. And the greater the value of the object or experience, usually the greater the price required. Subsequently, at times, parenting can be very hard work if you are fully committed, but those sacrifices also always give a return far in excess of what you put in.

I had not yet arrived at that point of realization that I would find years later when my wife and I brought our firstborn into the world. At this point, I was merely going on blind faith when I gave in to the prospect of having children. But when I thought of the possibility of my death and feared for what I would leave behind (i.e. nothing but an insurance payout), it was then that I really examined my soul and started asking what was truly important in life. It was then that I finally gave in on the subject of children.

My wife had already been ready for a while, but I had been skeptical and resistant, not even wanting to discuss the issue with her, mostly because I had experienced a very unhappy childhood and was pessimistic about my ability to be a good father. But at this point, considering the possibility that my life might be cut short, I was deeply touched by how unjust it would be for me to leave my sweet wife with all the sorrow of my possible death and little else to remember me by. At least, with a child in the house, she would always have a person in which to see something of me, something that would bring back the joyous memories of our best days together. I felt that I owed her this much.

Despite all the initial anguish, I ultimately didn't deploy. An experienced warrant officer was chosen over me for the deployment roster. In the always cautious world of army operations, the pragmatism of experience would win out over youthful enthusiasm when it came to choices for leaders to deploy with our unit. But the effect of the war and the change in my thinking was dramatic and lasting. For the first time, I had finally come to terms with the highest sacrifice that my chosen profession might require, and, realizing that risk, I accepted the possibility with humility, knowing that our great American freedom often required the blood of her patriots. I began living my life with renewed vigor, realizing that each day could be my last, since no one knows the hour that their life might be taken by the Creator.

So, for my wife and I, something good came out of that war. I had surrendered to the idea of being a parent and was now mentally and emotionally prepared for the challenge, and thus my wife and I embarked on the journey toward parenthood, trying in earnest to reach the miracle of pregnancy. God blessed us richly in this area as He did in so many things over the years. It was almost too easy. Not that we didn't have some worries and doubts in the beginning, thinking that it was taking too long in our limited perspective of our youthful years. But once we chose this road, we became more cognizant of the people around us who were also trying to have children. For some, the struggle was a long frustrating road, so we never took for granted the fact that my wife was able to conceive so quickly. We realized what a tremendous blessing this was and thanked God often for this gift. Within a year (early 1992), we received confirmation of my wife's pregnancy, and the joy of our firstborn—a beautiful son—followed in September 1992, and his birth would be followed by three more miracles in the succeeding years.

The Post-Vietnam Resurgence of the Military

Years passed. Our nation had won Desert Storm with relatively little expenditure of life, money and materiel, so the victory was considered glorious, especially given the cloud of Vietnam still hanging over the heads of many senior leaders in the military who had been junior leaders during Vietnam. Many of those commissioned and noncommissioned officers from the Vietnam-era military had vowed as they rose through the ranks that the mistakes of Vietnam would never be repeated. They never again wanted to fight a war like Vietnam where blood was shed for seemingly senseless reasons sometimes, where body counts were often the measure of victory, where our commitment to victory was not absolute, where our commanders were not given appropriate latitude to use their experience and expertise to conduct the war properly and with a clear goal for victory without undue interference from politicians, and where some of the leaders were not fully committed to professionalism and the welfare of their troops, not being servant leaders who put the interest and needs of the troops ahead of their personal aggrandizement or careerism.

As Jonathan Shay suggests in his 1994 book, *Achilles in Vietnam* (Introduction and Chapter 1)[9], the moral violation of poor leadership in Vietnam probably was a key factor in the numbers of Vietnam veterans who developed PTSD. In the moral chaos of war, the troops need to believe that their leaders are morally upright and will always do the harder right over the easier wrong, that the fighting is driven by a "just cause," and that their leaders will always treat their troops with compassion (knowing that these are the sons and daughters of America, the cream of our society, courageous citizen-patriot-soldiers).

There were some bad leaders who came out of that war which has been covered in numerous other books on the Vietnam War, but there were also many courageous, wise, and dedicated leaders who came out of that morally chaotic environment. And many of these leaders rose in the ranks to positions of power eventually where they could exert their moral influence in the military for a better world for all the troops to right the wrongs of the Vietnam era. Moreover, these committed patriots sowed the seeds for a better military (better trained, better equipped, and more morally sound) that we reaped in tremendous battle victories during Desert Storm and during the long wars of the current era in Iraq and Afghanistan. Sure, as in all groups of people, some have their various all-too-human flaws, but many of these officers and noncommissioned officers from that era saw what was wrong and were also fully dedicated patriots who have served their country honorably and well. They truly turned around the bad situation of the post-Vietnam military into a top-notch professional military that Americans can be very proud of.

Post-9/11 Wars

So the hard work of those post-Vietnam military leaders paid off in the amazing victory of Desert Storm, which began to banish the stigma of Vietnam. But despite our victory there, there was yet another war with this same dictator years later, one of the consequences of the horrendous, tragic 9/11 attacks on the World Trade Center in New York City and on the Pentagon. Some may say that the moral and rational connections between the Iraq War and 9/11 are a little fuzzy, but, all things considered, this was a war that seemingly needed to be fought with a madman dictator ever agitating below the surface of blatant, egregious military and diplomatic violation. Hussein was a persistent, chronic "thorn in the side" of America that just would not go away, and his antics were constantly testing the patience of the American public and our political leaders.

Some may say that President Bush did not build a compelling case or that he had faulty intelligence when he made the case for the invasion of Iraq. But hindsight is always 20–20. We can easily look back on decisions we or others have made and pronounce a profoundly wise judgment about how this or that should have played out, but in the immediate moment of these decisions of great import, we often do not have a completely clear picture of all the pertinent facts, nor do we have a perfect perspective of all points of view. So, we usually make decisions based on the best information that we have, our best understanding of the situation, and our best prediction of which choice will produce the best results. Life is always messier than we claim, pretend, or desire it to be, so it is inevitable that all of us will make decisions that will seem unsound in retrospect a little further down the road.

That said, I am confident that President Bush made the best decision that he thought was right at the time with his limited understanding of the situation and his concern about the potential misbehavior of a madman who may or may not have been sitting on a pile of WMDs. With that kind of threat and uncertainty, most people would choose the path that was safest for all Americans or that would most likely lead to the well-being of the majority. Surely, anyone with the full weight of the responsibility of the presidency and the understanding of the consequences of inaction (especially in the shadow of 9/11) would not dare to take unnecessary risks with American lives.

So, for better or worse, we invaded Iraq in 2003. Thanks to the advancements of television news coverage and the more media-friendly military leaders, this time we would watch this new war with Iraq play out over television, sometimes blow-by-blow, unlike Desert Storm a decade earlier.

At the time, I was stationed in Germany, my family and I having moved there shortly before 9/11. We followed the cable news accounts of the subsequent Afghanistan proxy war and the eventual larger American military presence in that country.

For those who are unaware, we have numerous American military bases throughout Germany and a few other European countries, complete with housing areas, military shopping centers and grocery stores, a little slice of Americana plopped right down in the middle of these European cultures, although there were certainly many adaptations, adjustments, or concessions to the culture around us within our gated and fenced communities. The military families who live on these bases experience the culture of their temporary host country to varying degrees. Some of our citizens, military families living within these communities, are more timid, fearful of embarrassing encounters as they try to speak the language or negotiate the different processes and cultural customs of such countries in which our troops are based.

But on the other end of the spectrum are people like myself, who see these challenging cultural encounters as a grand adventure, knowing that living in such a place is a unique opportunity not afforded to everyone. Living in these places also gives many wonderful opportunities for travel and seeing things and places that we will remember for a lifetime. People like me fit into our host culture as best we can, learning as many of the languages as we can in our travels, being receptive to new experiences, being open-minded to the many cultural differences, and always maintaining a humble sense of humor. We don't worry about making mistakes, knowing that the gracious citizens of our host country are usually very patient, understanding, and helpful, realizing that we are strangers in a strange land, and appreciating that we are, at least, making an effort to speak their language, participate in their cultural events and festivals, eat their foods, and shop at their businesses. A smile and an easy laugh can go a long way.

Unfortunately, our peaceful adventure in this foreign country took a dark turn after 9/11. The change was not due to the German citizens. In fact, the Germans were very gracious and sympathetic to our nation's grief. Not certain how they could help, many set up temporary shrines outside the guarded entry points of our various gated communities at which they would lay flowers, candles, or a variety of gifts and trinkets. Security became very strict around our communities for a few months after 9/11. There was a lot of tension among the troops and their families as we were briefed on the presence of other possible terrorist groups living in our host country of Germany that might take advantage of the chaos and shock of the moment to inflict yet another attack on our troops in Germany, their family members, or even American and German civilians who were working on the military bases but living out among the German communities and neighborhoods.

There was a lot of paranoia during those days as we had no idea what such an enemy might try who had already demonstrated the willingness to go to prodigious lengths of time, planning, and preparation just to inflict violence on thousands of innocent civilians in the 9/11 attacks. There were many reported incidents of close encounters thought to be terrorists or their sympathizers trying to harm or, at least, frighten our troops and their families to demoralize them. There were also a few incidents that turned out to be false reports of terrorism or, at least, misunderstandings, even normal heated encounters between people that had nothing to do with the terrorist groups.

For instance, I remember one incident that found its way into our various operational briefings or reports that I would get by virtue of my job as a strategic/operational planner participating in a planning group for the United States Army European Command (USAREUR) operations cell. My job dealt with human resource planning (unit manning, mail operations, casualties, etc.) for virtually all operations that USAREUR was involved in during that era (2001–2004), such as the ongoing operations in the Balkans that had started in the 1990's under President Clinton (Bosnia-Herzegovina and Kosovo). I even made a few trips via a US. Air

Force C-130 into those areas as part of my job, which was high adventure for a young major, not to mention the extra money on my paycheck at the end of those months that I visited these combat zones (all troops serving in or visiting for any length of time in these designated combat zones receive danger pay and pay no taxes on their pay for that month).

But part of my job was to screen the various classified reports that our military intelligence and operational planners would produce daily and to look for key events that my bosses would need to be briefed on, to subsequently disseminate out to our units, or which would require me to make planning and coordination for various military contingencies. In one of these reports during the frantic, paranoid period right after 9/11, I read about a high-speed encounter between an unnamed US soldier and a German citizen on the autobahn (the German freeway). The German national had apparently tried to pursue the soldier and had made threatening gestures and so forth. The soldier had described the other driver as having an Arabic appearance (i.e. dark hair and a darker toned skin). Of course, it is well-known that there are large numbers of Islamic people living in Germany in certain communities, mostly of Turkish origin, but it was also well-known that some members of the German-Turkish community had sympathies for the Arabic terrorist groups, being Muslims themselves.

Over the course of a few days, however, updated information was published on our secure message networks that changed the character of this exchange between the soldier and the possibly Turkish driver. As the rest of the story took form, it was evident that there was a traffic encounter in which the German driver perceived that the soldier had been discourteous or had not complied with the normal rules of the road (Germans are very particular about and get quite upset about when people do not follow the rules). Germans take their driving very seriously. In any case, as the story developed, it changed gradually from a possible terrorist incident into a simple road rage incident.

Nonetheless, it's important to understand the big difference in lifestyle and security that our "forward based" soldiers encounter in the various countries around the world as opposed to what they would experience if stationed in the states. As noted, our little military communities were spread throughout Germany at one time, each one with its own little microcosm of America, its own perimeter fence and active security measures a little oasis of America albeit a rigid military flavor. My family and I lived in one little post, but I worked at another about ten miles away; plus, I frequently had to travel to a few other posts in the area in order to fulfill the requirements of my job.

So probably all of our American troops stationed in Germany were briefed on the possibility that they could be targeted by terrorists, and there were certainly multiple opportunities for those unfriendly to the US to take out their grievances on us as targets of opportunity. Plus, we went to church in an English-speaking congregation that was nestled in the German community and with no special security procedures; they conducted services the same way other German churches did—without guards at the door screening visitors or any other type of security procedure.

As noted earlier, perhaps, the biggest security issue we faced was the large Turkish population in many areas of Germany, immigrants who had flooded in to take lower level jobs during Germany's boom economy of the 1970s through the 1990s. They tended to be Muslim, and, from my experiences, tended to be, at least, apprehensive, if not outright antagonistic, toward Americans. It was primarily this population and their connections to others in the Arab world that drove most of our security fears in this foreign landscape, although, to be honest, there were few real threats that developed out of this population over time.

All in all though, overseas duty was certainly not the same as in the States. In the States, you would assume that you were surrounded by friends and supporters (the Vietnam era, not-withstanding), but here, you never knew. The wonderful German people were very supportive, but you always knew this was not their war, and you knew you could not necessarily count on their support, especially when it came to sending their own youth to risk life and limb. Once their government made the commitment to do just that, you knew that protests against war would be much more forceful and frequent and would many times be conducted right at the gates of the posts you would have to drive through. Additionally, there has been a strong pacifist streak in the Germany population for many years. I don't know if this grew primarily out of the distaste for war after the disaster of WWII, or whether it was a tangential movement from the Vietnam protests and other cultural movements in the US or merely the desire to live peacefully and enjoy life once material success became permanent and widespread in Germany.

It was in this tense, sometimes paranoid, environment that I watched our cable news shows daily (either at home or at work) as we successfully negotiated uncharted territory in our war with Afghanistan at first and Iraq a couple of years later. I was amazed at our success as we used proxies to execute much of the Afghanistan war in 2001. Of course, the American-friendly Iraqi troops of the Northern Alliance had a big intellectual and strategic boost from our special operations soldiers who were strategically placed among their ranks as liaisons to coordinate weapons, ammo, air/artillery strikes or, more importantly, to advise these tribal fighters in the finer techniques of large-scale war that they lacked (even though some had experience from fighting the Russians in December 1979 to February 1989, following the Russian invasion and subsequent occupation of Afghanistan).

I watched our burgeoning involvement in Afghanistan with guarded interest as an American citizen and a little bit of apprehension as a military leader, knowing that our involvement in that war was relatively limited in the early years. I would be more apprehensive when we embarked on another war with Saddam Hussein in Spring of 2003, this time on his home turf, and this time with much larger numbers of troops than we had invested in Afghanistan (at the beginning, at least).

Like most caring military leaders, I was concerned about our troops as I saw the Iraq war play out over television. I was deeply troubled for our soldiers as the drama of the various battles was captured in real-time television news. I knew that I had served with at least some of those troops that were in those early battles, so the war felt personal. Regardless of whether I knew them or not though, these were all American troops, our sons and daughters, brothers and sisters, mothers and fathers. Furthermore, I could have just as easily been one of them, given the possible variations in career assignments. I also felt the war more personally now because of my greatly increased experience with troops, because of the greater weight of leadership as I rose through the ranks, and because of my realization of the sanctity of life with the birth of my four children.

Moreover, I remembered in the back of my mind that I had not gone to the last war (Desert Storm) and regretted somewhat the loss of opportunity to pay my dues and bear the same burden as my brothers- or sisters-in-arms, but I knew even in 2003 that it was likely I would eventually serve in this new war. Time would prove me right as over the succeeding months the war and the subsequent occupation unexpectedly (at least, to our military-civilian leaders) dragged on and quickly increased, with the formerly glorious victory now morphing into a longer, larger, and more costly commitment.

The day eventually came that I was on orders to a unit stationed at Ft. Bragg, North Carolina; it was on the short list for deployment to Iraq. I was on leave in conjunction with my move from my unit in Germany back to my new state-side assignment. I had tried very hard with limited success to disengage from my job in Germany in time to take a few weeks of leave. I had been under incredible amounts of stress from the high level of responsibility in the jobs that I held while in Germany, from the additional work that the war produced, from very demanding bosses, and from the stress of being a military leader in an army that was at war. That latter stress was somewhat intangible or hard to describe, but when you are a member of a force that is at war, you just feel the pressure of working a little harder when you know others are deployed and feel somewhat anxious if you are not there paying your share of the sacrificial duties inherent in a combat assignment.

In any case, I never found adequate time to unwind between these two assignments, and for two solid years, my nagging guilt at not being involved in the fight when my country was at war and the stress level from my increasingly demanding jobs had been building ever higher until the tension seemed almost unbearable. Increasingly, I hated getting up in the morning and hated going to work, and the stress level gave me a hair trigger temper that I tried desperately to control so that I would not take it out on my subordinates or my family. In normal times, I was the optimistic type who tried to find the good things in every situation. Moreover, I certainly didn't want to be one of those soldiers who lived overseas and constantly complained about wanting to go back to the States, all the while missing an opportunity of a lifetime for adventure in a beautiful foreign country like Germany. But this daily unrelenting pounding of stress and high demands of my jobs and my bosses wore me down over the period of two years. I came to the point that I would rather have died than lived, and although I wasn't thinking about suicide, I still developed a constant unhealthy desire for the escape of death.

It was during this time that, when I would arrive at work and walk toward my office building, I would usually gaze deep into the dense German forest on the other side of the perimeter fence of our compound, and, seeing the lush, peaceful foliage, I longed for an escape—any kind of escape. I truly understood the sentiment of the persona in Robert Frost's famous poem, "Stopping by Woods on a Snowy Evening." Like that man in the poem, I also had tremendous responsibilities that weighed me down, but I knew that I had a greater desire to fulfill those obligations than I desired escape.

> The woods are lovely, dark and deep,
> But I have promises to keep,
> And miles to go before I sleep,
> And miles to go before I sleep.[10]

Despite my iron-willed commitment to my duty, the simmering emotional cauldron within me concerned me, as I feared it would interfere with the obligations that I wanted to fulfill. This was not the optimal way to arrive at a new unit. I thought that a few weeks of leave away from the demanding army environment would clear my head and get me ready for whatever I faced in the new job. However, knowing that the deployment was inevitable, hanging over me like the sword of Damocles, I was unable to fully enjoy my leave or to let go of the building tension. Consequently, I never fully decompressed, leaving me sitting on a barely contained emotional powder keg when I reported to my new unit.

When I finally arrived at the unit at Bragg, I took over one of the main staff sections on the General's staff for a logistics unit that had several thousand soldiers in peacetime, but which would balloon to between fifteen thousand and twenty thousand troops in wartime. This was a high-powered, demanding, and prestigious job, but it was also an expected job for this point in my career as a major on the promotion list for lieutenant colonel.

Although the job was very important and prestigious, one which I deemed to be an honor and privilege, I found out soon enough that I had a very difficult task in front of me in assuming the duties of my new job. Unfortunately, I discovered many of the people in my new section to be dispirited, including the hardworking, highly intelligent, and very professional deputy who

THE LONELY ROAD HOME

had been left holding the bag for leadership of this section by the man whom I would replace. She was one of the finest officers I've ever worked with in my career. She was dedicated and demanding and had a heart and soul for the troops. Like me, she always thought first of the welfare of her soldiers above her personal interests. She actually did have a boss, the man I was replacing, who should have been doing the work that had been dumped on her and should have been working with me for the transition of leadership, but he was retiring and was spending all of his time on the transition out of the service.

Moreover, our unit's leadership was reluctant to hold his feet to the fire during the final months of his career. I assume they were reluctant because they believed that his long record of good service was too important despite his inadequate performance in the final hours of his service. I reluctantly agreed with my new bosses. I felt that a man does deserve honor for a lifetime of service, even if he doesn't carry the honor all the way to the end. In the end, we're all human, and we all let others down at some point.

Unfortunately, this man was not the only person who displayed bad leadership from my experience over the years of my army career. Thankfully, bad leaders such as this were in the minority from my experience though. I always felt that truly honorable army leaders—as covered extensively in army leadership regulations, field manuals—and the Uniform Code of Military Justice—should be servant leaders, trying always to rise above self-serving thinking and actions. They were supposed to always put the troops first—they eat first, get paid first, etc. Furthermore, when any subordinate troop is in a moral or life crisis, that situation should become the personal burden of the compassionate servant leader. The truly moral leaders realize that, although much responsibility is laid on their shoulders, the real debt for mission accomplishment is paid by the hard work of the men and women under their command.

Moreover, if the troops are cared for first and they truly believe that the leader has their best interests at heart, puts them first at all times, and takes care of their needs in the critical moments, then the troops will follow this leader to the gates of hell, so to speak. Likewise, given such high expectations in the military environment, moral failure by leaders is usually considered one of the most egregious of sins among troops, and one which leads to the greatest feelings of betrayal. This topic is explored so effectively in Dr. Jonathan Shay's *Achilles in Vietnam* (Introduction and Chapter 1) in which he writes about the moral violation, the betrayal, that troops felt in that war when many of their leaders failed them by self-serving, career-centered actions that strayed off the path of sound moral leadership.

In any case, when I took over this job at Fort Bragg to help my new unit prepare for deployment to Iraq, my poor deputy was at the upper limit of her stress level due to the overwhelming demands of a job (i.e. leading the entire staff section, one job level above her normal duties), which she had the heart and courage for but not the preparation or experience. She did an admirable job given her limited experience, doing things that were a couple of levels "above her pay grade."

Nonetheless, she was clearly close to burnout by the time I arrived in the unit and was at her wit's end. I felt that she was too young and too talented to go through that kind of soul-wrenching injustice, so the moment I walked in and recognized the situation for what it was, I wanted so badly to set things right and give her and the rest of my new staff a better example of what a good leader does. This moral situation notwithstanding, I had my work cut out for me. It's not an easy task to get a group of people ready for a combat deployment in the best of circumstances, but in addition to the mountain of obstacles I was up against, I was also fighting my own personal demons.

The days leading up to the deployment left everyone with heavy hearts. We knew what was coming, and like all normal people, we feared the unknown when faced with a seemingly gargantuan task. It was not so much that we feared what we would face when we arrived in Iraq, away from our home and our loved ones, since that is what the troops in the US military train for every day. Perhaps, our greatest fear was the impending moment of separation. We knew it would be painful, and we doubted our ability to get through that moment. From the moment that I had confirmation that I would be deployed, my heart was continually heavy. It did not help that I had just come from a very stressful job and from which I had not properly decompressed. But now, with my emotional reserve still exhausted from my previous job in Germany, I was faced with an even more daunting challenge in this deployment.

With my emotional exhaustion and the promise of more problems to come, I knew I had to go see a doctor for help from my crushing anxiety and depression. Unfortunately, I was afraid of asking for help because of the stigma associated with troops who seek or receive psychiatric help. With mixed results, Army leaders have tried in recent years to ameliorate this perfectionist, prejudicial environment against anyone seeking mental health treatment or showing weakness in any way. Unfortunately, everyone knows in the military culture that there is a general prejudice against anyone with a perceived weakness or any kind of bad mark on one's record. As one of my former bosses put it, "One 'awe shit' wipes out a thousand 'attaboys.'" The military, for better or worse, tends to be a perfectionist culture.

If you listened to the official line, you would think this was not true. In the military, we are always receiving briefings or classes on what to do if any military member needs help with family issues, psychological issues, drugs and alcohol problems, financial issues, etc. Moreover, at these briefings, they constantly stress the importance of being courageous enough to ask for help, but anyone who has been around the army for very long knows that people look at you and treat you differently once it is perceived that there is a weakness in you—or, at least, what they think is a weakness. There is a kind of egotistical, macho perfectionism that simmers below the moral surface in military culture. This is not a very healthy environment when you're working with real flawed human beings who need room to make mistakes without being crushed in response to their mistakes or weaknesses. This attitude is generally not very beneficial to the troops, but this is, unfortunately, the way it is in some units and among some leaders.

In entering a new job, the last thing I needed was the general perception that I was damaged goods or that I was trying to get out of a deployment. That said, I would rather have gone through my own personal hell quietly than admit openly that I had a problem. Of course, the danger to that approach and the outcome that I feared is that I would have probably held it all in until I reach the point of explosion or emotional meltdown. This last possibility worried me even more. I couldn't afford to lose control. There were too many people depending on me at work. My family, of course, depended on me at home, and many of these people were looking to me for an example of courage in the face of deployment preparation challenges.

Furthermore, given the leadership history in my new section, I felt compassion for my soldiers and felt compelled to ameliorate and heal any damage that my predecessor left behind. I wanted to restore their faith in their leaders, no matter what the cost was to me personally. Thankfully though, none of my worst fears materialized concerning the possible referral to psychiatry. When I worked up the courage to go see a doctor and tell her about my emotional/psychological issues, I was pleasantly surprised that she did not refer me to psychiatry but rather prescribed a low-level stress-reducing and mood-enhancing medication, Wellbutrin.

Thankfully, this medication worked well—for a few months, at least—until we deployed, and the adrenaline blast of my early post-traumatic stress disorder (PTSD) symptoms rendered it ineffective. But fortunately, this was long enough to get me and my team into Iraq and get us settled. In time, my emotional/ psychological problems would get much worse and develop into full-blown PTSD, but this would be after I was able to complete the majority of my responsibilities in getting my team through the most difficult transition periods, the time leading up to and immediately following the deployment.

Moreover, I'm almost amazed at how well the secret of my psychiatric issues was kept. I know there's much disagreement about privacy for mental health patients in the military community, and we'll probably never get to a perfect solution. One side of the issue is the concerned commander who wants to know everything that is going on with his or her people and everything that will affect his or her mission, and on the other side is the emotionally or mentally suffering patient who does not want the public stigma of being a "damaged" person. However, given the culture of military perfectionism, it is fully understandable as to why the soldier who is suffering mental health issues would be cautious about the demand for complete openness and, therefore, reserve the right to keep his or her issues secret so long as they do not affect his or her work performance.

In my case, I functioned very well during the day, but this is only because of the emotional machinations I went through in ignoring or packing away and refusing to admit certain realities. My willpower got me through, but my emotional reserves were not an endless well from which I could draw. I subconsciously knew that, sooner or later, I would have to deal with all the simmering, potentially explosive emotions under the surface.

Unfortunately, not all people felt as I did about the deployment (i.e. a feeling of duty and obligation to bear a share of the load when our nation is at war). Surprisingly, when a unit is scheduled for a deployment, various character flaws of some troops in the unit rise up to the surface, and we open a window into the soul of our subordinates, peers, and superiors. I don't know if this is a sign of cowardice (the most negative perspective) or simply the soldier's self-delusion about what military service really means (soldiers who are not fully committed to the notion of self-sacrifice). But often we find out the most shocking moral flaws or psychological problems about our fellow troops during these times of stress. I'm sure this is universally true for all people—that you don't really know them until you see them under extreme pressure.

Thankfully, most soldiers just "ruck up," "suck it up," and do their duty no matter how difficult the deployment may be for them personally and no matter what they may feel inside. I'm sure all of us in the military have, at least, some fears and doubts when faced with a deployment to a combat zone and separation from family, but being committed to duty and honor, most of us suppress these misgivings for a later time because we desire the greater good, mission completion, commitment to our fellow soldiers, respect of our family and friends, and service to our country.

Some, however, harbor secrets or seriously misguided internal thoughts, which drive them to dishonorable actions. Depending on your worldview, these flaws could be inextricably inherent to human nature, or such people are blameless due to the circumstances of their environment. If you take the latter position, you might think that, perhaps, they carry deep, painful, and humiliating secrets or wounds that eat them alive from inside out, things which they have never really faced and come to terms with. But more importantly, I believe, perhaps, they have never reached the moral decision point in which they realized that this is the hand that life has dealt them with, good or bad, and subsequently they commit to fighting against their personal demons and trying to make a go of their life and even make the world a better place in spite of their inner struggle.

Or some may take the opposite route of self-pity, and they succumb to the demons, angrily believing that the world around them owes them something for the pain they feel, or, in their anger, they seek revenge on the world and everybody in it for what they have suffered.

Bottom line, sometimes we just never know who the people around us really are until we see them in a crisis.

Building the Deployment Team

All of us felt the fear and anxiety about leaving loved ones, and we all felt some fear of the unknown and what might happen to us in a combat zone. Unfortunately, those who harbored their secret wounds and committed to the moral path of selfishness over duty would employ various tactics, no matter how outrageous, to try to get out of the deployment. One of my soldiers came to me and my deputy asking for relief from the deployment. Her reasons seemed to be valid and genuine rather than self-serving. She had gone through a deployment already, which had broken her emotionally. I'm assuming that she had developed PTSD and was already suffering much for her country. She had serious doubts about her emotional energy to survive another deployment.

Reading the anguished expression on her face and listening to her explanation, both my deputy and I agreed that she really was not capable of making another deployment. Her spirit was truly willing, but her flesh was weak from traumatic experiences she had endured in her last deployment. She had already done her part. I thought no less of her for knowing the measure of her limitations and recognizing the power of the emotional and psychological demons inside her from her previous combat deployment. So, we decided not to put her through that again if we could avoid it.

However, another of my soldiers who seemed to be sound in mind and heart repeatedly went on medical appointments, always returning with some issue that, if not resolved, would have kept her from deployment. We guessed from her actions and words that this might simply be an attempt at avoiding deployment, perhaps, not having confidence in her ability to endure it. But unlike her already deployed peer mentioned earlier, there were no significant physical, emotional, or psychological problems that prevented her from deploying. Rather, it apparently was simply fear and a lack of confidence that were hindering her. We faced a real moral conundrum with her because we feared that it might set off a domino effect if we let her off the hook. In any case, if she were allowed to avoid deployment for what would appear to be superficial or capricious reasons, it would set the wrong moral precedent in our section and unit, violating the army values that we prize.

To the uninformed, those army values that we were constantly reminded of and saw displayed on posters around most units are: loyalty, duty, respect, selfless service, honor, integrity, and personal courage. This soldier's avoidance of a deployment would have violated several of those values and would not have sat well with anyone possessing even an average moral compass and would have stood as a constant indictment and reminder to our troops that we (their leaders) had not done or were not willing to do the right thing, poisoning the moral foundations of our unit's morale.

Instead of making a big deal out of the situation, we simply let this soldier's peers work on her. Eventually, their various talks and pressure had a positive effect—perhaps overcoming her lack of confidence, perhaps reminding her of her moral obligations to duty and honor—but to her credit, in the end, she did the right thing. She got all of her medical issues cleared and, subsequently, went on the deployment with the rest of her peers. Moreover, she did a great job while she was in Iraq, serving very well and honorably.

As for the rest of my soldiers, some of them did not want to go and made their positions clear, but all of these soldiers, except for a couple of hard cases, would end up going anyway despite their initial misgivings. They were honest people that simply felt the fear we all felt about the unknown and about separation from home and from loved ones. But these candid soldiers were not the biggest problem. Our worst problem lay in the ones who stayed quiet and went about various appalling maneuvers in order to avoid deployment.

I had heard stories about this phenomenon from friends who had deployed to Desert Storm (1990–1991). Several of my friends told me about the lengths that certain troops would go to in order to avoid deployment. This included the antics of some misguided young female troops who openly advertised at the local club on Friday or Saturday nights their willingness to have sex with any willing soul, and, believe me, in the military or any group of young people, there are always willing souls. Their intent, of course, was to get pregnant before their unit's scheduled deployment. Said pregnancy would, they knew, immediately pose a road block to their medical clearance for deployment.

Knowing of this tendency among some troops who are morally "on the edge," I was watching out for signs of the same malingering behavior that might arise among my own flock as we prepared for our deployment to Iraq. I did not have to wait long. Of our troubled and troublesome soldiers, we had one who deliberately broke his wrist. The circumstances of his broken wrist were very suspicious. According to his report, he broke it going up the stairs, which did not seem to make sense. However, he was chagrined to find out that his wrist healed more quickly than he expected and that the doctors promptly cleared him for deployment. Having failed this ploy, he finally admitted to us that he simply did not want to deploy. Like all of us, he feared the unknown, but he was apparently unwilling to take any risks in his life out of selfishness, perhaps, fearing discomfort, fearing the limits of his own abilities, or fearing the loss of control of his life. In any case, we made it clear that this was his duty to his country and his legal obligation, one of the reasons he had signed his legally binding enlistment contract.

He probably thought in his immature moral reasoning that we were being cruel to him by forcing him to do something he didn't want to do (he clearly did not want to deploy), but we had a moral responsibility as military leaders (to our superiors, to our subordinate troops, and to the American people) to ensure that all of our troops carried out their assigned duties. Moreover, we had a moral responsibility to ensure fairness and equality among our troops and that the appearance of fairness was matched to the reality of fairness. We had to ensure that the other young soldiers who were doing their duty and carrying their share of the burden saw that everyone was obligated to shoulder their fair share of the load and that standards were enforced. If we had let certain people off the hook just because they were being too difficult, then we would be shirking our duty as leaders and would be treating our troops unequally by not demanding that these troublesome soldiers take up the same load carried by their peers.

While I saw this demand of standards and duty from my troops as an essential moral duty of leaders, I have been surprised to find throughout my career that there were sometimes other leaders who did not feel such a binding moral obligation to their troops. Surprisingly, I have run across a fair number of leaders who are readily willing to do the expedient thing rather than the harder right thing, often not punishing, correcting, or counseling a problem soldier to see if they could "repair" this person. They were, as they say, following the path of least resistance. I have seen time and time again how such leaders often would simply pass off their problems to someone else for resolution, avoiding the harder, more difficult work of real, moral leadership.

But, in my opinion, by transferring the problem soldier to another unit, another section, another platoon, or even putting them out of the service, such leaders were sending the message that these soldiers were not worth the time spent on fixing them. And they could end up sending a self-serving moral message to their troops that it's okay to shirk your duty in doing right if the task seems too hard.

Of course, there is a situation called a rehabilitative transfer, in which a soldier who has been punished is transferred to a new unit in order to start fresh. Moreover, it is true that there are some people who are too hard to crack, but, too many times, I saw leaders not even make a cursory effort to mold or shape the character of their problem soldiers. I guess we're all human in the end—prone to error. Still, I felt like a good leader should always make that effort, and often I would find that it doesn't take as much effort as they feared to turn a bad soldier into a good one. In any case, this is certainly part of a leader's moral responsibility to his or her people, to try to have an impact on their troops' lives, shaping them into better, more productive, more educated, happier, and more functional people if possible.

Unfortunately, I was faced with one of the harder cases in this one deployment-resistant soldier. When a broken wrist and a disingenuous confession of suicidal ideation did not work, I believe he purposely got himself arrested under charges of driving under the influence of alcohol, otherwise known as DUI. He thought that this charge would make him too problematic to deploy. Of course, in his youthful ignorance, he did not realize the Pandora's Box he was opening up by treading down this path.

What he didn't count on is that, in the military, if troops get into trouble with civil authorities, they often get punished in the civilian system and get punished a second time by their military leaders because they have brought discredit to their service and the moral values which all of the services embrace. There is even a charge in the Uniform Code of Military Justice (UCMJ—the code of law, passed by Congress, under which the military services operate), a sort of catch-all charge for all bad behavior which is not covered specifically somewhere in the UCMJ. This charge is labeled "conduct unbecoming." This is a critical moral concept in a quintessentially moral organization (the military) in which one does not live up to or properly represent the values of the service.

When this soldier's DUI legal ploy didn't pan out, he went back to the psychiatric route. Claiming suicidal ideation was the final trick that worked for him, although we noted and remarked that he seemed suspiciously cheerful, given his suicidal state immediately after being taken off the deployment roster.

Another of our soldiers tried various creative ways to avoid deployment. She too tried the psychiatric route, but her psychiatrist cleared her for deployment, saying that, in his professional opinion, there was nothing wrong with her, that she was clearly shirking her duty to deploy—"malingering" as we call it in the military. He didn't tell us how he came to this conclusion, and that would, of course, be privileged information, but my guess is that she made the mistake of telling the doctor point-blank that she did not want to deploy and would do anything to avoid it. At that point, her status changed from being a patient in need of care into being a malingerer, a coward shirking her duty. Subsequently, with no other tool or method to prevent her deployment, she performed an outrageous stunt that was obviously designed to make us all think that she was really crazy. She showed up one morning with her beautiful long hair cut into a Mohawk. That was the first and last time that I've seen any female with such a haircut, so this stunt did render its intended effect. But when this antic did not result in her name being stricken from the deployment roster, she then followed this unusual stunt by taking the lead of her other young colleague (mentioned earlier) by making a trip to the emergency room claiming suicidal tendencies.

On one level, I understand the actions of such soldiers. I don't believe that one can completely control his or her emotions when faced with a seemingly terrifying event. However, for most people, there comes a point when the noble side of our nature takes over, and we acknowledge the bad feelings, simply deciding to put our selfish and petty concerns aside to do what is right and proper, something called moral courage. Moreover, I don't think that these young soldiers fully understood the ramifications and repercussions of their actions. Obviously, if they were not fit for duty or if they refused to fulfill their duty, our only recourse would be to separate them from service in the army. And consequently, such a separation would not be favorable, hindering their chances to be hired for future jobs. Given their low skill level and penchant for avoiding unpleasantness, I could not imagine that their lives would turn out to be very good after they were kicked out of the service under dishonorable circumstances.

They could have gone the longer path by claiming vague medical ailments, faking an injury or pain whether based in reality or entirely made up, and they could have gotten a more favorable separation, maybe even a pension. But they were impatient and anxious to get out, fearing that something would go wrong or that their scheming house of cards would fall, resulting in the unthinkable deployment. So, they were willing to accept any discharge offered, whichever was quicker. In the end, these soldiers received negative discharges shortly after our unit deployed, which would, for the foreseeable future, presumably taint all their attempts at employment.

Eventually though, we worked through the mischief of these soldiers, and our deployment team was set, although my commanding general (CG) and his chief of staff continued to make strategic moves of people to plug holes in other subordinate deploying units, taking away a couple of my key officers late in the game and throwing a couple of big wrenches into the works of my deployment planning. Of what was left, however, I had a superb although small officer and noncommissioned officer staff—very bright, talented, and dedicated people every one of them—and we eventually gained some noncommissioned officer "diamonds in the rough" who were released from other sections for what were essentially personality clashes. Nonetheless, during this short phase immediately before and after deployment, we all settled down to focus in earnest on deployment preparation.

We tried to avoid thinking about the pending separation from our families as we prepared for deployment. It was tough when I had to tell my wife about the pending deployment. It was tougher still telling our children. My wife and I agonized over the right time to tell our children. I was especially distressed over the impact this message might have on their young minds and hearts. Eventually, my wife and I settled on a time and a setting, and we broke the disconcerting news of my deployment. The response from my children turned out to be exactly as I had feared. There were some tears. They all cried and worried about what might happen to me. They feared the experience of living without their father in the house. They had seen the news reports about soldier casualties. Of course, we didn't let them see the news after that for fear of worrying them needlessly (at least, at the time, I believed it was needless).

My wife and I set out to put the best face on the deployment. I searched for all the information I could find on the internet about Iraq, the country and culture, and the base at which I would be stationed. I was actually surprised, knowing the seemingly endless reminders in the military about informational security (i.e. keeping operational information out of the hands of enemy that could be used against us), that I could find maps of the base and aerial pictures as well as pictures on the ground of soldiers in their daily duties. Nonetheless, I was thankful to have this information and the pictures readily available since this did have some positive effect on my children. It is an all-too-human flaw to fear the unknown much more than is warranted. Sure, my children would miss me, but they would eventually adjust to my absence and would settle into a "new normal" for their everyday activities. But I know that the stress of separation was relieved somewhat by the consistent, regular connection to me through the modern miracles of virtually instantaneous communication via e-mail and weekly phone calls that I would make to my family.

For my part, I lived in a constant state of anxiety and dreaded the day we would be separated—the day I would actually walk onto that airplane and leave them behind for a year. Having been a very close family at the time, I knew it would feel like a piece of our hearts was torn from us. And a year seemed like an eternity at the time. In many ways, it would turn out to be an emotional eternity. In terms of the emotional and psychological impact on me, I feel now, many years after the deployment, as if I never completely returned. Some days, I feel as if I'll never feel completely at home again, never be able to consider Iraq as just a past phase of my life that is concluded, completely behind me.

To prepare for our imminent family separation, we were allowed to go on something called block leave. Block leave was typically two weeks of leave immediately prior to the final deployment preparation in which the majority of the unit members would simultaneously go on leave to spend time with their families. It was a sacred, inviolable time for soldiers and their families. Our block leave was a very enjoyable time for my family, every last moment cherished. We went to Tennessee's Smoky Mountains and visited many places around that state that we had wanted to see for a long time.

This time with my family would end too soon. I would return to my unit for our final deployment preparation. Some groups of the unit had already left, and I myself had only about two weeks until I would depart. Since everything had basically been done, all equipment had been shipped, all training had been completed, and all instructions for preparation had been followed to the utmost; there was really not much left to do until that final day of boarding that plane.

We returned to the time-honored military tradition of simply waiting. The result was that I had a flood of unexpected time to spend with my family in the dwindling days. Most days during this period, I only spent half a day at the office with very light work and then spent the rest of the day with my family. But, with the specter of separation, it became increasingly difficult to enjoy that time.

Finally, the day of separation came. I packed two duffel bags and a carry-on bag for the flight and immediate training needs after that. We made the last-minute preparations that morning with heavy hearts. The time came that we had to load up my military gear in our vehicle and leave for the Green Ramp at Pope Air Force Base (Pope is contiguous to Fort Bragg as this is where all the airplanes fly from for the parachute training and operations that Fort Bragg is so well-known for). The Green Ramp was simply a large warehouse with extra-wide benches to accommodate airborne soldiers with their bulky backpacks and packed parachutes for the gamut of paratrooper training.

The Green Ramp also served during wartime operations as the primary staging area for deploying units, since the large warehouse could hold hundreds of soldiers and their equipment (as well as family members who wanted to take advantage of the ever-dwindling minutes remaining with their deploying loved ones). Moreover, the warehouse adjoined expansive runways that could accommodate any size of military or civilian aircraft, including the chartered civilian passenger jet that was reserved for us and awaiting us just outside the warehouse's door.

It was a very surreal scene at the Green Ramp. A band was playing upbeat music, but nobody really listened. I don't think anyone wanted to be serenaded with cheerful music as their hearts were breaking, waiting for that heartrending moment of separation. Some soldiers had left their families at home, preferring farewells there with a very quick, measured break rather than the long, torturous, drawn-out farewell at the Green Ramp. There was some validity to this choice, since those ever-waning moments with our families seemed to drag out and intensify the pain. Many sat with their families either not talking or making idle chatter in order to avoid what was really on their hearts and to prevent the boiling cauldron of emotions from erupting. There wasn't much intermingling between the troops, since those with their families wanted to focus their time exclusively on their families. So those soldiers who were single or those who had left their families behind that morning and were already past that moment of separation sat quietly reading or lay sleeping on the large, wide benches.

I sat quietly with my family for the most part. I did try to make conversation, as did my wife, but it was very difficult. We took pictures of the family and waited. There were a couple of heartrending false alarms with everyone scurrying to gather their carry-on baggage only to be put back in the waiting mode minutes later. Then, there was the real, actual moment as our officer and noncommissioned officer leaders called us to formation. From that point, we would no longer be able to hold our loved ones–only see them. Soon, even that we wouldn't be able to have.

For that final moment just before the formation, family members desperately hugged each other with many eyes tearing up. The band continued to play lively, upbeat martial music. The brutal irony was too much, so we either laughed at the incongruity or ignored it altogether. Of course, as noted previously, some didn't have family there to bid them farewell, by choice, having left their family at home to avoid the long, drawn-out moment of separation. Others were alone by necessity, such as the single soldiers whose only family was fathers, mothers, sisters, and brothers, perhaps, in another state hundreds of miles away already. Many of these single soldiers were young troops, stationed away from their original homes, coming from all parts of our great country, so this deployment was just another step of separation, albeit several thousand miles further.

Ironically, there were some who seemed to take the whole scene stoically, or even amusedly. To some, this was just another deployment among others they had experienced. Some were going for their second, third, or even fourth times.

But finally, we were put into formation, with our carry-ons resting on the floor in front of each line (the other gear as well as the duffel bags had already been loaded onto the aircraft). Once we were formed up, there were a few short speeches given by our key leaders, and the National Anthem was played. Then, rank by rank, we formed a single line and filed onto the aircraft. I had seen a few big tough soldiers shed tears before the call to load, but as we actually lined up to load the aircraft, with families lining the path, I saw more tears. We loaded the aircraft and waved to our families. I kept a brave poker face because I didn't want to further burden my family or my troops, but inside my heart was breaking. How could I live without my beautiful, precious family and my beloved wife for an entire year? I couldn't even think about it because the burden to my grieving heart was too heavy to acknowledge.

Ironically, I imagine that most of us were actually somewhat relieved when we finally boarded the aircraft. We had finally gotten through that dreaded, heartrending moment of separation from our loved ones without completely losing our composure. But I suppose that most of us could still feel the seemingly endless emotional tension from waiting at the Green Ramp with our families and the ever-building physical exhaustion from that stressful event.

Trying to contain all of my negative, anxious thoughts, I took one of my Wellbutrin pills, hoping to take the edge off the tremendous emotional pain I was feeling. Then I settled into my window seat. I resisted looking out the window since it was on the side where the families had walked out to watch us board. It had seemed like an eternity, until the airplane engines throttled up to taxi down the runway. The aircraft started rolling away from the Green Ramp at 12:45, and after several short movements, redirections, and pauses of the aircraft as the pilot awaited permission to take off, we were airborne at 13:25 (1:25 PM).

When we were finally airborne, wheels up, I had gathered up enough courage to look out the window. As the aircraft climbed to about one thousand feet, I could see all the families standing outside the Green Ramp, their faces becoming ever smaller by the second. I tried to distinguish the faces of my own family members within the crowd. All families were waving vigorously. My heart sank at the sight. I did not want to think about either my pain or the pain that my family must have been feeling at that moment. I wondered how we were ever going to bear this burden of separation. Still, I was glad to have had my family at the Green Ramp. I wanted to spend as much time as possible with them, soaking up as much of their love to last me as long as possible into the deployment.

Then, the hard reality that this was the last time I would see my family for a very long time, a year which seemed like an eternity looking at it from the perspective of the very beginning, started sinking in. Furthermore, not knowing the future, I considered the dismal prospect that this might be the last time ever that I saw my family. I'm sure we all had that grim thought in our subconscious minds, although we would never have spoken it. But, at least, the waiting and preparation were finally over, and we had begun our year-long journey. We had taken the first step onto the road of our foreign, lonely journey. Our lives would be completely different for the next year, and we knew we would be completely different people when we returned. Moreover, although we would maintain as much as possible the relationships with our loved ones back home, the people we worked with would become our ad hoc families for the year ahead. For better or worse, our deployment team, my fellow soldiers all around me on the aircraft, were the people who were "there in the flesh," and we would all need each other's emotional and spiritual support to get through the tough times and experiences that were ahead of us.

The Journey Begins

After the emotionally draining drama of family farewells, most of us were exhausted. Soon after our takeoff, talk in the aircraft died quickly. With so much doubt, worries, and possibly even guilt in the back of our minds, we settled wearily into our seats, thankful that we had gotten through the intense emotional storm of separation. But from the moment that we first received confirmation of our deployment date until this day of separation from our family, about six months' time span, we had all been in the same dead, breathless sprint to the finish line, feeling as if we were running in the dark, not really certain where the finish line was or what the shape and direction of the road under our feet were. So, in our preparations, we metaphorically ran blindly and desperately onward with no idea when we had done enough to prepare or when we would reach that point of completion.

This frantic effort without certainty or finality and the pending separation from our families had been exhausting us mentally, emotionally, and spiritually. We were running on fumes and faith. Not only were we working very long hours on tedious details of preparation, but we also had work to do when we went home at night to prepare our families for the long separation. We had to figure out all possible contingencies that might occur in our absence and the strategies we would employ to resolve them. Simple things like powers of attorney would make a tremendous difference in the ability of the spouse left behind to conduct various household transactions with bills, paychecks, legal issues, or bank accounts. The totality of the personal and professional planning and preparation that goes into a simple deployment would probably be mind-boggling to the average citizen. Most Americans have only a vague sense of the tremendous sacrifices that our troops constantly make on behalf of their fellow citizens.

Then on the actual day of departure, we endured the hours-long, seemingly endless and soul-sapping farewell at the green ramp. It was a bittersweet relief to finally board the aircraft and begin our long journey because, at least, that would mean a separation from the previously frenetic way of life and beginning the journey so that we could eventually reach the end of it. Now that we had moved on to the next phase of our life, we hoped for a more orderly and rational existence than the whirlwind chaos of predeployment preparations. Savoring a chance to catch our collective breaths, I'm sure many of us were going over memories in our heads of special moments in the last few months spent with loved ones and possibly still grappling with solutions to mission challenges that we had yet to resolve despite all of our preparations. Otherwise, we were completely spent.

Even if this next step might be painful as we adjusted to the separation from our families, we knew that we had to go through this phase to get it over with. The sooner we got through this, the sooner we would be home. This was a pragmatic sentiment that we spoke so many times throughout the predeployment process, but it's so hard to make the heart follow the head. All of us, family and soldiers, had sought the wisdom of practicality while going through deployment preparations because we craved, at least, the ruse of purpose, meaning, and order behind everything.

After the chaotic storm of predeployment activity, what we needed most was a brief respite to prepare for the next step, an oasis, a pause to breathe. As we settled down for the flight, we ran into one of a number of minor controversies. For some, these controversies were mere annoyances. For others, they loomed larger in the imagination, signaling fragmentation in our unit and moral weakness in our unit's leadership or in the ultimate moral purpose of our mission. Depending on your outlook, it was a glass half-full or a glass half-empty.

Of course, the leaders could not be blamed for the rise of conflict any more than a parent can be blamed for the natural, inevitable quibbling among their children. Whenever you put people together, there will always be conflict on some level. The intensity of that conflict depends on the maturity and self-control of the people involved, the importance of the issues at stake, or even the general climate of the group, whether they have been building their cohesiveness and beginning to feel like a team. Nonetheless, we all knew we were facing issues of life or death in our combat mission, so the trivial could quickly become magnified in that morally dire environment

Some of these things might have seemed trivial to our leaders, but leaders sometimes forget that if such issues are not trivial to their people, then the matter is worthy of attention. Most people, leaders included, want to do the right thing, but awareness and consideration of others is something that must be cultivated and exercised, or it will easily atrophy. Moreover, all leaders, by necessity, must sort through the litany of issues that come into their purview and decide what is important and what is trivial.

In any case, our first minor moral challenge concerned the seating on the aircraft as we flew out of Pope Air Force Base/ Fort Bragg en route to Kuwait. To some, this would seem a trivial issue, but given the seriousness of the mission ahead, all things seemed to take on greater significance.

After finding my seat on the commercial chartered aircraft, I soon found out from others that there was a first class section on the aircraft. I had never thought about it. I hadn't noticed it when boarding, and, being used to traveling coach, I just automatically headed toward the rear of the aircraft.

In any case, I was generally not the type of person who was always scheming for or demanding privileges for my rank, although I knew others who did this. I had always avoided even the appearance that I was more concerned about privilege than about duty because I had learned how detrimental such actions can be to unit morale. Furthermore, once you get a reputation like that among the troops, it is hard to dispel, and it consequently makes your job as a leader much harder. But the troops always notice such things, even if you don't think they do. Plus, as a leader, one must always be cognizant that he or she is looked at by lower ranking troops as a model for good behavior, even if those troops do not work for you, so the troops in your unit do not have to work for you to be influenced by your comportment and moral example.

All things considered, even if there was not always a moral issue of egalitarianism in the inevitably moral environment of a military unit, in my opinion, things like comfort and privilege are relative. Like most soldiers, I'm not so soft or narcissistic that I think I must have a certain level of comfort, and I'm not so egotistical that I think the world owes me something. Moreover, I think of my rank and position more in terms of responsibility to others rather than privileges gained, so it never occurred to me to think about or ask about what I was not getting. I know when things are good enough, and that is sufficient for me.

Moreover, being accustomed to economy flight, all I wanted was a decent seat, which I had—back in a corner at a window where no one would bother me. The row only consisted of two seats, both of which I had to myself (the aircraft's seating was more than enough to cover the numbers of our troops flying, so there were quite a few empty seats). From my chosen seat, I could see outside, and the bathrooms were convenient. I was satisfied. Besides, I thought of the alternative—flying in the jump seat of a military aircraft (an uncomfortable canvas seat on a metal frame), which I had done too many times to count.

Of course, jump seats would come with the whole package of other factors of ambience—deafening noise of the engine and excessive cold or heat in the cargo area where you were riding.

Additionally, military aircraft just always seems more prone to the jerks, jumps, and jolts of turbulence. I'm not paranoid enough to think that the pilots might be making the ride more bumpy than usual for their perverse amusement at our expense, but, as they say, just because you're paranoid doesn't mean that people aren't out to get you. You just never know. So, suffice it to say that, knowing the alternative on a military aircraft, a normal civilian airplane with nice, cozy upholstered seats and cabin climate control would do me just fine.

There were a few other high-ranking, pragmatic, egalitarian leaders like me on the staff, and I saw them around the coach cabin, but, as we would find, there were many others who were more status (or ego) oriented. Even some audacious junior soldiers or lower ranking officers took seats in the first class section. Most of these were on the special staff or were even the enlisted security troops specially trained to protect our commanding general (or Praetorian Guard, as we sometimes jokingly called them). Of course, I knew how important our general was, given the size of our unit's mission and that the insurgents might deem him a high value target, so who's to say how much is enough?

The large personal guard force notwithstanding, I have to respect my general for getting out of the headquarters on a regular basis and sharing in the danger of his troops, visiting most, if not all, of the bases where his troops were stationed. He was definitely a man of courage and wanted to be seen as a soldier's soldier. He even instituted a staff ride-along program that got some of us out on convoys with the troops.

I volunteered to go on the ride-along early in our deployment though, as I believed it was important for our troops to see their higher ranking officers to be willing to share in their dangers. My convoy turned out to be high adventure over a day and a half as we stopped off at several bases, drove hundreds of miles on the Iraqi highways, and had a breakdown on an Iraqi highway, which made some of the troops nervous. However, it resulted in a serendipitous interaction with a small group of curious Iraqi boys who came out to investigate and attempt to talk to us. There was some danger involved in this convoy. We were hit by an ambush later on, which was set off by a roadside bomb or improvised explosive device (IED). Thanks be to God though that only a couple of vehicles suffered minor injuries and no people sustained injuries from the blast or the bullets.

But getting back to the conundrum of the aircraft seating, which was based on the rank and positions of some of these people who had boldly claimed first class seating privileges, I would venture to say that they seemed to have an excessive measure of self-importance, automatically assuming a sense of entitlement. Normally, it would have been easy to overlook these people, but in a tense environment like a deployment, even the minutest things can be magnified, leading to much gossip or talk among the troops.

But this one incident began to open our eyes to the differences of the people around us as well as to challenge our views of what we considered to be right and wrong. You may think you know people when you work with them, but when you live and work around them twenty-four hours a day, especially in a stressful environment, you find out some surprising things about them, things that maybe they would prefer you didn't know about and maybe you would prefer not to know about.

Those of higher moral sensitivity expected the whole to work together, one for all and all for one. And in many ways, we did achieve this. We accomplished much together that could not have been accomplished alone, and we achieved one purpose— to defeat the enemy and to supply those units that depended on us. But our success almost seemed like a fortunate accident sometimes. We had always expected the parts of the whole to work together, everyone dedicated to doing their part, the beehive metaphor. That was part of our necessary belief in what we were doing—that there was a bigger central meaning and purpose. This belief formed part of the comfort that enabled us to sacrifice ourselves, and even our families at times, and it was part of the faith that we clung to in order to ensure our safe return to the States. We had to believe that we were working for a higher purpose and that those around us were equally dedicated.

But in our current situation on the aircraft, it appeared that some were claiming undue privileges without having paid anything into the proverbial pot. So be it. The world is not completely fair. That's one of life's most prominent lessons, and it's something we learn to live with.

But one sore point at the end of our tour concerned the bestowing of awards/medals. There's nothing wrong with giving honor to all the troops for wartime service, but the medals or awards should be given out equally and should be commiserate with risk and effort, never driven by political machinations that reward certain members of a unit more than their peers or by personality considerations.

Unfortunately, the army (which I'm sure is also true in the other services) in our current wars has been either erratic about the award standards or excessively stingy with awards compared to previous wars and other eras. Others have written on this phenomenon, and the web site "The American War Library" has compiled some excellent statistics about the award inequity (http://www.americanwarlibrary.com/medals/armymedl.htm).

Some attribute this low level of award granting in the current Iraq and Afghanistan wars to a backlash from the supposedly excessive award granting during Vietnam. However, the claim that the awards granted in Vietnam were extravagantly high is very debatable. It is well-known that the Vietnam troops, regardless of service, sustained an unprecedented number of continuous and contiguous days in combat. A *New York Daily News* article about a recent (2011) Vietnam War documentary aired on the History Channel, *Vietnam in HD*, points out that "the average

World War II infantryman saw ten days of combat a year. The average Vietnam infantryman saw 240."[1]

Given these figures, then the troops in Vietnam experienced remarkably more days in combat, many times over, than our vaunted Greatest Generation of World War II veterans. Given the high level of combat engagement, a rational person would expect to see a high level of awards granted, commiserate with the amount of sacrifice that these troops made for their countrymen. Not to be misunderstood, I am not challenging the validity, honor, or equity of the awards given to World War II veterans. I am merely pointing out the flaws in the argument that Vietnam War troops were granted awards out of line with or not commiserate with standards of awards in other American wars.

Additionally, if the stingy, low level of award granting for the current wars is a deliberate reaction by military leaders to their perception that Vietnam War awards were "given out like candy," then our troops in the current wars of Iraq and Afghanistan are indeed being served poorly by their leaders, especially given the high number of combat days that these troops experience (comparable to the Vietnam War numbers by all accounts). As stated previously, our military awards system is imperfect and is run by imperfect people, so I expect there are many anecdotal stories of high awards given where they were not deserved or, at least, appeared to be undeserved, a much lower level of awards given than was called for, or even awards given for circumstances that were highly questionable, if not blatantly false. These things happen in our imperfect world.

Certainly, these are important moral issues that should be addressed by individual leaders as they encounter such moral conundrums during the course of their duties. As I noted previously, morality is indispensable in the military due to our higher responsibilities and due to our capability for violence or, more accurately, due to the human predilection to misuse violence and power when they are in our grasp. Given these truths, the essential morality of equity is sometimes easily dismissed in today's military, especially by people "playing favorites" or the elitist culture of "special" people that exists in certain high-level head-quarters and organizations. I imagine that this is not a problem peculiar to the military though.

Pleasant Surprise

But the inequities of the awards system aside, we would experience a serendipitous event during our journey to Kuwait. We had an unexpected delay in our journey to the combat theater that would develop into a much-needed morale boost. The reason for the stop was to refuel the aircraft and apparently the most convenient airport, given our flight plan was Bangor, Maine. This stop came after only a few hours in the air, so we were somewhat surprised to find that our first stride toward Iraq did not cover any greater distance.

When the pilot announced the need to refuel at Bangor, I'm sure that more than one person rolled their eyes. But we accepted this just as we patiently bore so many unexpected surprises in military training and operations. Our stoic, reluctant acceptance of this unexpected surprise stopover would change dramatically in short order though.

As we came off the airplane and entered the Bangor Airport terminal, we encountered a gauntlet of older veterans and other kindhearted military supporters who stood spread out along the ramp in an enthusiastic, high-spirited receiving line. They offered hearty encouragement, handshakes and hugs. They had carefully anticipated our arrival and were out in full force. It was humbling to realize that these people had gone out of their way and gone to so much trouble to be there and to be enthusiastically supportive, even though they had their own lives and families. We were truly humbled that anyone would care enough to interrupt their lives and do so much for us, especially given that we were complete strangers.

It was more than a little humbling. I'm sure many of us were already beginning to feel some loneliness without our families, but we accepted these feelings as an ugly but necessary hardship that came with military life. But to find that these complete strangers identified with our trials and tribulations in service to our country and cared enough about us to go far out of their way to encourage us was beyond words.

In addition to the tremendous morale boost of the receiving line, these people also readily met pragmatic needs. They offered all members of our unit access to cell phones paid for by their organization, but many of these phones were clearly their own personal phones. There was no doubt that these wonderful people understood and cared. This was so unexpected, especially since it was not in an area of the country where one expects to find such strong military support or exuberant expressions of patriotism.

The moral-boosting delay was a pleasant surprise, but we still had much traveling to complete. After a couple of hours, we reboarded our aircraft. The jet started moving at 1645 (4:45 PM), November 17, 2004, and liftoff was at 1655. Thanks to our pleasant reception, we embarked with a reinvigorated sense of purpose. This just made us more eager to get to Iraq and do our jobs, knowing that we had the hearty support of many fine Americans.

After several more hours and a bleary wakeup, we arrived at Rhein Main Airbase at Frankfurt, Germany, at 2300 (11:00 PM) Eastern US time, November 17, which was 0500 (5:00 AM) local time, November 18. This was our second refueling and crew change. It was here that I remembered my watch's ability to keep two different time zones that could be looked at with the touch of a button. On one, I programmed Iraq time, and on the other, I programmed Eastern Time, which would be the time at my family's home in Hope Mills, North Carolina, just south of Fort Bragg where my unit was stationed. For my entire deployment, I always kept the Eastern Time Zone on my watch. Somehow, it made me feel closer to my family. At various times of the day while I was deployed, I would press the button, look at the time, and try to imagine what they were doing at that time back home.

At Rhein Main, we had a two-hour layover. The plane was cleaned and refueled. I got two AT&T calling cards for later use in calling home. We had already been told that there would be calling centers in Kuwait and Iraq from which we could reach home. And while we were waiting to reboard, there was an Internet area at the terminal, so many of us were able to check e-mail. I was pleasantly surprised to see that there was already an e-mail from my sweet wife, Lesia. She told me how they had watched the plane go out of site. Then, all emotionally exhausted from that morning, they returned home and watched movies the rest of the day. I felt a deep sense of sadness and guilt that they had to go through that emotional pain.

Outside the terminal at Rhein Main, the German morning was just breaking. It was a typical, gray, late fall day as I had experienced so many times in my eight years in Germany over three tours (1979 to 1981 in the Nuremburg suburbs, 1988 to 1991 in the Stuttgart suburbs, and 2001 to 2004 in the Heidelberg suburbs). I briefly fantasized about leaving the terminal and taking off through Germany. I know and love the country very well and can speak the language quite tolerably. But it was only a fantasy. I knew I had an obligation to fulfill, and I truly wanted to fulfill it, no matter the difficulty.

In my trepidation between my desire to fulfill my duty and my desire for freedom from this burden, Robert Frost's words from "Stopping by Woods on a Snowy Evening" kept coming back to me.

> The woods are lovely, dark and deep,
> But I have promises to keep,
> And miles to go before I sleep,
> And miles to go before I sleep.[2]

Weary but duty-bound, I continued to keep my promises—returning with my comrades to reboard the aircraft—when we finally got our call after a few hours. We settled back in with a new crew of pilots and flight attendants. We started taxiing at 0730 local time (0130 eastern), November 18. It would be four hours and forty-two minutes of flying time to Kuwait. We had just a few more hours in the safe, predictable, controllable sanctuary of the aircraft. After that, we would be off to the challenges of training and ultimately the challenges of our mission engagement.

The Purgatory of Kuwait

At 1430 local (0630 Eastern), we landed at an airfield (Ali Al-Salem) in Kuwait which was a mere oasis of concrete and a couple of buildings in the middle of the sandy expanse. My first impression was that everything looked bleak and lifeless, but this was from a limited perspective of a neophyte just glimpsing or coming into contact with a foreign landscape, so my initial perceptions did not have the full verity of context or experience. I could see a concrete runway, airport buildings, and sand. Nothing else. It looked so foreign to me like an alien landscape from a far-flung planet, so diametrically opposed to the lush landscapes that I was accustomed to from my boyhood experiences in Georgia, my current home station in Kentucky, or my numerous travel experiences all across the United States and Europe. It was so foreign to me that it could have been another planet.

From there, we would be bused out to Camp Virginia, Kuwait, a destination for most US (and even many allied) soldiers while acclimatizing, completing perfunctory training, and waiting for operational permission and transportation to enter Iraq. The camp was built on a few square kilometers of a typical Arabian, sandy, barren desert, a vast beach without an ocean, seemingly in the middle of nowhere. The camp had the proven capability to host around ten thousand soldiers in its busiest moments, usually during periods of transition between incoming and outgoing units, which glanced off of each other like great tectonic plates.

The camp itself was a small town. It was comprised of an amalgam of simple wood-framed buildings, metallic-framed Quonset huts and large tents, many of which had been locally purchased. The canvas of the tents was known to be cured with kerosene, making them quite flammable. The structures in the camp included: a laundry tent, a supply depot, restroom and shower trailers, tent housing of various sizes, all with climate control appliances. There were also tent operations cells set up for work with computers and phones (which proved to be rather ineffective in reaching key personnel or leaders in the unit that we were soon to relieve). Additionally, there was a, small PX (post exchange—a military convenience store), the telephone center (from which we could make calls back to the states), the internet café, the movie tent, and the personnel processing tents.

There was a respectable amount of the latest technology at Camp Virginia with the climate control units for the tents (providing both air-conditioning during hot days and heating during cold days), the generators powering electronic AC 120-volt devices with outlets and lighting in all the tents, the Internet café giving fast and easy access to e-mail and Internet in general, the sizable phone bank, the movie tent playing the latest movies on a large screen, and the generator/lighting composite units, which provided area lighting at key facilities, housing areas, the restroom/shower trailers, etc.

These night area lights were quite essential, since this was a desert without any built-up areas nearby, no trees, no buildings, and no significant landmarks in general. The nights became inky-black (without the urban sky, light pollution, that is so familiar to most stargazers.), making visibility and navigation in the dark difficult, or even impossible for even the most experienced soldier. Furthermore, it is too easy to become disoriented in a desert environment in daytime, and even more so at night. Thus, the meagerly dispersed, generator-fed area lights were a tremendous blessing in being able to navigate the camp at night with little effort and finding whatever or whomever you wanted or needed.

The variably colored portable toilets were generously dispersed at key locations around troop housing, dining, working, and entertainment facilities. These were an occasional, and often essential, necessity that we would have to endure as our primary restroom facilities while in Kuwait (and to a partial degree while in Iraq) were unpredictable, although our base in Iraq had enough brick and mortar facilities that you could easily avoid ever using the portajohns if you were absolutely averse to such facilities.

Another common sight around the camp besides the porta-johns, tents, and buildings were the many pallets of bottled water, which were strategically positioned, tactically dumped at nexus points for high traffic areas across the camp. In this environment, hydration was a constant necessity to avoid being a heat casualty. Unfortunately, this water (being left out in the hot sun) would often be lukewarm. Moreover, it had a heavy mineral content that was causing kidney stones among many troops—myself included.

In any case, although we had been briefed about staying in Kuwait, we clearly didn't grasp what that meant in terms of time expended and the inevitable and unpredictable training discomforts. Our time in Kuwait ended up being a lot longer and being a more tedious experience than we had anticipated. In order to get to Iraq, Kuwait is a necessary rite of passage. It offers a safe place for acclimation and adjustment to the region's environment and time zone so that the troops will be minimally disoriented when they finally arrive at their various operational bases for their combat mission in "the box."

But all the romantic Hollywood illusions of war notwithstanding, we would learn quickly that war had a healthy measure of boredom, downtime, and tedium. And we also learned that much of our duties in war were not as urgent as certain people sometimes try to portray them. Urgency is usually driven by the unknown or by anxious leaders, who tend to fear any aspect of war that they do not thoroughly understand or control. Once the unknown becomes known, we tend to relax, to settle into routine.

For now, we were already strangers in a strange land. This part of Kuwait in which we were training was several miles south of the Iraqi border. Since most of southern Iraq was arid desert with few towns, and maybe a few clans of Bedouins, the camp was considered fairly safe territory. Any significant incursion by Iraqi insurgents would have to cross many miles of open desert where they would be naked to all of our passive, stationary, and active human or technological intelligence gathering capabilities. So it was a pretty low threat environment.

But it is always better to be safe than sorry, and military culture usually does not casually permit unnecessary risks, always expecting the unexpected, and trying to prepare for the unpredictable. Moreover, with the omnipresent international jihadist fighters who were constantly streaming into the region for their Islamic jihad fight against the infidels, we might encounter an extremist threat virtually anywhere at any time. Consequently, we usually required armed and armored escort for any troop bus movement, or even smaller leader movements, to other Kuwaiti locations, even though this was considered safe territory. And all transportation was by ground since our unit did not yet have dedicated air assets (army helicopters), since all those assets were committed to the fight within the box (the Iraqi borders, regions, and towns).

Our main focus while in Kuwait would be the training. While transiting Kuwait into Iraq, all soldiers underwent extensive compulsory training, even though we had achieved most of the same training before departing our home base. Most of it seemed logical, necessary, and useful, but there was also a fair amount of annoying military filler and redundancy that seemed to have little purpose or little added value. It was somewhat frustrating to some troops to repeat many mundane, tedious training tasks, which we had recently completed back at Fort Bragg, but it was doubly frustrating to experience the long delays in getting into Iraq and engaging our mission after we had been told repeatedly how urgent it was for us to be there yesterday. Most of us gamely or stoically accepted these experiences just as we patiently endured many things in the military because, after a few years in the service, you just become impervious to unexpected and annoying events (or people) as you realize it's just part of the culture.

In any case, this last-minute training was one final check to make damn certain soldiers were ready before they crossed that line into the box where the stakes became life or death. So the training did take on a new sense of urgency. Also, the training landscape would bring us much closer to the terrain and weather of Iraq than would our home station of Fort Bragg, North Carolina, with its balmy weather and pine trees. It goes without saying that the training was important, but I think it was equally important to our leaders for us to acclimate to the region, the heat, the cold, the aridity, the dust, the new time zone, the change in creature comforts and infrastructure, and, of course, the separation from all those whom we loved.

Camp Virginia, Kuwait—Life in Tent City

About 1700 hours, after a long, monotonous bus ride, we finally arrived at Camp Virginia, our new home for the next two weeks. We had the luxury of a shave and shower, which was very welcome after our almost twenty-four-hour odyssey by aircraft. We would also be able to get out of our duty uniform and into our physical training uniform, which is arguably more comfortable. There were also some very Spartan entertainment and communication facilities at Camp Virginia, among which was a post exchange where we could find a few creature comforts and a free Internet area (which was usually too crowded, so many used the pay-as-you-go Internet café).

Also, we were released without specific guidance to a number of tents where we could stake out our own personal area with our cot and military gear, but we were pretty much left to fend for ourselves in finding a good sleeping spot among those tents.

Ironically, with all of the tedious planning that we did, we didn't focus too much on the transitional stage in Kuwait. I think the amount of time spent there and the requirements that we had to check off before going over the berm caught many by surprise. Most of the soldiers were in football-field-sized tents with dozens of people. In such an environment, it was difficult to sleep owing to the infinite variability of people's habits. Additionally, some people were simply disoriented, so they would walk in and out of the tents at all times of the night.

Still, others had no sense of manners or common courtesy for their fellow soldiers, talking out loud and turning on lights when they came in at 0200 or 0300 hours. Some were more careful, using flashlights and trying hard to move quietly. Of course, if you're tired enough, it's surprising what you can get used to. One issue that we had to get used to was the separate female tent. In their wisdom, the leaders had placed all female soldiers in one tent and all the males in the other tents. There are good reasons for this. Both genders needed a little more privacy without the opposite gender present. Also, there was always an unpredictable threat from some male soldiers away from home and girlfriends or wives to sexually assault female soldiers.

But the main issue for the command was to avoid even mutual hookups among male and female soldiers. Such sexual relationships can cause numerous morale problems within the unit. We even had one suicide once we were in Iraq from a soldier distraught about the combat environment and the relationship that he had developed with a female soldier. Of course, I was to have my eyes opened when some of my female soldiers informed me about certain incidents with other females who appeared to be hitting on them. I guess that, since soldiers are people too, there is no way to totally avoid any and all misconduct and wild ideas or lifestyles.

But we all accepted the issue of the separate female tent as a necessity. It was somewhat inconvenient when one was trying to contact a female soldier for legitimate mission reasons, or even just trying to see if the soldier was in the tent while you were checking on the welfare of all of your soldiers. That is, it was inconvenient for people who were trying to be conscientious and trying to respect the female soldiers' privacy. As I soon found out, some of the males didn't worry about inconveniencing anyone. Some simply charged into the tent without the typical loud warning "male in the tent" that would precede entering and normally followed by a short pause to allow women to cover up if they were in the process of changing or allow them enough time to object and tell you to wait. But among the problems with males coming into the female tent, there were male soldiers who simply spent too many hours there with their female friends or girlfriends. I felt sorry for the female soldiers. Even though they ostensibly had their separate and private tent, in effect, they had very little privacy.

For the male soldiers, the situation was better since males were in the majority anyway and had more tents to choose from. Ironically, the female soldiers tended to be much more respectful of our privacy than some of our male soldiers were of theirs. But we would all suffer from the same biological issues, regardless of gender. For instance, I would not get much sleep that night because, like many others, my biological clock would take several days to even begin to reset. Also, I was anxious to contact my family to let them know I had arrived in Kuwait safely, so I was willing to sacrifice a little sleep to get the comforting contact of my family's voices. Moreover, I was just too pumped up about the overall experience and the tasks ahead of us.

Although I was still adjusting to the separation from my family, Kuwait offered a new adventure, something I had never experienced before. Initially, I had a sense of exhilaration from the strangeness of everything. I did manage to send my wife an e-mail within hours of arrival to the camp. Then I was fortunate enough to run into an old friend who directed me to a much smaller tent where he was sleeping, and, with my arrival, there would only be eight people in the tent. This smaller, more comfortable sleeping arrangement would be much more conducive to relaxation and sleep, although that was not the biggest of my worries. However, it also afforded me the luxury of relative privacy, something that would be a rarity for the next twelve months ahead of me.

For the first full day, I was still jet-lagged, so I got in a few catnaps before it was time to get up again. Then I got up early at four thirty in the morning local time, donned my physical fitness uniform, which would give me some physical comfort and the comfort of anonymity. For an officer, it can sometimes be annoying to constantly respond to the military courtesy of saluting and correcting those who didn't salute, etc. Sometimes, I just preferred the anonymity of just being a regular Joe.

The phone and Internet facilities were a half-mile hike across a sandy field (and I use the word *field* very loosely—it was just an open area of ground upon which nothing had been built). Walking across this sandy area in spite of our great level of fitness was really challenging. It was like walking three or four times the distance because you could not get good traction on the deep, lubricious, mutable sand.

Upon arriving to the phone center, signing in, and getting into a freed-up booth within a few minutes, I was able to get a call through to my wife, Lesia. I talked to her and the kids briefly. They would be going to bed soon just as my day was beginning. It was a strange thought that most of my day would be played out before they were finished with their night's sleep. We spoke for a few minutes and then said our good-byes. These short phone conversations were always bittersweet. I got a little moral boost as well as emotional and spiritual comfort from hearing my wife's voice and the voices of my children, but when it came time to say good-bye, I felt a wave of deep anguish rush over me, a small piece of that painful departure day separation. I missed them so much. It felt like a piece of my heart was missing, but like most of my fellow troops, I just packed away the bad feelings and refused to acknowledge them because dwelling on them would just produce unnecessary anxiety.

Shortly afterward, I had to go to our first morning formation. But there were too many questions unanswered about our schedule or our eventual entry into Iraq, so there was nothing for us to do after this formation until 12:50 PM. I went back to our tent and tried to take the guilty pleasure of a nap. However, I was soon reminded that I would not have much control over my own schedule. I ran into my boss on the way to the 12:50 formation, and he was his usual nervous, frustrated, boisterous self. To his defense though, this would prove to be a frustrating place. The camp was, as I noted, very Spartan. There were few communication facilities, which would make it hard to contact our own people inbound to Kuwait at this camp and, likewise, those we were due to replace in a few weeks in Iraq. And the small camp was big enough to make it a challenge to cover all possible places where you might be looking for someone. All too often, you might arrive at a particular place looking for someone only to find out that they had been there but had departed a few minutes prior. So, you were forced to continue this cat-and-mouse game of trying to find someone, even though you knew it was futile.

After our 12:50 formation, we were directed to take care of certain administrative processing to get our combat zone allowances and to get ready for our entry into Iraq. We went to a large tent building with desks and a hard floor of plywood where we filled out some family separation paperwork and other such forms. These forms would make sure that we got all our combat pay allowances, which would prove to be very substantial no matter what rank you were. After that, instead of returning to my tent, I tried to track a few people in the ongoing cat-and-mouse game. With no established way of communicating with each other and the fact that no one had anticipated this difficulty, there was no plan in place to ameliorate the problem.

Over the days though, we developed habits such that you could determine when best to find anyone at a given location. Plus, we did have a central, somewhat Spartan workspace with an actual office, chairs, and computers for each section, so we finally got a schedule established for this area to be manned at all times of the day. Additionally, as you would expect with any army unit, there were always briefings that we had to conduct. They were primarily just "dog and pony shows," as we say in the military, but the briefings gave a sense of comfort to our constantly worried senior leaders who had nothing else to do here in the transitional stage but worry. So we did the briefings and were glad that there wasn't anything more serious to be concerned about at present.

Adjusting to the new environment and the absence of family and various creature comforts and getting through training and into Iraq safely were concern enough. But without more significant work to occupy us, the days seemed to drag by interminably, even though it was only a couple of weeks. The problem was that we didn't know how long we would be there, and we were very anxious to get on to the real mission. A lesson which I had already learned from my years of army duty, a lesson I would encounter many times prior and since, was that the unknown is usually the most demoralizing problem that soldiers can face. No matter how hard you try to prepare for the unknown and fill in the blank spaces, there are always things that you couldn't foresee, and there are always things that make no sense anyway until you experience them for yourself.

The training too was ill-planned in some cases partly because there were several lower level leaders who were arguing over who was responsible for the actual training, scheduling, and coordination of it. You would think this would be one of those details that would have been discussed among the thousands of things we addressed before leaving our home station, but as with all things in the military, in spite of all our training, discipline, and professionalism, we are still people and, therefore, inherently flawed and prone to mistakes. In any case, now that we realized the omission, instead of certain people just stepping up to the plate and accepting responsibility, you had various NCOs and officers engaged in a turf battle. Granted, part of the whole argument was valid, since we were all a team and we had the legitimate moral expectation that all team members would step up and do their job. But unfortunately, there was a fair number of people in our unit that just did not care about anything that could not be pinned on them directly as their responsibility. Some of them were always working angles. They were more worried about showing how smart or important they were than they were about their responsibilities, the mission, and the team they were a part of. Such is life.

Unfortunately, we would find out that some would choose to help themselves before they thought of others. Perhaps, they were overwhelmed like everyone else was, but this gets to one of the things that really differentiates the character of people in such an environment. It's so easy to put on a façade of being a good leader or a good soldier in the rear when you never have to pretend for very long, but when the pressure is on in a combat environment, it becomes almost impossible to pretend anymore. You no longer have the various crutches or escapes that might help you maintain a façade back at the home station.

Additionally, we all faced the same problem of lacking our normal moral support structures and people. You no longer have the comfort of your family and friends, except for the ones that are in your unit. You no longer have the relief of, at least, the nightly and weekend escape from the pressure cooker of a job and maybe a good stiff drink, or two, or three. The high-ranking general officers over the theater had put puritanical standards in place, which put alcohol off-limits for Iraq and Afghanistan presumably because they were more worried about offending the sensibilities of the Muslims in these countries than they were about the comfort of their troops. I believe this is the first time in military history that our troops have been completely denied the comfort of alcohol during a war.

And ironically enough, I'll bet that most of the higher-ranking generals who set this policy do not have to give up alcohol for very long, since they have their many flights back to the States or other friendly areas where they can drink. For example, in the June 22, 2010 *Rolling Stone* article on General Stanley McChrystal[1], he and his staff made time for pubbing at Kitty O'Shea's in Paris, while none of the soldiers under his command back in the combat zone would have even been allowed one single beer. In fact, if any had been caught with alcohol in the combat zone, they would have been harshly punished under the UCMJ, while some of their general officer leaders were apparently living it up.

In addition to the denied comfort of alcohol, troops generally never have any real rest while in the box, since they can never fully relax during the day from all the stress and danger and can't completely relax at night with the constant possibility of mortars and rockets at any given time and the sporadic invasion of their sleep time for various operational reasons at any hour of the night. Throughout our deployment, I would be awakened many times at night to answer questions or deal with situations that just would not wait. Moreover, you never have any real peace or quiet, even in your sleeping quarters with the constant barrage of noises in a military environment.

Among the sounds you hear are the sporadically inbound helicopters and the ever-constant generators running to power up the numerous pieces of equipment, to power the combat command and control centers, and even to power the living quarters and the few creature comfort facilities that are available. There is also the constant sound of the crunch of gravel and military vehicles moving here and there at all hours of the night with various missions being run out of and into the gates of the compound. The sound of all this reaches into every corner of the small base, since the various staging areas for vehicles are, due to necessity, always near the sleeping quarters and the command and control centers. There are the unpredictable, sporadic sounds of explosions from incoming mortars and rockets launched by insurgents into the base from outside the wire. There are the sounds of the various sirens to warn of incoming mortars and rockets and, afterward, to notify everyone when all is clear. There are the sounds of munition explosions almost every day as confiscated arms caches are destroyed at designated munitions disposal sites. There is occasionally the sound of weapons firing if you live near the ranges on base or if you live near the perimeter where they occasionally fire at attempted incursions, or what even appears to be an attempted incursion. There is even the occasional sound of misfired weapons, since everyone is moving around on base with weapons loaded with ammo. Lastly, there are the sounds of weather, such as the strong winds during shamal season or thunder and lightning strikes during the short rainy season in winter. In time, you forget what quiet really sounds like.

Without even the possibility of peace and quiet, there is never the comfort of any real, significant escape, since noises, dangers, and demands of your time and effort are always on you or they can spring upon you when you least expect. It is no wonder then that so many develop PTSD, even if they never leave the relative safety of the base perimeter. Even if you are in that relatively safe environment, you are still bombarded night and day with danger and sensory stimulation, things that take away your peace, almost ensuring that you never relax. Since you never relax, this sets up the pressure cooker inside your body with adrenaline constantly pumping, and it is this constant state of arousal that can easily lead to PTSD as our fight-or-flight processes get stuck in the on position. Of course, this constant state of arousal can happen to anyone in a high pressure environment other than combat zones where you never completely relax, never quite feel safe. It can happen in abusive environments for women or children. It can happen to the police officer who patrols or works in dangerous areas for extended periods of time or to the paramedic who deals with trauma on a regular basis for, perhaps, months at a time with little relief.

In all these cases, the hypothalamus located in your brain recognizes the danger situation and sends a signal to the adrenal glands, which sit atop the kidneys. It tells them to release certain chemicals (such as adrenaline/epinephrine/norepinephrine), which tell all your bodily systems to get ready for explosive fight-or-flight demands and gives the muscles their strength and quickness to react to this danger. The glands also release cortisol, which primarily makes your various body organs and systems release energy or convert other compounds to energy in the form of glucose, the sugar that your muscles can quickly burn for whatever action is needed. What normally happens with the average person is that the adrenaline and cortisol rush only last for a set period of time, maybe a few minutes until you are out of danger. Then the body gradually takes these chemicals back out of your system allowing you to relax. However, with the person under extended pressure, under continuous, relentless adrenaline surges without relief, he or she can eventually develop PTSD as the body becomes hardwired in this constant state of arousal.

Of course, while we remained in Kuwait, we had not yet reached the real pressure cooker of living in the combat zone. We still had a few more days to endure our mundane, boring, but safe purgatory.

In the meantime, not all was bad about our stay in Kuwait. There were times of humor and laughter. One amusing incident occurred to me one night on the way to the telephone and Internet areas to make contact with my wife. It was funny and not funny at the same time. I was walking alone, my mind drifting, leaning into the strong wind, and just focusing on keeping my balance between the wind and the shifting sand. I was doggedly trudging through the darkness toward the area light outside the phone center a third of a mile away. All of a sudden, I was aware of a liquid droplets blowing against my leg, which seemed very strange given the arid desert that was all around me. It was then that I realized a truck was driving along beside me, upwind with about a thirty-foot separation between us. I thought at first that there was some fuel or other such liquid blowing off of the truck. Then I realized—this was one of those trucks that pumped out the port-a-potties to keep them clean. The instantaneous horror and disgust of what was spraying on my legs forced me into a desperate scramble to get out of the target area. For one brief moment, I was the fastest man alive.

Finding Beauty in the Desert

Not all about Kuwait was bad. In spite of my growing annoyance with the sand that got into anything and everything—oddly, even things that were very tightly wrapped—there was still something beautiful and serenely peaceful about the sparse desert environment. I remember one training exercise in which we had to go to the field, which was just another sandy, barren desert area a few miles away from the sandy, barren desert where our camp was situated. Normally, when one refers to the field, he means that he is leaving a comfortable place with walls, furniture, and climate control, and going to an uncomfortable place somewhere out in nature. Of course, there was no forest here, but it was hard to distinguish between the comfortable and the uncomfortable—the home base and the field. When we did go out, it didn't seem that much different from being at Camp Virginia in terms of scenery and creature comfort, unless you want to consider the steadily building stench of unbathed soldiers who go through sweaty training without access to showers. However, one can quickly get used to his or her own stench and that of others. You don't even notice it after a while.

The first day out in the field, we trained on weapons and then we bivouacked at the training site where our instructors (civilians who were retired soldiers) would be out bright and early the next morning. There was only one tent that was large enough for maybe half of the group. Others found space on the backs of vehicles in the surrounding area, especially the beds of the large troop transporter trucks. Everyone instinctively suspected that being on the ground in this environment might not be ideal, given the stories we had already heard about vipers, rats, wolf spiders, etc.

Those in the tent felt that they had scored a victory. They could sleep on the carpets that were on the floor or on the platform tables. Plus, they had a heater. This being the winter, the desert could be quite cold at night, since there were no trees and no buildings or asphalt/concrete to hold in the heat built up during the day. What the tent people hadn't counted on though was the presence of mice that were attracted to the concentrated area of food droppings from people eating there on previous training sessions. One of my officers later related to me the night's excitement when a few mice decided to investigate the sleeping visitors as they searched for food.

For my part, I was not quick enough to find a good place, but I finally found a place in the back of an uncovered Humvee. I snuggled up into my sleeping bag, glad to be out of the cool air. I had closed the opening of the bag and buried my face inside where I was cozy and warm. But I soon found I couldn't get to sleep, my body clock still adjusting to this new time zone. Opening my bag back up and exposing my face, I began to look around. For the first time, I noticed that a full moon had risen almost directly overhead. Gazing at the beautiful moon, the clear, starry skies and the glowing landscape of dunes, I felt a sense of peace at the beauty, as if God was there with me in person and talking to me, whispering to me through all of this stark, quiet beauty that He loved me. I prayed a quick prayer and closed my eyes, dropping quickly into a deep and peaceful sleep.

In addition to this amazingly beautiful night, two days later, I experienced another interesting incident that would remind me that there is beauty everywhere on this amazing earth that God has created. During another training exercise, part of this field time, we were lined up in a convoy of some twenty vehicles. We were waiting to enter a training area of makeshift buildings that were designed to look like an Iraqi village where we would perform a live fire exercise. Live fire exercises consisted of a set number of scenarios, with participants firing (only at designated safe areas in which there would be building mock-ups and people-shaped pop-ups). The mock-up buildings were on both sides of the road. In order to keep soldiers from firing dangerously or indiscriminately from their positions on the vehicles, we were each assigned to fire on only one side of the road, and we were instructed in precisely what time frame or conditions we would be firing (our "rules of engagement"). We were not allowed to switch from one side to the other once we were assigned a position. Also, as part of the exercise, when we entered these areas with the mock-up towns, we had to positively identify a threat before we could fire on the pop-up. For instance, we had to look for a gun or other such indicators of hostility. Some of the pop-up targets would be civilians without weapons, whom we were, of course, not supposed to fire at. We were trying to train up to the established rules of engagement for the area we would be operating in and learning to distinguish at instant glance civilian from enemy combatant.

We were forced to wait a couple of hours to begin this exercise since a very strong sandstorm had cranked up shortly before our arrival to the training area. We had pulled on our heavy goggles and tightened down the straps as tightly as they would go (sand will get into anything). We all had either wrapped the long T-shirt material scarf around our heads or wore the balaclava, which could be wrapped around the face and underneath the helmet and then tucked around the goggles so that very little, if any, skin was exposed to the sand. It was important to protect the eyes and the mouth, especially when these sandstorms picked up.

The visibility was down to only about thirty to forty feet. I sat immobile, alternating between looking down and watching the sand that followed the ground, writhing and undulating like some kind of snake or dirt river, or watching the brown wall of sand, marveling at its impenetrability and wondering just how long the storm could last. As I was watching and waiting like some kind of a specter, a Bedouin shepherd suddenly appeared from out of the wall of sand and moved slowly across the dirt road behind our convoy, his sheep stumbling behind him and around him. His sudden appearance and the incongruity of such a pastoral scene of a shepherd and his sheep made the scene so surreal. I noticed that, unlike me and all of my comrades, he merely had part of his headdress wrapped around his mouth, but he had no protection for his eyes. He seemed impervious to the stinging sand and so cavalier and at ease with the sandstorm— just another day for him.

At the same time, he seemed amused by our careful (and futile) attempts to block out all of the sand. A brief exchange took place between the shepherd and one of our sergeants who had walked out to engage the man. Of course, neither spoke the other's language, but I have found from all my travels that there is a universal language that transcends all language and cultural barriers—a friendly smile, a non-threatening body language expressing curiosity about and respect for the other person, and maybe a handshake. Before the Bedouin departed, our sergeant offered him some bottled water, a simple gesture of friendship, a small gift that the man accepted graciously. Then, as quickly as he appeared out of the wall of sand, he and his sheep disappeared again, as if they were stepping into a cloud. The suddenness of their appearance and departure made it seem as if they had all been a dream, a conjuration of some powerful genie from an Arabic folktale.

The sandstorm eventually abated, and we were able to commence our training. With the greatly increased visibility, I now saw with admiration that the area we were training in had undulating hills, unlike the flat, sandy desert back at camp. I was surprised at how beautiful it was. Also, I remember noting at certain flat places in the terrain, where the land was flat for several miles in one direction, that the blue of the sky was reflected in a mirage, making it appear as if there was a vast, beautiful sea less than a mile away. It looked like a placid sea of glass—peaceful and serene.

In the Queue for Flight to Iraq and a Miracle

After we returned to home base from our training, we found out that we were already in the queue to begin movement into Iraq. This would entail taking a C-130 from Ali Al Saleem Air Base in Kuwait and flying an hour or so into Balad Air Base just north of Baghdad, Iraq. I think it was an hour-and-a-half flight. But to make the trip, we had to be scheduled onto a flight and hope that the aircraft would neither be on deadline for repairs nor would we be bumped off of the flight for people or materials that were higher priority. Both of these occurrences were distinct possibilities.

But there was another issue that I had to confront. I had to decide who would go with me to Iraq on the first flight. Since I would be one of the first from our unit bound for Iraq, I was only allowed to take one person with me. Unfortunately, I had two key leaders whom I needed with me—my deputy and my sergeant major. Moreover, I was concerned about how my choice would appear to whichever one that I did not pick to go with me. They both held critical positions and were indispensable to me. Both were highly motivated, very intelligent, well-accomplished, and capable professionals, but the last thing I wanted was a morale issue as soon as I hit the ground with either one feeling insulted by my choice. In the end, I chose based on the knowledge and skill sets that I would immediately need when we got on the ground in Iraq, and both of them handled the situation graciously like the true professionals that they were.

About this time too, I had another more pressing problem. In my second week in Kuwait, I developed a backache—or, at least, I thought it was a backache. I took some anti-inflammatory drugs (ibuprofen) that I already had in my backpack, but the pain became more and more intense over the days. I went to the doctor who gave me a strong muscle relaxer and some very strong pain medicine, but somehow the pain managed to break through all of that, leaving me unable to sleep, work, or even think.

Finally, I made a more insistent trip to the medic. The navy was running the small hospital there. A young navy doctor came over to examine me. After a few questions, he asked me to point to the place where I was feeling the pain. He then told me to relax just before he rendered me one of the most painful sensations I'd ever experienced. He proceeded to dig his thumbs into the spot where my kidney was. A bolt of pain shot through me as if I'd been stabbed by a large jagged knife. I jumped a foot off the table, and, from my obvious pain as well as my frantic reaction to that pain, the doctor ingeniously concluded that I probably had kidney stones. He said that they had diagnosed several cases of people passing through the area with kidney stones, and his theory was that the problem was due to the bottled water we were drinking, which had a very high mineral content.

It was nice to know what was wrong, but now I was very concerned. What would happen to me if there were indeed kidney stones? I did not want to be medevaced anywhere after only having been in the theater for two weeks, and I was also doubly concerned with how it would look to my people and others if I were medevaced out. I did not want to give out any appearance or suggestion that I was apprehensive or unenthusiastic about my mission in Iraq (i.e. that I was malingering). Plus, even if medical treatment were not avoidable, what would my people do? I'm sure they could have figured it out, but they had already gone through too much with my unprofessional predecessor, poor leader that he was. I knew they could have muddled through, but I did not want them to be leaderless at this critical juncture no matter what I had to do.

I prayed very hard to be delivered from this, and I told my wife who prayed for me and had others praying. Unfortunately, within twenty-four hours of telling my wife about this ordeal, I was notified that I was on the manifest for the aircraft flight into Balad, Iraq, the following day. I was still in extreme pain, but I also still had a determination not to let anyone down. So, I had a decision to make. I either had to hide my pain and get on that aircraft as planned, or I had to make an issue of my problem and possibly get medevaced. I was so acutely aware of how this might look. I didn't want anyone to think I was shirking—not my subordinates, not my boss, and not my peers. This last thought weighed the heaviest on my mind and heart and subsequently convinced me of what I had to do. I decided that, pain or no pain, I was leaving for Iraq the next day.

That night, our flight was confirmed. We would definitely be on the flight the following night. So, we passed a restless night of anticipation and got up bleary-eyed the next day. We tried to stay occupied during the day, restlessly conscious of the fact that we might be departing any moment (the exact time of the flight not yet being established). That evening, the time finally came for us to load our baggage and equipment. The austere contract busses were lined up outside our tent city, awaiting the loading of our baggage—two duffel bags of equipment and a carry-on or backpack for most of us. We loaded up and then departed for a much-longer-than-expected bus drive to Ali Al Salem Air Base. We had military police or Kuwaiti army escorts the entire way. Nothing was left to chance, even in the friendly "safe" area of Kuwait. In fact, we had been told about an incident that had occurred less than a year earlier in which a soldier was gunned down during a supposed traffic stop by a terrorist impersonating a Kuwaiti policeman.

So nothing could be left to chance. Our escort took us to a transit point near the airfield where we got out, used the bathroom, smoked, and chatted while waiting for the approval to enter the base and the final escort that would get us to the flight line. Like many of the leaders, I stood off by myself. I preferred to stay alone and think with so much on my mind, the mountainous list of tasks I would have to accomplish upon arrival into Iraq to get my people housed, get them oriented to our work spaces, and get them trained and motivated for their jobs and the overall mission. And as if I didn't have enough to think about, my back was still throbbing with excruciating, stabbing pain. I tried to move as slowly and carefully as possible to keep from setting off the spasms of pain.

After almost an hour in our assembly/waiting area, we finally got our escort and permission to enter the base. We were all getting a little frayed around the edges from the long day, but we kept our heads in the game. Soldiers endure amazing amounts of pressure for long periods and learn to still keep their composure despite the pressure, knowing that they have important tasks to accomplish, momentous responsibilities to their unit and their country, a deep commitment to their comrades, and even the inevitable danger that might pop up at any moment to which they might have to respond.

Once we moved onto the air base, there were still a couple of groups in front of us for priority of aircraft. To make good use of the waiting time, we worked on palletizing our large baggage (duffel bags, etc.). This entailed loading baggage on top of a wooden pallet tightly and structurally interlocked for stability, and as evenly balanced as possible. Any shift in the contents of one of several pallets on board an aircraft could cause a problem for the stability of the aircraft. Everyone seemed to be chipping in regardless of rank. I didn't want to appear selfish or arrogant, so, in spite of my excruciating pain from the kidney stones, I gamely tried to help out in carrying a few of the heavy bags to the pallet.

A strange thing happened at that point. I felt the stabbing, excruciating pain with every stride and began to think that this might not be such a bright idea. I prayed one more prayer silently in my head. Then, all of a sudden, the pain vanished. At first, I thought it might be a trick of my imagination, so I cautiously continued work with the bags, moving very carefully with each lift and toss, expecting at any moment for the horrendous pain to return. But the pain never did return. I could probably attempt to devise a rational explanation, but I remember the exquisite brutality of the pain and the inadequacy of the pain medications to bring me significant relief for several days as well as the inexplicable, sudden cessation of this horrible pain. Knowing all this, I just can't accept any frivolous explanation. I believe that whatever was wrong (most likely a kidney stone) was miraculously taken away by God in a humble display of His tremendous power and His boundless love for me. In any case, I was so relieved that the problem was gone. I would not have to seek medical help for resolution of this problem and would be able to fulfill my leadership responsibilities to my people and my unit without distraction.

In short order, we had all the bags stacked and balanced. We then threw a heavy cargo net over the top of the mound of equipment and baggage and cinched it down on all four sides very tightly. Once this process was completed to the satisfaction of the Air Force troops who were supervising our work, then everyone could go off to rest in the waiting area and await our call for our flight.

The rest area was two large Quonset huts beside the lot where our pallets rested, waiting to be picked up and transported to our aircraft. The huts had cold water, dozens of nylon army cots set up for the troops to rest, and power for lighting and electronic devices, which a small group of soldiers had already taken advantage of as they gathered around the small screen of a laptop to watch a DVD movie. Perhaps, more importantly, there was an opportunity to eat. There were boxes of various Meal, Ready-to-Eat or MREs stacked in one area of the hut so that we could indulge as we desired, satiating our hunger from the busy activity of palletizing and the long day. MREs are generally pretty good given the constraints in which they must be prepared and packaged, but soldiers will always take part in the time-honored tradition of griping about the chow. Subsequently, some anonymous, sharp-witted soldier had, at some point, humorously dubbed them "Meals Rejected by Everyone."

Since our pallet had been inspected by the Air Force flight crew and deemed to be sufficient, we were released to the temporary oasis of the Quonset huts, our holding area and an opportunity for well-needed rest, although I didn't understand for the life of me how anyone could have rested. I was still too pumped up on adrenaline, anxiously wanting to get out of Kuwait and to reach Iraq so that I could begin my deployment mission and responsibilities.

After what seemed like an eternity, the group in front of us was called on the loudspeakers for their flight. After two more eternities, we were called, upon which we scrambled for our bags and the Quonset hut's exit. Once outside and in the lot or makeshift assembly area, we were loaded onto a bus with an airman driver who was part of the airfield control personnel. Our pallets would be picked up and delivered to our aircraft in short order. After a painfully slow ride and another forty-five minutes of waiting, an airman finally guided us onto the airfield at Ali Al Salem Air Base within a short distance of our waiting C-130.

At this point, we were given a few instructions and were released to disembark the bus and quickly grab our carry-on bags or backpacks that had been held in the bus's stowage compartment, to march in an informal line, and to lean forward into the winds of the powerful, hot prop wash from the spinning propellers as we walked up the ramp into the rear of the aircraft. Walking into the back of a C-130 is like walking into a very hot hurricane. It's always a relief to finally get through the force of the hot blast of the prop wash so that you can walk upright and without encumbrance again. And it's a relief to fight your way through the gauntlet of rules, regulations, and requirements to finally board a military aircraft and settle into the comparatively comfortable jump seats with the assurance that you have finally begun your journey to reach your destination.

A C-130 is not the most comfortable of conveyances, but, so long as the turbulence is not too bad, it's a reasonably good ride. The bad part is the cold or heat in the cargo/passenger area. Sometimes, the cooling and heating systems aren't that great. And sometimes, the pilots have to conserve energy for whatever reason and divert it from the climate control systems. Of course, there might be one other explanation—that the crew just got some perverse pleasure in screwing with the passengers—but I prefer not to believe that one.

In the cargo area of a C-130, there are aluminum-framed rumble seats that can be folded up or disassembled depending on the use of the aircraft (i.e. for paratroopers on a jump, for regular troops flying into military operational areas, or for carrying pallets of cargo of virtually anything to wherever those supplies might be needed for either military or humanitarian purposes). Sitting in the jump seats is relatively comfortable so long as you aren't packed together with other troops like sardines in a can with your knees touching and bent rigidly and uncomfortably for a long flight. If that happens, your misery index rises very rapidly and remains high until the aircraft touches down and vomits you out onto some runway where you are eternally grateful to the Lord that you have survived.

We were fortunate though. The entire middle section of the aircraft (which could have been set up for more seats for the sardine effect or for more equipment) had been disassembled, leaving us plenty of leg room, so now all we had to do was to put the earplugs in tightly (the C-130 is very loud in flight). And, perhaps, we might actually get some sleep on the short flight to Iraq.

Finally, some twelve hours after we left the dismal confines of Camp Virginia, we were rolling down the runway for a one-and-a-half to two-and-a-half-hour flight to our home for the next year. The length of the flight would depend on anti-aircraft threats. Occasionally, you might be in an aircraft that gets a radar lock-on. The C-130s at the time were equipped with flares, which could then be fired from the sides of the aircraft. These flares would create a heat signature that would attract any inbound heat-seeking missiles, diverting them from locking on the hot exhaust of the aircraft. It's always a little unsettling to be on board an aircraft when they start firing these flares. And although I would experience over time a few flights in which the flares were employed, fortunately for us, this flight was entirely uneventful.

Arrival in Balad, Iraq

We arrived in Balad, Iraq in the dark, almost 1200 hours at night. We were all very tired and disoriented. We walked from the aircraft to a large reception tent. We filled out some paperwork, signed some papers, were greeted by our counterparts whom we would replace, and then we set off to reclaim our baggage from the pallets we had earlier assembled and which had been off-loaded from the aircraft.

After retrieving our bags, we loaded them onto the waiting busses or trucks, and then we were off to the battalion headquarters to meet a welcoming committee. This would be a short meeting, since we were absolutely exhausted, and it was late at night for them as well. You can ride the adrenaline wave for incredibly long periods of time when it is required for training or mission events. But sooner or later, everyone hits the wall. Most of us had hit the wall finally. I made some polite conversation with my counterpart, found the master of the keys, and got my quarters assignment, a small prefabricated room or hut (like a small recreational trailer) grouped among similar huts for high-ranking personnel. Thankfully, I didn't have far to walk. Also, we were thankful that many of us would end up in the prefab huts that had recently been erected. The army was doing its best to get people out of the dusty tents. One thing I've discovered over the years is that the army is always good at improving bases in combat zones or operational areas of the various foreign countries where we have combat or humanitarian missions. And they don't stop improving until the base is quite bearable—not as good as being at home but not bad, all things considered.

I quickly found my hut and my bed. I would be sharing the hut with another officer of equal rank, but each of us actually had our own room. We even had a small bathroom and shower that we would share. For the first time in weeks, I could actually use a porcelain toilet as opposed to the ubiquitous porta-potties that we had become accustomed to in Kuwait. My room had some very simple furniture, but it did have a bed with a mattress. For the first time in weeks, I would be on a mattress instead of a nylon cot or a floor. Things were not looking too bad. Living conditions were not as bad as they could have been. I had finally made it out of Kuwait. I was no longer bedeviled by the pain in my side. Plus, I had finally survived the chaos and the long gauntlet line of military requirements and processes required for entry into the combat zone of Iraq. I felt like I had already been tried in the fire, being a survivor of the seemingly endless, tedious requirements and processes that apparently conferred upon me the genial but certainly undeserved privilege and permission to graciously enter the exalted kingdom of combat. Nonetheless, I had finally arrived at my new home for the next year. All things considered, I knew I could be worse off, so I was relatively happy at my present circumstances and found no trouble getting to sleep at the end of this whirlwind day.

The Iraq War, Our Mission, and the Telling of History

To fully understand our deployment, you would have to comprehend some contextual, background information. The occupation of Iraq started in summer 2003 after the invasion and combat operations related to the invasion drew to a close (March 19, 2003 to May 1, 2003). Upon conclusion of this short war, it became readily apparent that the civilians who led us into this effort to invade Iraq and the top-level military leaders did not have a good plan of what to do once they defeated the organized forces of the Iraqis (this has been extensively covered by such authors as Thomas E. Ricks in his 2006 book *Fiasco*[1]). Also, our military and civilian leaders made some pretty bad mistakes in the beginning, such as the extensive de-Baathification program (i.e. refusing to work with anyone who was a member of Saddam Hussein's or Iraq's Ba'ath Party).

From the *Encyclopædia Britannica* online, accessed March 6, 2014, the Ba'th Party, also spelled *Ba'ath*, is also known by its more formal name the "Arab Socialist Ba'th Party or Arab Socialist Ba'th (Renaissance) Party, Arabic Hizb Al-Ba'th Al-Arabī Al-Ishtirākī…"[2] It was an "Arab political party advocating the formation of a single Arab socialist nation. It has branches in many Middle Eastern countries and was the ruling party in Syria from 1963 and in Iraq from 1968 to 2003. The Ba'th Party was founded in 1943 in Damascus, Syria, by Michel Aflaq and Salah al-Dīn al-Bīṭār, adopted its constitution in 1947, and in 1953 merged with the Syrian Socialist Party to form the Arab Socialist

Ba'th (Renaissance) Party. The Ba'th Party espoused nonalignment and opposition to imperialism and colonialism, took inspiration from what it considered the positive values of Islam, and attempted to ignore or transcend class divisions. Its structure was highly centralized and authoritarian."[3]

Saddam Hussein was the formal leader of the Ba'ath Party in Iraq, and it is probably this fact which motivated military and civilian leaders of the Iraq War to reject any participation of these former officials, reasoning that they may have been complicit in Hussein's tyrannical rule of the Iraqi people. Presumably, they were making the correlation between these political and government leaders and the Nazi leaders in World War II Germany, many of whom were actually complicit in war atrocities. However, this was not a safe assumption, given the history which we now know about the brutal rule and harsh tactics that Hussein inflicted, even on those who worked close with him and were in his "circle of trust." In that environment of brutality and fear, hardly anyone could be considered to be a free agent acting with complete liberty and autonomy.

In any case, the refusal to include any former Ba'ath Party members in the new Iraqi government and army meant that there was an immediate shortage of experts for most of the critical jobs necessary to run the country after the initial 2003 invasion. Moreover, with all of these former governmental and military leaders out of a job, many of these people subsequently turned into insurgents, since they didn't have anything else to do with their time, and, in addition, they now had an "axe to grind" against the Americans for being arbitrarily kept away from work to support their families.

So, our efforts to reconstruct Iraq without any trained leaders to work with turned out to be quite problematic to say the least in the early years. Over time, it became apparent what a big mistake that was, and they gradually ameliorated the situation but not before some significant growing pains and serious military problems such as fighting and winning the insurgency with, at times, counterproductive tactics that turned many Iraqi citizens against us for a few years.

I served in Iraq during one of the periods of post-combat occupation (or nation-building) with the 1st Corps Support Command (also known as the 1st COSCOM), which would deploy into Iraq beginning the first week of December 2004. At that time, we would assume the mission from the 3rd COSCOM, commanded by Brigadier General James E. Chambers. Our mission would end sometime at the end of October and early November 2005 when we handed the reins to our successor, the 13th COSCOM commanded by Brigadier General Rebecca S. Halstead.

The 1st COSCOM was based at Fort Bragg, North Carolina. We were part of the vaunted 18th Airborne Corps, which included the 82nd Airborne Division at Fort Bragg, North Carolina, the 101st Airborne Division at Fort Campbell, Kentucky, and the 10th Mountain Division at Fort Drum, New York, as well as numerous non-divisional units like ours. Each of those divisions is designed to have their own logistical support that is internal to their structure and organization, but our unit (1st COSCOM) had, as its primary mission, the task of supporting all the large nondivisional units (that did not have this internal logistic support) under the 18th Airborne Corps umbrella (including an intelligence brigade, a military police brigade, and other such independent units not within one of the divisions). Our mission, however, would eventually reach far beyond the boundaries of just our parent corps and its units until we were providing logistics support virtually to every corner of Iraq, even to many units that were not traditionally in our mission description.

Prior to our deployment into Iraq, our unit, like all units coming into the theater of combat operations, had to go through a long list of training tasks while staying at Camp Virginia in Kuwait. Camp Virginia was the typical dusty, sandy desert that most people think of when they think of that area of the world. We arrived at Camp Virginia on a flight aboard a chartered commercial aircraft from Pope Air Force Base (which is right next to Fort Bragg) about mid-November 2004. We trained for about two weeks. Then our unit members were bused incrementally in several large groups out of Camp Virginia to Ali Al Salem Air Base in Kuwait and then flown to Balad Air Base, Iraq, one of the largest US military bases in Iraq. The group I was in arrived at Balad on December 1, 2004.

For our mission, upon entry into Iraq, our headquarters would be at Logistics Support Area Anaconda, which was in the general vicinity, community, or metro area, if you will, of Balad, Iraq. Wikipedia gives an excellent explanation of what our base was, its history, and its importance to operations throughout Iraq:

> Joint Base Balad, formerly Balad Air Base and Logistics Support Area Anaconda, or simply LSA Anaconda—formerly known as Al-Bakr Air Base and known in popular media as Camp Anaconda—was one of the largest United States military bases in Iraq during the Iraq War. It was formerly the largest Iraqi Air Force base during the Saddam Hussein era...Located within the municipality of Yethrib, the installation is known officially as Joint Base Balad, formerly LSA Anaconda and Balad Air Base. The name of this base in the Saddam era was Al-Bakir Air Base...This base [hosted] several Army and Air Force units, as well as small attachments of US Navy personnel...As of early 2007 the base was the central hub for airlift and US Air Force operations in Iraq, it was also a major transshipment point for US Army supply convoys.[4]

Also, to situate the city in Iraq and to give context to my readers of where exactly we were in the country, the same article in Wikipedia notes that the city of Balad is a short distance outside the perimeter of our base:

> Balad is a city 80 kilometers (50 mi) north of Baghdad in the Salah ad Din Governorate, Iraq. It is located within the borders of the so-called Sunni Triangle; however, Balad is a primarily Shiite town of approximately 100,000. It is the principal town of the Balad District.[5]

Our base was about a half mile off of the historic Tigris River, and the river was our source of water for all of the base's inhabitants.

In addition to all of the army logistics units at Balad (it was one of the largest logistics support bases in Iraq, if not the biggest), there were also some Air Force units. There was an Air Force drone mission (which I'll discuss a little later in this chapter) being flown out of the Balad Airfield, and the airfield was also used for deliveries of payloads and personnel via C-130 and C-141 as well as a stopping-off and refueling point for these and other aircraft. Additionally, there was a unit of Air Force F-16 fighter jets and many army attack, transport, and recon helicopters, all of these aircraft providing support for ground force operations.

Balad also had probably the most advanced combat hospital in Iraq. Normally, soldiers, marines, sailors, or airmen serving in the theater of operations were sent to Balad with very serious wounds for any medical procedures or surgery necessary (they had a large surgical team here) to stabilize them before they were medevaced (medical evacuation) via C-130 or C-141 aircraft to the military hospital at Landstuhl, Germany, a very large full-service regional hospital capable of handling virtually any type of wound or complicated medical procedures and surgeries. Once the troops were stabilized enough at Landstuhl, they would then be medevaced to the Washington, D.C. area to Walter Reed Army Hospital for further treatment until they could be released to a regional hospital in their home state or at their military base from which they deployed.

The Weather

Balad Air Base was not as barren as the sandy desert environment in Kuwait. There were quite a few trees, but the ground was mostly very fine river silt dust, which became sticky like peanut butter whenever it would rain (which was only for a short period from January through February of each year) but would frequently be whipped up into choking dust clouds during windy periods such as the shamal season. Our unit's constant and never-ending gravel distribution operation (in which we laid gravel over the various dusty fields around the base to keep the dust down) was somewhat effective over the course of time in controlling the ever-present problem of blowing sand or dust.

When we arrived at the beginning of December, the weather was fairly pleasant, mostly cloudless and very cool, ranging from rather mild sunny days in the '50s to very bitterly cold nights in the '20s and teens.

We only had one thunderstorm that I remember, but it was quite memorable. The storm blew in on Christmas eve. I was among a group of leaders who had volunteered to take guard duty along the perimeter fence and the guard towers during Christmas eve through the evening of Christmas day so that the lower-ranking troops could get a break, enjoy their Christmas meals, and, perhaps, call their loved ones. During the thunderstorm on Christmas eve, a lightning bolt struck a tree near one of the guard towers where a friend of mine was standing watch, as he reported to me later the next day. The strike was about a mile away from my quarters where I was sleeping, but it was so loud that I thought an insurgent had driven a vehicle-borne bomb into the gates on that side of the base. I had heard enough of artillery, aircraft bombs, tank munitions, mortars, claymore mines, hand grenades, etc. throughout my military career that I could readily identify from the sound what type of explosive had gone off, and this lightning strike was so loud that it sounded like a very large bomb blast.

Ironically, I would have a basis of comparison a few months later when I was waiting in the line outside one of the base's five dining facilities for my dinner. While we were waiting in line, a vehicle-borne bomb was driven into one of the gate areas and set off near the dining facility. You never forget that sound, but surprisingly the lightning strike on Christmas eve had been louder than the vehicle bomb.

Besides the cool, dry weather in winter, there was also a short rainy season as mentioned above. We even had snow flurries one time in late December, although very little stuck to the ground. As for the rest of the year, the weather begins warming up around April to May until it gets extremely hot during the months of June through September with many days above 110 and even 120. As hot as that sounds, you generally get acclimated to the heat. The air is a lot drier in that climate, so it doesn't feel that bad, unless you have the unfortunate misery of being on a convoy in a vehicle during the middle of the day with no air-conditioning, then it is quite miserable. Fortunately, we had air-conditioning in most facilities to include sleeping quarters, and we did eventually get air-conditioning on most of the vehicles, but it sometimes did not help much since the hatch on many of these vehicles had to be open with someone manning the gun turret atop the Humvee or the various other vehicles that had been fitted with cupolas and heavy machine guns.

Loaded for Bear and Enemy Activity

Rain or shine though, the US military's mission continues on, and for the 1st COSCOM, that mission would be commanded and controlled from the sprawling base at Balad for the next year. Moreover, that mission would grow tremendously from what we were designed to handle under our established organization. By the time our mission reached its greatest expanse, we were providing theater (i.e. country-wide) logistics support to units operating throughout Iraq, and even some in Kuwait, as our normal wartime mission greatly expanded upon our arrival in Iraq starting at the beginning of December 2004.

Moreover, our unit leaders changed the name of our daily "convoys" throughout Iraq to "combat logistics patrols," which more aptly fit the combat realities and the aggressive posture, weapons, and equipment ("loaded for bear" was a common phrase thrown around during briefings) which our support soldiers were required to assume for their missions during our tenure starting December 2004 and continuing most of the year of 2005. In the guerilla warfare conditions under which our soldiers were operating, virtually all the roadways in Iraq, over which our soldiers were driving, turned into frontline combat.

It's important to point out here that our unit was not comprised solely of logistics soldiers. We also had two Brigade Combat Teams (BCTs—independently operating major combat units comprised of about 4,400 combat, combat support, and combat service support soldiers) working for us, doing traditional infantry wartime missions. Thankfully, our unit did not sustain an extremely high rate of casualties (as compared to the casualty rate in our most recent significant modern war in Vietnam), even with the daily combat missions of our two BCTs and our nearly 2,500 vehicles traversing the Iraqi roads and highways daily.

But the relatively low casualty rate was not for lack of trying on the part of the insurgents, as we would find out over time. The average of insurgent attacks on all US forces in the theater during our deployment to Iraq (December 1, 2004 to October 28, 2005) was roughly six hundred daily. (Note to reader: this statistic was pulled from a briefing chart in my notes, among hundreds of briefings that I sat through while in Iraq, so this statistic was from officially compiled statistics during the war.) This number includes all attacks of improvised explosive devices (IEDs or roadside bombs), mines, snipers, ambushes, grenades, mortars, and rockets, and it counts all attacks on convoys, bases, ground and air vehicles, and troop formations. Our units and leaders were constantly in a battle to thwart the technology and techniques of the insurgents, to determine tactics and techniques to circumvent enemy attacks and known danger areas, to harden our vehicles in order to prevent casualties, and to develop technology to detect the IEDs, jam their radio signals, or to design better vehicles that would dramatically improve survivability for our troops should we be hit by the IEDs.

I knew about the danger in an intellectual sense before I even left home, but I couldn't grasp the reality of it until I actually experienced it. I had seen glimpses of the violence during our video conferences with the unit we were to replace while we were still back at our home station. Sometimes there would be an air raid warning in the middle of the briefing. We could see our counterparts on the big-screen television scrambling to don helmets and body armor as the siren wailed in the background. Seeing that made me keenly aware, if only in an intellectual sense, of the reality of the danger that we would eventually face when we got to Iraq.

Once we were on the ground, the first siren that we heard (the first week of December 2004) was quite jarring with its deafeningly loud, spine-chilling wail. We all hurried to get into our protective gear (full battle rattle), and we scrambled for protective cover. We watched with surprise at how our predecessors moved more slowly, almost bored with the entire process. In time though, we would become inured to the warnings like them, especially given that the sirens most times came after the rounds had already landed and exploded, so there seemed to be very little preventive or defensive power in the warnings.

There was always the possibility of follow-on rounds, but that happened only one night, as I can recall, in the entire year of our tour. Most times, the insurgent attacks on our base from outside the perimeter fence were quick in and quick out, designed to minimize the possibility that they would be spotted and, hence, caught in the act, captured, and turned in by American-friendly Iraqis or by our own troops, allies, or various governmental paramilitary friendlies (security contractors, dark operators all along the spectrum of combat, Delta Force, CIA, SEALs, Special Forces, etc.). I think the fear of being caught was so paramount in insurgents' minds that they could only bear a quick one, two, possibly three rounds or rockets lobbed up into the air from their firing point in a Hail Mary tactic (a wild lob of the round up in the air toward our base) followed immediately by a desperate scramble to pack up all equipment and evacuate the area before anyone in the surrounding community or any units operating in the area were any the wiser.

Over the course of a year, we would hear the numberless sirens going off (both the attack warning siren and the subsequent "all clear" siren) during several weeks-long stretches at least once a day as the insurgents' gnat-like persistence sought to bring a little taste of terror into our lives. Attacks were so frequent that our base came to be known as "mortar alley" or "mortarita-ville." Mostly, the attacks were by mortars and rockets. There was one car bomb at one of the gates in an attempt to breach the gate defenses. There were, tragically, some Iraqi soldiers killed by the vehicular bomb, although no Americans were injured or killed. But the explosion could be heard in any part of the base within two miles—a large, heavy thump that was a little bigger than the usual mortar and rocket explosions and the controlled blasts that were a regular occurrence when our forces destroyed captured arms. I was standing in line at one of the dining facilities on the side of the base near the explosion, about a half-mile away, and we not only heard the blast but also felt the shock wave immediately following the blast.

Most of the strikes missed serious targets; exceptions were when a few mortars hit some aircraft on the airfield one day. One evening, apparently a former soldier with the Iraqi army, someone who had some real skill, walked several mortars in a straight line in a field bounded by work buildings and sleeping quarters, and even hitting our headquarters building where people were at work (although thankfully no one was injured). After walking in the mortars, this man then threw a couple of wild shells, both of which passed over our sleeping areas and landed harmlessly in sandy fields. But this was a close call with everyone escaping injury by the grace of God as He was ever watching over us. All of us realized how narrowly we had missed a serious mass casualty event.

Of course, there was little we could do about these sporadic attacks. There was never any predictable pattern to these attacks, as they occurred virtually any time of day or night, being from an infinite choice of firing position and being fired during any type of weather, so coming up with preventive or precautionary measures was difficult, if not impossible. We almost always ended up reacting to an attack that had already happened. This was probably the biggest challenge of addressing the sporadic indirect fire onto our bases. These insurgents were not stupid. They figured out that if they repeated any pattern, location, time in their attacks, then we would find them by putting tactical units on the position quickly enough to catch them.

Nonetheless, there was a unit during our tenure that actively worked on the technology to shoot down these mortars and rockets while they were in flight, thereby preventing any damage to facilities, equipment, vehicles, generators, etc. or preventing any threat to the troops. Since the Desert Storm era in the early 1990s, we have been working with this "umbrella" technology of radar identification of incoming rounds and reactionary, preventive rounds in response to shoot down the incoming round and/or to calculate the location of the enemy attackers and knock them out with rounds from friendly artillery units or friendly military aircraft. Much of this technology has been developed in coordination with the nation of Israel, which has had to live with the problem of sporadic terrorist indirect fire (mortars, rockets, and artillery) inflicted on the civilian population for a few decades now.

I don't think they ever successfully shot down an inbound mortar or rocket during our deployment (2004–2005) since they were still developing that part of the technology, but their radar systems, which traced the rounds, were very effective technology, often giving us early warning before the base's much slower reactionary siren system sounded to warn us about the rounds that had already landed.

Wikipedia has a good short article on this air defense artillery system.

> C-RAM is an initiative taken in response to an operational needs statement made by the Multinational Force Iraq (MNF-I). The directive arose in response to the increasing number of casualties caused by attacks using rockets, artillery, and mortars in Iraq. The land-based *Phalanx B* was subsequently deployed in Iraq in the summer of 2004 [during our unit's deployment]. It protected the Green Zone and Camp Victory in Baghdad, Joint Base Balad near Balad, Iraq, and was also deployed by the British Army in southern Iraq.[6]

In addition to the threat from indirect fire, there was always conceivably, at least, a threat from a breach of the security fence around the base. Thankfully, we never had a breach of that fence because it was pretty heavily guarded, and the fence itself was a pretty significant obstacle to attempt to breach. Plus, it would have been very difficult for anyone to cross the couple of hundred yards of uncovered ground outside the fence without being spotted. And it would take them several minutes to try climbing the perimeter fence. Moreover, if they were not cut up pretty good by that time, then they would be easily spotted by any two of the guard towers within vision and subsequently shot by a 7.62mm machine gun or a 50 cal, not to mention the various shots by all the SAWs or M-16s. They would probably look like Swiss cheese long before they even got over the fence.

Unfortunately, this airtight security did not extend "beyond the wire." Throughout 2005, as we were conducting the bulk of our mission, the insurgency really got going and was responsible for some heavy casualties for our logistics soldiers who were constantly on the roads in order to support the one hundred thousand-plus US troops (not to mention all our allies) that were spread throughout Iraq. Our logistics soldiers were basically sitting ducks, easy targets for the insurgents. Eventually, we would get all our vehicles sufficiently armored and would find better ways of spotting IEDs, jamming their frequencies, and clearing routes, etc., partly as a positive outcome of the booming drone program.

These drones flying constantly throughout Iraq could put eyes on every inch of roads virtually around the clock, so if they spotted someone stopping along a highway and doing something that looked unusual or suspicious, they could look a little closer and, if necessary, relay the information to the local BCT to go and check it out, or, in some cases, they could fire missiles to take out the threat.

Wikipedia has a good article on the unit, the 15th Reconnaissance Squadron of the US Air Force, that was running the drone program during our deployment to Iraq. The 15th was flying MQ-1B predator drones on combat missions during our time, having a tremendous impact on the threats to our soldiers, and this unit's successes were often reported in the intelligence portion of our evening operational briefing. The Wikipedia article notes that:

> From July 2005 to June 2006, the 15th Reconnaissance Squadron participated in more than 242 separate raids; engaged 132 troops in contact-force protection actions;

fired 59 Hellfire missiles; surveyed 18,490 targets; escorted four convoys; and flew 2,073 sorties for more than 33,833 flying hours.[7]

Tragically, even with all of the excellent technology on our side and the dedicated troops such as the 15th Reconnaissance, we still lost many good and brave soldiers during the insurgency, even if we did learn and improve our technology and tactics, eventually beating the insurgents at their own game and many times catching the insurgents in the act as they were setting up roadside bombs or setting up mortars or rockets to fire upon our troops or our bases.

Suffice it to say that danger was ever-present throughout the country every day regardless of your job. Moreover, although our support troops may not have sustained the same rate of casualties as the traditional combat fighters (infantry, armor, cavalry, etc.), these noncombat soldiers were constantly in combat situations throughout Iraq during their daily missions, especially given the Iraqi insurgents' preferred tactic of attacking the thousands of convoys that traversed the Iraqi roads in any given year.

Consequently, our unit (1st COSCOM) had at least seventeen killed in action (KIA) whose death were due to enemy fire, most from IEDs during our year-long mission. We also had at least 267 wounded in action (WIA) whose wounds were sustained as a result of enemy fire in addition to over 1,389 wounds, injuries, or illnesses not due to enemy action but rather a secondary result of merely living in the continual hazards of a combat zone (all statistics from my notes during my Iraq tour of duty). Furthermore, our unit sustained at least twelve deaths from non-hostile (i.e. other-than-enemy action) but which were arguably attributable to our tactics in response to the general enemy threat and the specific, known, ever-changing tactics of the enemy.

The First Corps Support Command

Given our unit's size, the size of our mission, and the level of violence that we were facing, our unit name was a bit misleading—at least, as our combat mission expanded, as we assumed command and control of two combat brigade teams (BCTs—combat units of about three to five thousand soldiers), as our mission expanded to include logistics support to units throughout Iraq, and as these missions required aggressive convoy security to prevent or inhibit enemy attacks on our convoys. In other words, even though we were not considered combat troops in the traditional definition, we were, nonetheless, conducting combat missions. Moreover, we ended up supporting many more units than we were commissioned for, equipped for, or organized for, but, to the credit of our amazing troops and many good leaders throughout our organization, we got the job done nonetheless.

Our unit name (a "command") suggests a small organization between brigade-sized (roughly 2,500 to 5,000 troops depending on organization and capabilities) and division-sized (10,000 to 15,000, again depending on organization and capabilities). However, once we got into Iraq and began to assume our monstrous breadth of missions at brief periods during our deployment, our unit crossed that threshold in numbers of assigned troops to become almost a corps-sized unit (normally 20,000 to 45,000 troops) with a mission that reached throughout the country instead of a limited regional mission that a division-sized or smaller command unit might have.

In fact, our commanding general, Yves Fontaine, spoke about our mission on a C-Span program during our deployment. Many people may not be aware that C-Span ran a series of video conference briefings during the Iraq and Afghanistan wars, which gave various leaders in the theater, whose units were fighting or enabling the fight, a chance to speak to reporters and the American people to tell their unique stories and the unique stories of their units, essentially a real-time history in the making. Our unit's (1st Corps Support Command or COSCOM) commanding general, Yves J. Fontaine, conducted one of those C-Span briefings on August 12, 2005 (over eight months into our mission) entitled "Operations in Iraq." The video can be found on the C-Span web site. The caption/explanation posted with the video synopsizes the general substance of the briefing, which explained our mission and a little about the conditions we were operating under:

> General Yves J. Fontaine, commander of the 1st Corps Support Command, Multinational Corps—Iraq, briefed reporters via satellite link from Iraq and provided an update on ongoing logistical operations in Iraq. He also responded to questions from the reporters.[8]

The introduction of the briefing was done by Bryan G. Whitman, a career member of the Senior Executive Service (the civilian equivalent of the flag or general/admiral level of military officers), the highest level rank of civilians serving careers in the government, just below the political appointees serving whatever presidential administration at the time.

Mr. Whitman, at the time he introduced General Fontaine, was serving as "the Deputy Assistant Secretary of Defense for Media Operations. In that position he was responsible for all aspects of media operations for the Defense Department. He also served as a senior spokesman for the Defense Department and oversaw all media functions to include oversight of the Pentagon's Press Office and all visual information programs and activities."[9]

In his introduction of our commanding general, Mr. Whitman said:

> Welcome to the Pentagon briefing room today. Our briefer today is Brig. Gen. Yves Fontaine. Who is commander of the 1st Corps Support Command of the U.S. Army's 18th Airborne Corps, which is currently deployed in support of Operation Iraq Freedom. General Fontaine's command

provides the logistical support for the Multi-National Forces Corps in Iraq. And so, in doing that, he operates throughout the entire theater [Iraq and Kuwait]. He has more than 20,000 U.S. soldiers under his command, as well as works with contractors and partners with Iraqi units that are out there to provide logistics and support. And he is certainly the right man for the job. He has an impressive list of previous assignments and accomplishments prior to taking on this challenge...And I'm reminded I'm sure as a logistics old adage...: "Amateurs talk about tactics and professionals talk about logistics." And I think the essence of that is that it is a very difficult job when you talk about maintaining equipping arming feeding the number of forces that his command is responsible for doing so every day and doing it in the superb fashion that they are.[10]

Much of the script from that C-Span briefing made it into an article authored by General Yves J. Fontaine and Major Donald K. Wols, who was his secretary of the general staff during the deployment (SGS–a position which is like a military aide, but encompasses many more wide-ranging duties and responsibilities). The article, which, as noted, contained most of the information from the C-Span briefing, was entitled "Sustaining the momentum: the 1st Corps Support Command in Iraq." In that article, they explained the tremendous mission that our unit was accomplishing:

> The 1st COSCOM's mission was twofold: to provide logistics to the Multinational Corps-Iraq (MNC-I) in order to maintain the corps' momentum and to partner with Iraqi logistics forces to develop the Iraqi Army logistics system. To carry out that mission, the 1st COSCOM was organized into "five corps support groups (CSGs), one area support group (ASG), one brigade-sized corps distribution command (CDC), and two brigade combat teams (BCTs), for a total of nine brigade-sized units.

The COSCOM consisted of 40 percent Active Army Soldiers, 34 percent Army National Guard Soldiers, 25 percent Army Reserve Soldiers, and, eventually, 1 percent Iraqi National Guard Soldiers. COSCOM personnel totaled close to 18,500 Soldiers at any given time, and up to 25,000 during surge periods, and were based in five geographic logistics hubs. Approximately 9,000 civilian contractors augmented the COSCOM logistics structure in the supply, services, and maintenance fields; they were part of an Iraq-wide civilian logistics support force of more than 30,000 personnel.

These CSGs, in turn, supported all of MNC-I, affecting virtually every unit in Iraq. Additionally, these CSGs "also partnered with three Iraqi motorized transportation regiments. The ASG ran the garrison activities at one of the largest support bases. The two [Brigade Combat Teams] provided base security and escort-and-security support for over 150 combat logistics patrols (CLPs) per day; these patrols put nearly 2,500 vehicles on the road daily. Altogether, over 4,600 Soldiers were traveling on the roads of Iraq every day in more than 300 gun truck missions…On an average day, the 1st COSCOM delivered 1.3 million gallons of fuel, produced and issued over 3 million gallons of water, processed hundreds of requests for repair parts, moved 110,000 cases of bottled water and 200,000 meals, and provided materiel management for over 30,000 pieces of equipment.[11]

The article goes on to explain the basing of our forces and the main threats to those forces:

Concurrently with setting up the CSS structure for successful operations, the 1st COSCOM established efficient and effective standards and conditions to protect its forces, both on and off the forward operating bases (FOBs). The COSCOM understood the two main threats to its Soldiers to be indirect fires into secure bases and the improvised explosive device (IED) variants encountered on the roads.[12]

Finally, three of our CSGs had a very substantial training mission for three Iraqi motorized transportation regiments, the Iraqi National Supply Depot, and two regional base support units, and this training mission put us beyond the scope of traditional logistics or war fighting and into the realm of nation-building.

The Power of Enablers

As explained by General Fontaine, our huge conglomerate logistics and combat unit had impacts on virtually all units throughout Iraq, and even had many counterinsurgency (winning the hearts and minds of the Iraqi people) impacts during our missions and during our various outreach projects. During our tour, we won the hearts and minds of the Iraqi people in our operational area by completing many "quality of life" projects affecting thousands of average Iraqis. Moreover, this was a couple of years before General David Petraeus had his day in the sun in which he was given the entire credit for the salvation of the Iraq War and credit for being the first and only one to use a counterinsurgency approach prior to the surge of troops, January 2007 through July 2008.

Of course, I'm sure that there are people who will still argue that Petraeus saved the day, even though many units of all sizes throughout Iraq were doing the same counterinsurgency missions and projects that Petraeus was commended for, reaching out to the local communities, their people, and their leaders to build trust while conducting missions. Moreover, units such as ours were doing numerous quality-of-life enhancing projects and engaging in social and professional outreach to all social levels of Iraqi people and leaders long before Petraeus's surge period. I know that there are other books suggesting that these quality of life or counterinsurgency missions did not take place before

Petraeus's time in command, but after reading a few of those books, I also noted that they did not cover all units operating in Iraq. Specifically, they seemed to miss critical enabler units conducting combat missions, such as the 1st COSCOM, giving little or no mention to them.

In writing the various military histories of Iraq, I'm not sure how you miss a critical logistics unit of fifteen to twenty thousand soldiers that is conducting combat missions and providing the gamut of logistics (beans, bullets. maintenance, fuel, etc.) to units throughout Iraq, but I guess everyone is human and prone to error from time to time. Unfortunately, most military histories focus primarily on the "trigger pullers," the combat units, when they write the history books. But any soldier who has served more than a few days knows how dependent he is, especially during combat on the many enablers: the medics, the cooks, the mechanics, the truck drivers, even the humble personnel clerk who greases the wheels of the big military machine with the morale-critical human resource services.

If you want to know how important the enablers are to the war machine in any conflict, just look up the incredible story of the "Red Ball Express" during World War II, which is told so well on the US Army Transportation Museum's web site.[13]

Of course, most of my readers will probably be familiar with the story of George Patton's thunderous, lightning-fast charge across France with his tank units after breaking out of the hedges of Normandy in July 1944, chasing after the rapidly retreating German units. But I doubt very many of you will remember or hear about the critical and amazing Red Ball Express logistics supply juggernaut that made Patton's victories possible, although there was a movie released in 1952 about this incredible logistics feat simply entitled *Red Ball Express* and starring Sidney Poitier, among others.

The US Army Transportation Museum web site tells us about the amazing accomplishments of the logistics soldiers that made the Red Ball Express run:

> After the breakout of Normandy in July 1944, an acute shortage of supplies on both fronts governed all operations. Some 28 divisions were advancing across France and Belgium, each ordinarily requiring 700–750 tons a day. Patton's 3rd Army was soon grinding to a halt from lack of fuel and ordnance. The key to pursuit was a continuous supply of fuel and ordnance, thus leading to the Red Ball Express. The Red Ball Express was conceived in a 36-hour brain-storming session. It lasted only 3 months from August to November, 1944, but without it, the campaign in the European Theater could have dragged on for years. At the peak of its operation, it was running 5,938 vehicles carrying 12,342 tons of supplies to forward depots daily.[14]

In short, the Red Ball Express was a truck supply route traversed by thousands of army supply trucks, driven by many thousands of humble logistics soldiers, mostly African-American troops, who did miraculously courageous work to keep the logistics transportation line of fuel, beans, bullets, etc. running nonstop so that Patton's tanks could move. Any military historian of the Normandy campaign who is worth his salt would tell you how critical the work of these support troops was to the glorious victories that the tankers claimed. Even today, looking back, the feats of those support troops seem almost incomprehensible, what with the amount of war materiel they moved in such a short space of time.

As I've found out many times over the years of my undergraduate, graduate, and personal research, historians frequently overlook certain facts when they don't fit a predetermined narrative (such as the History Channel's highly entertaining and compelling *The Men Who Built America* series, which presents a story that is just a little too neat and tidy).

Like those brave troops on the Red Ball Express, we were having a tremendous impact on the theater mission in Iraq (as noted previously in the "Sustaining the Momentum" article), and we were also having a counterinsurgency or quality-of-life impact on the population of Iraqi citizens around our units and bases. To give you an idea of the impact we were having, another excerpt from the article by General Fontaine and Major Wols lists some of the projects:

> The 1st COSCOM, like other major support commands, also found opportunities to enhance the lives of the Iraqi people living around us. It provided oversight to reconstruction efforts that were extremely productive. These efforts included construction of over 24 water filtration systems, which provide clean water to over 20,000 Iraqi citizens; distribution of humanitarian aid packages, containing such items as clothing, school supplies, hygiene items, and toys, to over 18,000 Iraqis; and funding for the construction of three new health clinics, 16 new or renovated schools, and 65 kilometers of road projects throughout our area of responsibility.[15]

The Telling of History

This leads to an important point about the US military, and even about the telling of history, especially military history. I have tremendous skepticism about the common theory and narrative that "great women and men drive history," which I often see in historical accounts and documentaries (such as the History Channel's *The Men Who Built America* series). I freely admit that these Carnegies and Rockefellers are unusual and talented men who do have some influence over events, but I also have a sneaking suspicion that they are merely the right person at the right time, showing up just in time to ride the wave of historical forces, the circumstances of which are already in motion. And it would seem that these forces are being driven by movements among the common people, likely even inspired and empowered by a divine hand. Of course, I'm sure that there are exceptions, certain people who did seem to exert great influence, but since no man or woman is an island, we are all dependent on others no matter how great, rich, or famous we may become.

In any case, this skepticism of the "great men and women" theories of history is not unique. The great Russian novelist Leo Tolstoy in his magnum opus, *War and Peace*, waxed philosophical views about the forces that drive history, given that the great Napoleon, at the height of his power, seemed almost powerless to influence events or prevent the unfolding disaster that befell his armies upon reaching Moscow (June to December 1812). How else can we explain the unusual disintegration of his armies at the highest point of their glory and power?

In Chapter 1 Part 13 of the Constance Garnett translation of *War and Peace*, Tolstoy writes:

> The combination of causes of phenomena is beyond the grasp of the human intellect. But the impulse to seek causes is innate in the soul of man. And the human intellect, with no inkling of the immense variety and complexity of circumstances conditioning a phenomenon, any one of which may be separately conceived of as the cause of it, snatches at the first and most easily understood approximation, and says here is the cause...But one had only to look below the surface of any historical event, to look, that is into the movement of the whole mass of men taking part in that event, to be convinced that the will of the hero of history, so far from controlling the actions of the multitude, is continually controlled by them.[16]

Of course, Tolstoy then, later in the novel, attempts an explanation of the forces that drive history, which does nothing more than kick the can down the road. He attributes the drive of history essentially to the will of the people, but he does not then explain what drives the will of the people, leaving it to chance (or fate?), so his explanation, in the end, is not complete. But many others have struggled to explain the forces that drive human history, and even human individual action. The Greek poet, Homer, in his epic *The Iliad*, struggled alternately to explain human action as a mysterious conjunction between free will and fate, even though these two forces would seem to be at odds with each other.

I write all this to state that it is, at least, questionable that people like former General David Petraeus drive history. Not to detract from the value of his service to our nation, but his service should not be given any greater significance than many lower-ranking people who serve at important jobs at all levels, serving sacrificially and honorably in many mundane occupations throughout our various military branches of service to little fanfare or recognition. Such high-ranking men and women are to be commended for their accomplishments, but they are no more important nor is their service more honorable or commendable than that private, airman, seaman, warrant officer, sergeant, or petty officer who sacrifices his or her life, time, and comfort many times over during the course of their tour of duty or career. Without the millions of sacrifices of these lower-ranking troops, the great leaders who ride the crest of glory in the history books would be as lost as Napoleon was when his army disintegrated in the latter half of 1812.

Battles on land, air, or sea are more dependent on the hard, dedicated teamwork of millions of our homeland's sons and daughters of all ranks working together professionally and honorably, daily fulfilling their duties sacrificially on behalf of their fellow citizens.

Of course, you could have found plenty of people who believed in the greatness of General Petraeus before the Paula Broadwell scandal broke in May 2012. Since then, you would be hard-pressed to find a few. What changed? We found out that he was no more than an ordinary person like the rest of us, subject to the same weaknesses as the rest of us, the same excesses, and even the same sins. Moreover, if he is no more in control of himself than the average person, it would seem to be, at least, questionable as to the extent of his influence on events in Iraq during the surge.

It is important to remember this so that we can give credit where it is really due. Instead of lavishing praise on these people "at the forefront of history," we should, instead, thank the common daily heroes, America's sons and daughters who have purchased the great blessings of liberty and ensured all the great victories and many thousands of smaller successes of our US military forces ever since the inception of our nation (for example, the Revolutionary War battles at Lexington and Concord). Sure, these famous people play their part, but it is the simple, humble, unknown heroes by the millions throughout our history that have secured our freedoms, paying tremendous debts of blood, sweat, tears, and even their very lives when necessary.

That said, heroes at all levels in our unit certainly played their part during our deployment, even if there will be no great books written about them. However, in the end, we will—all of us— at least, have the satisfaction that we went when called and did our part.

I've already explained the part that our unit, over overall team, played during our combat tour, but, perhaps, I should explain a little about the mission and contribution of my own team, the dedicated troops who were in my section, fulfilling our duties in our little slice of the mission pie. My job while I was in Iraq was as the chief human resources officer or G1 for our command. This was a very significant and challenging job, since my team of officers—noncommissioned officers—the lower-ranking enlisted soldiers, and I were responsible for all casualty tracking, all awards, morale and welfare programs, the very critical rest and recuperation program (R&R, which rotated each soldier back to the States for fifteen days of leave at home), manning, replacements, personnel accounting, some coordination of various personnel services, finance, mail, and conducting briefings twice daily on combat operations with the rest of the staff.

These briefings gave us a chance to disseminate useful operational information for the awareness of the entire team, and updated the commanding general on the status and conduct of our various logistics and combat operations, and even gave each staff section a chance to report on what they were doing and how well they were contributing to the overall mission. Moreover, the briefings also gave our commanding general the opportunity to give us further guidance as necessary for mission accomplishment.

I had a team of about twenty-five people for our staff section's mission. Most of my duties were confined to the offices we worked in at Balad, but I did get "outside the wire" several times to include a few flights and one convoy. The combat I saw included the sporadic rounds of indirect fire (mortars and rockets) launched into our base throughout our tour of duty, a couple of near misses in aircraft that I was flying in, and the improvised explosive device (IED), which hit the vehicle that I rode in while I was out on convoy. By the grace of God, we were unharmed by the IED attack, but there were shrapnel marks on the sides of the two vehicles that were hit, deep and long enough to let us know that we had escaped by the "skin of our teeth."

Life in "The Box"

Upon arrival into Iraq, our team took on the full weight of our mission, replacing our predecessors in about one week's time doing what we called a right-seat, left-seat ride (a process in which we first observe our predecessors at work, then do the work with our predecessors looking over our shoulder and advising us, and then perform the duties solo). We were a little bit ahead of schedule in assuming our mission from our predecessors, but this was a demonstration to the commitment, preparation, and high morale of our unit. And, having assumed the mission, we began to settle into life in our piece of the combat zone on Balad Air Base.

To further explain what life was like during our deployment, I should explain one unofficial term that we commonly used in discussing the mission. "The box," as we sometimes referred to the combat zone, was so dubbed because the area of operations on military maps was usually delineated somehow by clearly marked lines, generally bounded by north, south, east, and west lines so as to resemble roughly a box shape. Of course, these boundaries were important to establish where we were operating and where we weren't, partly to ensure that the entire mission and the individual parts of it were clear to all units operating in the combat zone, partly to avoid unnecessary civilian casualties (or even fratricide), and partly to clearly define the space in which we were operating so that military planners and those executing the battle plans would stay within their own lane (i.e. to avoid chaos).

But as simple and well-defined the geometric space of the combat zone might be, the actual operations going on within that box were far from simple. As such, military plans tend to be long (often hundreds of pages) and tended to be extremely detailed, covering every single bit of minutiae as possible. Thus, as you would expect, planners trying to plan for something as monumental as a combat tour would want to know as much as possible and to prepare as much as possible.

Unfortunately, we would learn in time that we couldn't anticipate everything, no matter how hard we might try. There are always too many hurdles to overcome and too many tasks to accomplish in the time given. We, along with our unit leaders, planned out as best we could, but all of us learned the lesson that I'm sure so many before us have had to learn. One can only cram so much into the preparation, and one can only plan so much for an experience that he or she has never encountered. The human imagination most definitely has limits when it comes to forecasting the future in military operations and in most, if not all, areas of life.

Furthermore, we could simulate; we could read lessons learned from others who had deployed; we could conduct our weekly teleconferences with those "in the box," although they tended to be of very limited value; we could gather some information on internet searches; and we could practice our missions and tasks under similar conditions (staff exercises, live fire exercises, and even site visits to Iraq by key leaders and staff). Overall, we could do any number of things to physically prepare and plan for our combat mission ahead, but the actual experience will always be different from the speculative imagination.

Moreover, we hoped to learn from our predecessors, but their experience would be unfortunately of limited value not because of any weakness or flaw on their part or ours. Their reality during their deployment would, in countless ways, be different from ours. Their missions would be different. Being a unique team comprised of unique people and a unique unit (as we were), they would interpret their missions differently from the way we interpreted ours. Their leaders would make different demands, and our enemy would even use different tactics with us.

Perhaps, the greatest single indicator of how different the deployment of our predecessors would be from our deployment was their freedom of mobility on the Iraqi roads without significant threat of attack. During our predecessors' tenure, the Iraqi insurgency was still in its beginning stages; the attacks were much more erratic, much less effective, and more time had lapsed between the attacks compared to what we experienced from the Iraqi insurgents when we were fully in control of the mission. For much of their tour, our predecessors were able to travel from our base to Baghdad (approximately a fifty-mile trip) in unarmored vehicles.

This is not to say that they did not experience any danger. They did have sporadic mortar and rocket attacks, although of less frequency than we did, and they did suffer one horrific incident in a single mortar attack in which one of the itinerant workers from the Iraqi population had disguised his evil intent in getting onto one of the work crews that daily came on base. This particular terrorist brought a global positioning satellite device (GPS) and plotted the exact coordinates of a popular gathering area beside the base's fast food restaurants. He then used this information to launch a bloody attack later that evening from a hidden location outside the base, lobbing mortars back onto the base in his preplotted fire point established by his GPS, and regretfully his firing hit the target with tragic results, with several US troops being killed or injured.

I never heard how they unraveled the entire story of what happened, but our security services and intelligence sections somehow pieced together the story, and subsequent changes were made to the Iraqi worker program and the screening of workers coming onto the base to prevent a recurrence like this one attack. Furthermore, in spite of the greater rate of attacks upon us during our deployment than our predecessor had sustained, we, thankfully, never experienced a mass casualty event such as this one tragic attack.

Ironically, however, as we would find out in time, our security situation was much more hazardous overall, with more frequent rocket and mortar attacks on the base than our predecessor had sustained. Moreover, our unit suffered far more casualties overall than our predecessor during the execution of our numerous daily logistics missions due to the burgeoning insurgency movement, which became more aggressive and more effective with the passing of each day, most of the wounds and deaths coming from the roadside bombs or improvised explosive devices (IEDs) that would kill or wound so many of our logistics soldiers while they drove on the Iraqi roads and highways.

The main reason why our predecessors experienced a less dangerous security situation was because of the initial disorganization of the insurgency groups, but that would change in time. During our time, Iraq would be a sort of "school for terror," with jihadist fighters streaming into the country from throughout the region. The supposedly disorganized rabble that was not to be feared after our overwhelming victory over the Iraqi army (March 20, 2003 to May 1, 2003) got to work pretty quickly after the Iraq War was publicly declared "mission accomplished." The insurgency kicked off in full swing during our tenure. We could go nowhere without armored vehicles and heavily armed convoys. Even then, we seemed frustratingly incapable of thwarting the roadside bomb attacks or their efficacy, especially since the insurgents were constantly improvising their tactics and technology.

Even I, a high-ranking staff officer typically found behind a computer at a desk or in meetings and briefings, found myself in a completely unremarkable convoy on a route that was not very heavily traveled, yet we were unexpectedly hit by a roadside bomb and small arms fire in an ambush. Our convoy was on a less operationally used route, but we were still attacked. This incident, among many others, showed how widespread and effective the insurgency was as it gradually increased during our tour with more and more horrendous results.

So the value of our predecessors' knowledge about operations was of limited use. They faced a different problem set (tactical situation) from us. Their talents and limitations would necessitate that they approach situations differently than our talents and limitations would. And with our infinite differences, we would arrive at totally different conclusions and solutions than those people who came before us. Sure, there are things on the tactical level that soldiers might be able to replicate between units, but there are many higher level issues or lessons learned that didn't transfer too well.

Even the demands and understanding of our allies would be different. Our interpretations and relationships with sister units and units from other nations would be different from our predecessors simply because we were different people. Our predecessors worked primarily with a US National Guard unit (a brigade combat team or BCT) from Pennsylvania, and we would work with this same unit for a short while as they finished out their tour. During the major part of our tour, we would work with National Guard BCTs from Texas and Hawaii. And during operational briefings, it became very clear that these two units from two very different states would reflect the culture that they had come out of back home, resulting in very different approaches to the mission by these units as they processed the mission through their very different cultural lens or perspectives.

This is part of the serendipitous experience of serving in the US military. It is an amazing cornucopia of cultural backgrounds, ethnic groups, etc. This is true of active duty troops in all the services, and it is certainly true of Reserve and National Guard troops who typically reflect the culture of whatever states, regions, or territories from which they originate.

Plus, our mission would necessarily differ from our predecessor because we would be forced to make constant small adjustments to our mission execution as subordinate units were constantly changing out with other units. The changes of units and missions, as scheduled by Army planners and leaders, was conducted with an incremental schedule that was designed to gradually change one unit at a time to avoid too much impact to the mission at any given time or place. In other words, the risk was spread out by not having all units within an organization change at the same time, so with each new unit would come a unique approach to the mission that was a little bit different from its predecessor.

Lastly, much of our mission would entail building and training the new Iraqi armed forces on a democratic model, a mission which our predecessors had not gotten very deep into.

The bottom line is that the possible experiences and interpretations and abilities our predecessors faced were infinitely different from ours. There was no way around this fact. It is simply part of life. It doesn't matter whether the subject is a military unit's changeover or some major transition in the corporate world. Such change will always be dependent on the infinite human factors involved.

Unfortunately, this fact makes for a somewhat difficult transition, since predecessors' "lessons learned" (as I have found out from personal experience) are of somewhat limited use. It would be nice to have a reliable, immutable body of knowledge that is expert and irrefutable and that applies equally to all personalities, all perspectives, all cultural experiences, and all the possibilities of enemy operations. But nothing in life is that simple, and when you look at issues of war, what was previously already difficult is even more confusing in the chaos inherent in war.

Among the unpredictable things about our deployment was our expectations of what the country of Iraq would be like or what the experience of living in that country would be like. I had preconceived notions about both Kuwait and Iraq as sterile desert places, which turned out to be wrong. Kuwait did, indeed, match many of my images of a harsh, barren, sandy desert. Yet, sometimes it seemed like the aridity, sand, and seeming loneliness were just a façade, hiding something more vibrant just underneath the surface. It reminded me of several lines from the song "A Horse with No Name" by the popular 1970s folk-rock group America.

> After nine days I let the horse run free
> 'Cause the desert had turned to sea
> There were plants and birds and rocks and things
> There was sand and hills and rings
> The ocean is a desert with its life underground,
> And the perfect disguise above.[1]

I was certainly disabused of my false notions about the desert one day during our training period in Kuwait when we had an unexpected rain. Within hours, there was a carpet of small grasses and flowers in numerous areas. I was so surprised to see that life hovered just below the surface of human observation and that it sprang out so bountifully and so quickly with the least provocation of water. And, of course, my experience of seeing the Bedouin shepherd appear out of the sandstorm shattered my view of the Kuwaiti desert as a lonely place. By the time I left Kuwait, I had developed a Scheherazadean, romanticized view of the desert.

My preconceptions about Iraq would be shattered as well. When we first landed at our base in Iraq, I was so surprised to see countless trees scattered throughout the base. There weren't as many trees as I was used to seeing at my southern home in the States, but neither were there so few as to suggest that the land was infertile or harsh. My impression of the base from my observation of the vegetation was that of a lush oasis. For example, just outside the perimeter fence on one side of the base lay a dense palm grove with richly green palm trees growing so close together that it seemed impenetrable. Many times, I had fantasies about wandering among the groves in the moonlight, but I knew that would have been a foolish fantasy to fulfill, since those groves frequently hid the guerillas that shot the almost daily mortar and rocket rounds into the base.

To add to the impression of the oasis, I knew that the historical Tigris River was less than a mile away. With modern technology, it would be so easy to transport that water and turn the base into a garden, but that was not what we were here for. Most of the base's soil was really made of fine, rich river silt, even though it appeared to be just dry, infertile dust much of the year. Given the right amount of water consistently delivered, the ground would gratefully yield anything you wanted, and the palm groves outside the perimeter of our base fence were proof of this fertility. But even with water, the task of maintaining plants still would require persistent effort to stay ahead of the ever-encroaching, ever-hungry aridity of the desert air.

All things considered, I was glad to be out of Kuwait. Now, my people and I were able to start our jobs and start the clock ticking that would eventually wind down to our day of departure. While we were in Kuwait, there was always the nagging feeling that we were suspended in time. We were neither here nor there, neither home nor away. Even with the danger looming in Iraq, it was preferable to this in-between existence, this purgatory.

We would even find out in time that there were many reasons to prefer Iraq. There were certainly better facilities (for eating, sleeping, showering, etc.), and there were more opportunities for leisure diversions or for communications with home. So, at the least, being in Iraq, we would be happy to escape the austere facilities of Camp Virginia, Kuwait. There were some pleasantries too, which we didn't realize we were missing until we got to Iraq. There was a coffee shop in the Air Force compound on our base, which served all manner of cold and hot coffee-based beverages almost as good as Starbucks.

Despite the pleasant surprises, this wasn't home. And no matter how hard we might try to see this place in the most optimistic light, we couldn't help but process it through the lens of home.

Everything was a comparison to what we experienced at home, so there was always a part of us that would miss home. The surprising thing about missing home though is that there are many things you never notice until you no longer see them or have access to them, so many things you take for granted, and when you begin to miss those things, they can take on much greater significance, even the most common and ordinary things.

What I missed most was the lush vegetation of a temperate climate such as I was accustomed to at home. In Kuwait, there was the promise that paradise might be one good rain away as we found out when a couple of rains during our stay there produced a bounty of flowers and grasses literally within minutes. In Iraq, there was much more promise of the bountiful, green pastures that we knew at home, but everything depended upon a regular supply of water pumped up from the Tigris River east of our base, since the sky rarely produced rain, save from the short rainy season in winter.

We watched with amusement for several weeks at one point during our tour as workers at one of our entertainment facilities tried in earnest to grow a small patch of grass outside of their building. They started their effort with sod, and God only knows where they got sod from in this dry environment, but the initial project looked very promising with the grass seemingly responding well to the new environment. But over time, the dry desert air got the upper hand, since, despite their best efforts, the grass started turning browner and browner at a certain point, eventually dying off completely.

But not all of Iraq was like this moderately arid environment. In one of my excursions outside of our home base, we flew to a base about thirty miles south of Mosul, which was operationally known as Q-west or sometimes Key West. This was formerly one of Saddam Hussein's air bases known as Qayyarah Airfield West, but since that name was a mouthful, it had been shortened to Q-west.

Upon landing at the airfield of Q-west, I was so overjoyed to see grass (for the first time in several months) everywhere in this temperate environment that I took multiple pictures of it as if it had been one of the great wonders of the world.

Besides grass though, the one thing that I missed the most from home was trees. I've always loved the shade, strength, and unshakeable stability of a good, large, old oak tree or any tree, for that matter. I spent so many of my boyhood days in the woods out in nature that it became like a second home to me. I took countless nature walks, sometimes just to explore the large wooded area behind our home and to find areas into which I had not yet gone. This wooded area began in a small stand of trees behind our house, but it was contiguous to the much larger wooded area at the end of our street, several thousand acres of undeveloped land, barely touched by human activity. The deep and dark sanctuary of the forest was, as I found out, an excellent place to think, to relax, to solve problems, and to provide adventure for an active teenage boy. This wooded area was so large that one could wander for hours in almost any direction without even running across the smallest sign of civilization.

There was something primal and refreshing about the forest. I loved the sounds of the birds, the lush foliage, the crunchy sound of the fallen leaves beneath my feet, the various animals and insects that I would encounter, and even the earthy smell of the various plants. I loved the solitude, the peaceful quietness. Out there, I could actually believe in the unique, special individuality of life when there was no one else around. Moreover, walking through the woods, I could better hear God speaking in His "still, small voice" (1 Kings 19:12).

I would also come to enjoy the deep, lush forests of Germany years later when I was stationed in that country. I had spent many hundreds or, perhaps, thousands of hours in German forests either running (I was a long distance runner for much of my adult life) or walking alone or with my family on our many excursions around Germany.

In Iraq, I would not have the comfort of that sweet escape into the forest, but going into combat in Iraq, I had absolutely no regrets about serving my country under these dangerous and austere conditions, since I had committed my life to that service. Nonetheless, the two things I really hated having to lose during my deployment were the comfort and love of my family and that escape into the forest, the solitude to think. During my year-long tour, I was only able to find short periods of comfort in the sporadic bits and pieces of communication with my family, but there was never any forest at hand in which I could wander and think, step back from life and reassess my circumstances. I was never able to take a break to regroup, catch my breath, lick my wounds, or regather my thoughts. There were very few opportunities to decompress in the entire year, and I think this was a major factor contributing to my continually building post-traumatic stress disorder (PTSD) symptoms and that of others around me (some researchers put the incidence of PTSD among our current generation of warriors in Iraq and Afghanistan as high as twenty percent).

I've learned in the military that I can take almost anything, endure almost any stressful or dangerous situation for a period of time, so long as it was followed by some kind of escape, uninterrupted rest period, or leave time to be away from the stress and regather my strength. Therefore, I was very grateful for my fifteen days of rest and recuperation (R&R) leave in the middle of my combat tour, very grateful to see my family. Those fifteen days, however, were just a drop in the bucket compared to the continuous and hammering onslaught of stress and violence almost every day.

For the sake of full disclosure and naked honesty, I should say that we were not constantly under the threat of harm. However, the enemy was so unpredictable and so incessantly trying to harm us by the regular, almost daily, attacks of indirect fire (rockets and mortars) throughout our year of duty that we could never, at any moment, be assured of safety. Moreover, my team and I were twice daily reminded of the ongoing, tragic, and relentless violence experienced by the troops under our command as we tracked and reported all the casualty, hospital, and medevac statistics.

Suffice it to say that we were all experiencing a relentlessly harsh pounding by the stress of simply living in this war zone: the long hours of duty, the inadequate nights of rest, the contiguous string of hard days on duty, the violence or the threat of violence, the desert, the sun, etc. And this continuously pounding, hammering stress can easily develop into PTSD, depending on the life experiences of the individual, his or her personality, maturity, family background, education, and unique ability to take on and process the gargantuan monster of stress. Not all people who go into a war zone will develop PTSD as a result of this stress or traumatic experiences, but the countless factors that go into who gets it and who doesn't would probably be impossible to calculate.

As for me, like many of my peers, once I landed in Iraq and assumed my mission, I got very few opportunities to escape the pressure cooker, and these meager opportunities were certainly not enough to completely dispel the continually building pressure of emotions. There was a rapidly filling powder keg of emotions inside of me that would develop into PTSD shortly after I arrived into Iraq.

From my research, I have learned that a major factor in the development of PTSD is the constant, unrelenting rush of adrenaline and cortisol, the fight-or-flight chemicals that are supposed to help save you from harm but which can turn into the enemy when there is no decompression time in a safe place to allow the chemicals to return to normal levels.

All things considered though, I much preferred Iraq over Kuwait. There were a fair number of indigenous trees, which seemed to flourish fairly well without much attention. There were a few palms here and there, and being an animal lover, I was pleasantly surprised to find that there were many signs of animal life around us.

Throughout my life, I've always enjoyed nature, whether running or walking through the lush foliage. The many lush forests of Germany gave me immense pleasure for the eight years of my life that I lived there. From my experience in temperate forests though, I've become accustomed to serendipitous discoveries of all sorts of animals, insects, and so forth. Although Iraq was by no means devoid of animal life, it initially seemed at first glance to be barren. But over time, I would find out that this sparse environment was teeming with life.

Cats were plentiful on the base. You don't typically think of them as wildlife, but since they were, for the most part, feral, they could easily be classified as wildlife. Some people fed them, although we were warned officially to stay away from them. I can understand why our leaders would want us to stay away from these animals because there is no telling what diseases we could have picked up. However, it is extremely difficult to control human nature. Upon seeing one of these common furry little animals, most people are, at least, curious. Not having seen such domestic animals in quite some time, a comforting sight that reminds us of home, there was an overwhelming desire to get close to the animal, somehow recapturing something missed from home. I had heard about roaming dogs on base too, but I never once saw one.

In the August 28, 2005 edition of the base newspaper, *Anaconda Times*, there was an article entitled "How Much Is That Jackal in the Window?" which is about the base animal control officer, Jeremy Parkinson, who was working for the contracting company, Kellogg Brown & Root. Of course, the title was meant to be ironic, since it was a play on words from the familiar children's song, "How Much Is That Doggie in the Window." In the article, Parkinson noted that "the main threats in the area were the dogs, cats, and jackals."[2]

He further noted that when he first arrived on the base, about the same time that we assumed the mission from our predecessor, "the dogs and jackals were running in packs of twelve to fifteen and were scaring a lot of people." Surprisingly, I never saw any of these packs, nor had I heard of them, but then I guess with a very large base like Balad with thousands of acres, there were many places they could roam while only being seen sporadically by a small percentage of the base's population.

The article went on to say that "the animals were breaking into a warehouse here, feeding off of the Meals, Ready to Eat and had become so accustomed to the people on LSA Anaconda, the dogs were no longer scared to come close to them."

Over the period of six months, Parkinson, according to the article, was able to capture most of the animals in the packs, but he noted, "The dogs, cats, jackals, foxes, and mongooses are still a threat, but the threat is not as serious as it was in the beginning."[3] That was the situation at the end of August 2005, just a few months before we would redeploy home.

Off base, dogs were a common sight as I learned from my convoy to Scania (Convoy Support Center Scania, also known as Camp Scania, was near the village of Nippur along the main supply route that we called Tampa and about a hundred kilometers south of Baghdad and forty kilometers southeast of Hillah). I remember with amusement the first dog I saw off post. We were convoying to Scania, and the area we were passing through seemed particularly hot and arid. However, the Tigris must have been fairly near, since there were shallow pools at varying distances from us to the sides of the road. As I stared out the window daydreaming, I noticed a dog sitting in a puddle of water, with just the few inches of his backside and hindquarters underwater. I had to laugh at his ingenuity and the absurd and unexpected sight of a dog sitting in a pool of water.

Other animal sightings were not so amusing. In one town we drove through, I saw a dusty field littered with many carcasses of dead dogs and a few other animals thrown in. It amazed me that people would just throw the bodies into this field where they would rot openly.

We had been warned about animal carcasses. They were such a common sight that one might not pay attention to them at all. However, the insurgents would occasionally put the roadside bombs (IEDs or improvised explosive devices) inside the carcasses. I could never understand this. I had thought that touching a dead animal, especially a dog, would be such a vulgar and irreligious act that it would be repulsive even for a Muslim to imagine doing it. But I guess a man filled with hate can do almost anything imaginable.

I never saw the famous, gigantic camel spiders. Many of my friends had brought back humorous camel spider stories from the first Gulf War, so I expected to encounter these ominous creatures at some point, but that never happened. Moreover, I never saw a single scorpion either, although I had heard of a few unpleasant encounters from fellow soldiers in our unit. I'm not overly frightened by spiders, although I prefer to avoid them. So the fewer arachnids/arthropods I encounter, the better.

The largest extent of my experience with any insect was the ant—the ubiquitous ant. Many give their admiration to the roach for its survival skills, but I can't imagine that they outdo the ant. I have seen ants all over the world, and I have a love-hate relationship with them. One can only admire their determination and industry, but that determination can get them into your house in very unwelcome intrusions. Thankfully, although I did see them many times and places around the base, they seemed to stay in their place and avoided mine.

Mosquitoes were somewhat of a problem, although they were limited as to when they could come out due to the heat and aridity. Being so close to the Tigris and its marshes though, we found that the mosquito population could quickly explode, so something had to be done to control them. Civilian contractors handled a spraying program for the base. You could see the trucks moving slowly on many summer nights, blowing out clouds into the air, which would settle gradually back to the earth. I had never seen such a spraying program since I was a child in New Orleans in the mid-1960s. When I lived in that mosquito-ridden city, I constantly saw the trucks driving through all the neighborhoods, blowing an oily, smoky substance in the spring and summer evening air, which was, I assume, formulated to kill off, dispel, or discourage the mosquitoes.

The most common insects in Iraq, however, were the sand fleas. In some areas, infestations were horrendous. The fleas loved the ubiquitous sandbags, especially when the bags rotted and burst open after months in the blazing hot sun. Ironically though, in spite of the threat of sand fleas, the burst sandbags often brought forth attractive grasses and flowers, which seemed to flourish in the damp sand. But seeing the beauty from the burst open sandbags (which were there to save our lives) caused a bit of cognitive dissonance—like seeing a flower growing out of a carcass.

Among the wildlife I observed in Iraq, I also never saw any of the famous snakes or vipers. I'm quite glad of that though. With the circumstances that we lived in and the dim lighting and so forth, an encounter with one of them could be instantaneously life-threatening. Of course, this is assuming that one even had an awareness of the snake's presence. Many times, I stumbled across a pitch-dark gravel parking lot at 0500 to get to the gym. I could not even see the ground under my feet. I had an ugly fantasy that snakes could be hiding down there in the dark and dust, but as I had learned to do with so many other unpleasant things, especially during military training, I just ignored it, refused to acknowledge it, and pretended that it wasn't real.

But not all of the animals were so demure. Bats, surprisingly, were so intertwined into our lives. They lived in a compartment just under the eaves of our headquarters building. They would come out at night, swooping, flowing out in waves just over our heads as we walked away from our work areas toward the dining facilities for our supper. The bats' departure in the evening gave some an eerie feeling, as they feared that the swift little creatures might miscalculate in their close fly-bys and strike us on our heads, get entangled in our hair, or whatever. But, of course, these fears never came to fruition, no matter how close the bats might get. To them, we were just various obstacles around which they had to navigate to get to their feast of flying insects, and being so close to the Tigris River, the bats never had a shortage of food.

We had a love-hate relationship with the bats, since they were so creepy but at the same time entertaining and beneficial in keeping down the insect population. They never bothered us, but, as you well know, they are the stuff of legend and myth. Even though they might not do anything to harm you, the sight of one of these creatures is normally enough to make most people's skin crawl. But you couldn't avoid the fact that they were fascinating. Many times, other people and I stopped to watch them swoop and dive after insects in the glow of the security lights at the entrance to our headquarters compound.

In the dim light, you wouldn't really notice the presence of the bats' dinner (insects) until you got around the bright force protection lights, which were comprised of small generators powering what were essentially stadium lights on twenty-foot poles. These lights only shined in one direction, but they were unbelievably bright. Looking from the back of the lights into the illuminated areas, one could see the huge multiplicity of insects flying about, attracted by the bright light. And, of course, the bats, although avoiding the main area of the light, would flit about the periphery and cull the bugs that were either going into or away from the light.

I don't remember seeing many birds, although you could certainly hear them about you on a cool morning, before the worst of the day's heat took over. I remember noticing one time a bush near the post exchange (the PX, which was our own miniature version of Walmart) that was infested with small birds. It was utterly amazing to see the bush, which was no more than eight feet high and four feet in diameter, with the songs of scores of birds coming out.

The rest of my interesting nature experiences consist of seeing pelicans nest on top of telephone poles with their automobile-tire-sized nests right on top of the pole. I also saw goats and donkeys primarily around the villages. I never saw a rodent but did see the occasional lizard.

That was the extent of my experiences with the wildlife of Iraq. My most memorable experiences of nature though were weather-related. Beautiful sunsets were a common occurrence in the fall, accompanied by unbelievably large and full autumn moons dominating the sky. There were times when the weather was amazingly beautiful with the autumn moon hanging in a perfect, serene sky and with the air around you a virtually perfect temperature.

One night shortly after we arrived—it was early December 2004—we were returning from our evening meal, and I was deep in thought, maybe thinking about home. Something prompted me to look up, and I was instantly enchanted. It was twilight, with the deepening, darkening blue of the sky turning into a purplish blue streak stretching almost down to the horizon with just a small band of yellowish light interspersed as you gazed toward the rapidly sinking remnants of the sun. The moon hung low, not far above the horizon on the twilight side. The temperature was a balmy seventy degrees with a nice, easy, slightly cooler breeze. I realized that I had experienced few evenings that were so beautiful, calm, or peaceful at home. This is not to say that I considered my deployment home preferable to being with my family, but I realized then that this desert land possessed its own version of beauty.

Despite these beautiful moments, there were times that the weather took a very ugly turn. While everyone else back home was experiencing winter with its cold and snow, we only experienced the cold at first. It could get very cold in the desert with very little vegetation to hold the heat in, the mostly flat and open land leaching all the heat into the sky very quickly after sunset. I was very grateful for our wooly jackets and gloves.

But the cold was not the dominant feature of the winter season. Soon, the rain came. The dusty soil could not hold the water deeply as it would in a more temperate climate with a well-developed soil and vegetation base. So the water sat on the surface in the six to twelve inches of fine river silt to become what many of us called peanut butter mud. It had amazingly viscous qualities and was extremely difficult to clean from anything. As a result, the mud got onto and into everything.

We (the leaders) took guard duty on Christmas day from the lower-ranking soldiers, which was right at the beginning of the rainy season. It was a developing tradition and a good, sincere effort at showing the troops that we cared about their well-being. However, regardless of the motivation, this was serious duty. It wasn't just a walk in the park. This was just before the insurgency took off. We didn't yet know the extensiveness of the enemy's capabilities, and Saddam Hussein was still out there. You couldn't help but wonder and worry about the worst possible scenario. Would the insurgents try to infiltrate the base while on your watch? You could never be sure.

So, for guard duty, we had to get into full battle rattle, as soldiers call it. That's with the helmet, flak vest or body armor, the harness (belt and suspenders), which we call LBE (load-bearing equipment), weapons, ammo, and rucksack (if required, with additional equipment or clothing). We stood inspection at 0600 that morning with functions checks for the weapons and distribution of ammo. There was a steady drizzle pretty much the entire day. Despite the dreariness of the weather, I felt very upbeat about the opportunity to serve on guard duty. I love to do physical things, and I enjoy helping people.

We went out and did a four-hour guard shift, and it was completely uneventful. It just seemed strange to be in a guard tower though, looking out over the Iraqi countryside (mostly farmland in our area) with a loaded weapon ready to fire on a Christmas day. No regrets, just seemed strange. Hopefully, the lower-ranking troops that we replaced were getting a little rest, some good food, and were calling home.

With the steady drizzle though sooner or later, you were forced to step in the peanut butter mud as you traversed the base to and from your quarters, work area, dining facilities, worship facilities, gyms, or even the port-a-potties. But once you first placed your boot into the mud, the mud clung to your boots like a syrupy glue, making them feel like lead weights until you scraped it off somehow. Cleaning it off your boots was like trying to get a piece of double-sided tape off your finger. As soon as you took the tape off with one hand, it was stuck to the other. And there was nothing you could use to scrape off the mud anyway, since the mud was everywhere and on everything.

And there was no avoidance of it no matter how hard you tried or what route you took. Various fields all around the base formed a sea of the sticky mud usually between you and some very much desired item, building, or service. It could be the phones, the PX, or, unfortunately and ironically in many circumstances, the showers. To get to the showers, you would have to pick your way through the mud and get it all over your boots or athletic shoes, slopping out over your ankles. Thankfully, there was a shower on the other end. As you were coming out squeaky clean, you were immediately confronted with negotiating the sticky mud. Thankfully, the rainy season only lasted a few weeks, and the base dried out relatively quickly in the arid environment.

The summer heat was another thing altogether. Some optimistic people try to dismiss the desert heat by saying, "It's a dry heat." That only carries so much weight. The arid environment also sucks moisture out of you a lot quicker, requiring constant hydration just to keep up. Also, when you're wearing a heavy uniform with sleeves down, a helmet, along with heavy, stifling body armor, load-bearing equipment (LBE), weapons, etc. At that point, almost anything above ninety degrees Fahrenheit would be challenging. Add to that the necessity of walking most places on base and then push the temperature above 120 degrees on a string of days during the summer months, with even the nighttime temperatures remaining above 100.

Worse yet, you could be one of the soldiers who had to walk patrol on combat missions or one of the many soldiers buttoned up inside an armored Humvee for numerous hours of the day for patrol or escort duty. For those soldiers on wheels, they could be lucky and be up in the hatch where they, at least, got a steady flow of air. Although that air was so hot, it felt like a furnace, and it was so dusty that you had to wrap something (balaclava or bandanna) around your face just to be able to breathe for the duration of the dusty trip. But to be up in that hatch, of course, meant being constantly in danger from the stray sniper or the constant unpredictable terror of the roadside bomb.

As if the brutal heat needed any help in creating misery, the shamal comes blazing in toward the end of summer. It was a hot furnace blast of wind, which whipped up the dust into endless curtains and individual grains of sand and dust, slapping your face and writhing at your feet like rivers of dust. The individual shamal storms could vary from several hours to several days, and the break in between storms was uncertain. The desert dust already got into everything, but with the force of the wind it was even more intrusive.

Amazingly though, the shamal events could be very beautiful. At times, the dust-filtered sun cast an exotic orange tint over everything, and some of the bloody sunsets looked sublimely apocalyptic. And there were days in which the dust hung finely in the air like a fog, creating a beguilingly mysterious landscape from the ordinary and mundane buildings and vehicles on base.

Interestingly, despite all of the extremes, there was actually a brief respite from the weather extremes in spring and in fall. The temperatures could be fairly moderate, and there was no rain or strong heat. During those days, I sometimes thought of Nebuchadnezzar wandering in the hanging gardens of Babylon, enjoying the sensual enticements of his Persian paradise thousands of years ago.

I can remember walking to dinner one particular night in the spring when the temperature was very pleasant in the '70s. A slightly warm breeze was blowing, and a bright full moon hung in the sky just over the tops of the buildings on the horizon. A rare and serene sense of calm settled upon the base. It was one of the most beautiful evenings I had seen anywhere.

Quality of Life

Our living experiences were not only defined by the environment and the creatures in it. And, thankfully, once we got settled in, our quality of life was not too bad. Probably the biggest morale boost was our three daily meals—we ate a broad variety of international dishes while in Iraq. The army cooks were in charge of the feeding programs, but many times all the workers would be contract workers either from the US or from third nations such as India. We had a lot of Indian workers, and they even brought much of their culinary knowledge of their native foods into use to the appreciation of the troops. Soldiers are generally very adventurous when it comes to trying new things, especially food, so eventually the Indian cooks established an Indian cuisine night, which was a big hit with the troops. We also had a very popular Mongolian grill night and "surf and turf" night with steak and seafood, including lobster.

For breakfast, we had the standard bacon, eggs, sausage, hash browns, pancakes, grits, biscuits, juice, fruit, coffee cake, donuts, yogurt, cereal, and milk. For many of our meals though, the cuisine was general American cuisine. There were usually a few choices on the long order line for main entrees (such as meatloaf, spaghetti, fried steak), and there was always a short order line for burgers, hotdogs, and sandwiches, along with the accompanying French fries, chips, etc. Additionally, there were always healthier options for those so inclined like salads, yogurt, etc. And for desert, there were always a variety of good cakes, cheesecakes, cobbler, ice cream, etc.

For drinks, we had milk, coffee—all the standard soda beverages that you would find at a convenience store in the States. We even had near beer, a beer with very low alcohol content, so that soldiers could still enjoy the taste of a beer without the problem of violating the general order prohibiting the manufacture, sale, purchase, possession, or use of alcohol while anywhere in Iraq.

Like most large bases in Iraq, we also had access to some restaurant or fast foods that are common in the US, such as Burger King, Pizza Hut, and Subway.

For entertainment, most soldiers would go to the recreation center where they could watch a broad variety of movies on the big screen TV there or where they could play any of a few dozen board or card games, musical instruments, or pool, foosball, or Ping-Pong.

We also had a few Internet cafes where the soldiers could access the Internet, including e-mail, so that they could contact family and friends. There were also a couple of large phone banks, which could connect to any phone number in the US, or even some foreign countries where we had troops and their families based. Skype was not real well-established at the time, but we could easily, without too much waiting, get a phone call back to the States or get an e-mail out. We just had to be cognizant of the time difference between Iraq and the States. I would often talk with my wife when her day was beginning and mine was ending or vice versa. In addition to these methods of communication, we also had very good mail service, and we often got care packages from home from our friends and loved ones, or even from complete strangers many times, as the American public was very supportive of our troops.

Religious services were very well attended on base as you would expect of troops living in such trying conditions. I attended one general Protestant service at which we always had good praise music and a good sermon. I also attended a gospel service most Sundays. That was a very rousing, charismatic service with lots of very physical expressions of religious fervor, speaking in tongues, etc. This was a new experience for me, since I grew up with relatively conservative and moderate Baptist services in the south.

There was also a very well-attended Catholic service every Sunday that many of our troops attended. Additionally, there were various prayer and Bible study meetings during the week. As for other religions besides Christianity, there was a mosque on base left over from its use during the days of Saddam Hussein, but it was fenced off and put off-limits for everyone on base. There were Muslim services conducted on base, but I never attended one and never saw one. I think there were also Jewish services conducted on base because I saw flyers posted on various bulletin boards.

Impact of the Stress

Danger, of course, was also one of the defining experiences of our life in Iraq. In time, the constant threat of injury did take its toll, even though we became accustomed to the frequent sirens. For my part, since I had to report and track the casualties, I prayed frequently that we would avoid casualties. But God in His mysterious wisdom had a different perspective and allowed some casualties in our units on a regular basis. I could have seen these as simply numbers that I had to report, but I felt each one personally (largely because that was the personality that God gave me), especially when our leaders required personal information on each one. I was required to track down and report information on marital status and children, parents, addresses, etc. I was forced to confront and engage the humanity of each one and confront the magnitude of loss (in my own way, there is no way that I could imagine what the weight of the grief would be to each family, yet the mindless guilt for each one began to eat away at my conscience as if I could have done something to prevent their injuries or deaths).

Although I arrived in Iraq with a strong sense of God's presence and protection, in time, I would have my faith seriously challenged as I began to question God. Partly driven by my guilty feelings at surviving when so many patriots, fellow soldiers, were dying or being seriously wounded by enemy attacks every week, I began to feel like God had let me down by not protecting our soldiers. Of course, this was presumptuous on my part to think that I knew God's will for all of our people, and it was presumptuous to believe that our soldiers could escape harm when all other units were taking casualties. Moreover, we were more likely to take those casualties, since our soldiers were constantly on the road delivering supplies throughout Iraq or escorting convoys. If I had had more faith, I might have trusted God, who saw the big picture that I did not see, and might have trusted that each of these casualties, although I might not understand why, somehow fit into the bigger plan for our unit, our country, and all of humanity. These things are too complex and mystifying for me to understand in my limited perspective.

Driven by my building feelings of guilt though, I pushed myself harder and harder, working longer and longer hours and feeling as if I was not putting enough of myself into the organizational pot of duty and teamwork. Eventually, in my obsession over this building "survivor's guilt," I completely disregarded my personal health, working myself to exhaustion, which necessitated a trip to the emergency room only a few weeks into our tour of duty. I had quickly lost twenty pounds during this period since I was too stressed out to eat, feeling as if I didn't have time to leave my work place. But the trip to the emergency room had a beneficial outcome as I finally came to grips with the realization that I could not do absolutely everything and that I had to take care of my body in order to be able to accomplish my mission and to be there for my people.

Military City Living

Besides the danger and the ever-present stress, there were other aspects of civilization that defined our existence while we were deployed. One was the constancy of building projects, new quarters, new roads, new working facilities, etc. Trailer cities were springing up overnight as these prefabricated houses were being brought into the theater for our soldiers' living and working quarters. They were the perfect solution. They were quick and easy to manufacture and were more than ample to stand up against the harsh elements of the Iraqi weather. They were also easy to transport and were relatively cheap. In some locations, they had even started to stack the discrete housing modules three and four high with accompanying stairways being added to access the higher rooms. I don't know how safe these stacked-up quarters would be with the threat situation at the time, but I often wondered what it would be like to live in these higher level boxes with an excellent view out over the base and the palm groves outside the perimeter, perhaps, even being able to see the banks of the Tigris river to the east of our base.

It's interesting to watch a community grow, regardless of the type. And our community did grow, like a miniature version of manifest destiny. There was always some building project, always some improvement. One constant example of our attempt to tame the land was gravel. Gravel was everywhere, and the trucks were constantly bringing it in. In fact, the gravel program was so important that one part of the evening brief to the commander every evening was about how many loads of gravel had been brought in that day.

And for the soldier, the gravel was one of the most omnipresent facets of life on the base. If you didn't hear the generators, you most certainly heard the gravel crunching under your feet or under the wheels of vehicles traversing the base. Walking in gravel is a bit of a challenge, like walking in sand, but despite the unpleasant side effects, the gravel offered many benefits. It cut down on the expanses of mud (during rainy season). We were very thankful for the gravel when the winter rains turned the mud into that gooey, sticky peanut butter-like substance. Also, during the many days of blowing dust (during the hot, dry summer or, worse, during the shamal), the gravel worked in our favor, holding down much of the fine, light river silt and keeping it out of our eyes and mouths.

Noise is unfortunately an indicator of the level of civilization. The more technology or industry we have, the more noise generally. We could seldom enjoy the peace of birds or crickets chirping or the pleasant swish of the wind through the few trees and bushes. Our most constant aural companions were the crunch of the previously mentioned gravel and the high-pitched whine of the ubiquitous generators. We were also sporadically serenaded with the shrill whine of the attack siren, the overwhelming roar of soldier banter in the cramped space of the dining facility, the staccato sound of helicopter blades from incoming aircraft (mostly bound for the base hospital), the whine or roar of military vehicles going by, and the numerous booms or dull thuds of exploding ordnance, whether from a controlled explosion of captured ammunition or from some mortar lobbed over the perimeter fence by some anonymous insurgent farmer.

But not all noise was unwelcome, even if harsh and loud. Ironically, one of the greatest sources of noise and pleasure of amazement were the F16s that took off from our base. They created tremendous amounts of noise. Everyone for miles around knew from the roar of the jet engines when the jets were preparing to take off. I loved watching them, hearing the deafening roar of their engines, rocketing down the runway in the darkening twilight, their lights flashing from between the buildings blocking our view of the airfield, as the jets taxied down the runway. Then they would suddenly flash above the level of the single-story rooftops beside the airfield, making a sharp angle up into the sky. Like flaming, shooting stars, they shot straight up into the sky, screaming with strength and power disappearing from sight within minutes. I imagined that they were like a gigantic fist thrust up into the sky by some invisible god.

I never got over the amazing sight of the jets taking off. They reminded me how, years before in the early 1980s, I had watched in amazement at the incredible maneuverability of the tank killer A-10s during large military exercises in Germany. Sometimes, we would be driving in convoys of military vehicles, wending our way through the southern German countryside on the way to our training areas when all of a sudden the A-10s would pop over the crest of some small hill and into our view seemingly so close that you could reach out and touch them. Just as suddenly as they had appeared, they would drop out of site and sink back into the valley behind the treetop foliage like a snake wriggling through the brush.

The Facilities

But all of man's amazing technological advances aside, perhaps, the highest form of civilization has to be the humble toilet. I remember seeing Roman ruins in Germany when I was stationed there and hearing about how the Romans had their wood and stone structures for toilets with the steady flow of water going through and using their individual sponges on a stick for hygiene. For Americans, we've reached (we think) a much higher level of civilization with porcelain toilets and soft toilet paper, although some Europeans may still see us as slightly backward, since a bidet is not a very common fixture in American bathrooms.

But Americans definitely love their comfortable bathrooms. I remember reading about how American soldiers during WWII were impressed with the level of civilization when they entered

Germany because the Germans had more familiar and more advanced porcelain facilities, just like the troops were accustomed to back home in the States.

As with many such conveniences, you never really appreciate them until you have to do without. In many of the temporary situations that soldiers find themselves in, the modern marvel called the port-a-potty is a dire necessity. It definitely beats having to do one's "business" in the woods as I've had to do a number of times while hiking the Appalachian Trail as a teenager. However, depending on the situation and one's attitude, the port-a-potty can either be a godsend or another torture on one of the lower levels of Dante's *Inferno*.

One has to keep in mind the additional level of difficulty for a soldier using one of these portajohns. The soldier may be in full battle rattle with body armor, weapon, ammunition, helmet, and load-bearing equipment (belt and suspender system for connecting grenades, canteens, first aid pouches, ammo pouches, etc.) on top of the actual uniform. So, in addition to considerations of security for the weapons and ammo, one has to negotiate the removal of all this gear in order to answer the call of nature. This stuff is heavy, bulky, and dangerous, and it can be difficult to take off in an urgent situation; however, I have frequently been amazed at the ingenuity and agility of a frenetic soldier with a full bladder.

Sleep

In considering civilization's enticements, one cannot overlook the importance of the sleeping situation. For sleep, hard-walled, climate-controlled rooms are very nice. You never know how nice until you've tried to catch a few minutes of sleep sitting in a foxhole on a hot summer night of military training, with sweat trickling down your back and flies or mosquitoes buzzing around your head, or you've tried to sleep on a hot, dusty roadside or the many other inconvenient places where our troops are forced to sleep in occasionally due to operational demands. In Kuwait, we had the large tents, which could accommodate dozens of soldiers, or the small tents, which could accommodate fewer than a dozen soldiers. Thankfully, by the time we passed through Kuwait, all tents were connected to large commercial air conditioners, but those were very noisy for the people in the tent, and it was very hard to control the air temperature in a porous tent with people constantly going in and out, not to mention getting the temperature at a level that was acceptable to a dozen biologically unique soldiers. Thankfully, when we arrived in Iraq, the military was quickly advancing on its project to get soldiers into hard facilities—either prefab or traditional construction.

Privacy is great too, but it is relative. I guess as long as one is limited to a small group at the very least and has time to be alone occasionally, he or she can enjoy some privacy. Military training usually doesn't offer that ideal situation. However, our living situations in Iraq were better, with most living with no more than four people and the higher-ranking (officers and noncoms) having either single or shared facilities with one other person.

For sleep though, the thing that I unexpectedly missed the most was the mattress. As a soldier, I've learned I can sleep on almost anything, and I can almost sleep standing up. I've had many restful nights on a dirt mattress (i.e. the ground). Optimally, we try to, at least, have cots for soldiers on an operation (where semi-permanent facilities are possible). The nylon cot is not bad when you're tired, but the height of civilization is a good mattress with just the right mix of sheets and light or heavy blankets.

In Kuwait, I had slept for the past few weeks on a nylon cot in a tent. The tent's air conditioner ran full blast during the day to keep up with the tyrannical heat. At night, all that desert heat vanished into space without vegetation to hold it in (that part of Kuwait was barren—a long-standing army tradition is to find the most undesirable piece of land in any region and put a base on it). As a consequence, our concern shifted immediately from the miserable heat to the bone-jarring cold. The cot offered no insulation against the dramatic drop in temperature, and, even with a good sleeping bag, I discovered that the thin nylon shield of the cot did nothing against the cold.

My first night in Iraq, I was able to sleep on a bed—a soft mattress, a comfortable bedding—in a hard-walled room with climate control. I was quite content.

Additionally, being stationary and with a space to call our own, we could begin to "feather our nest." We would be here for a year, and we'd be without the comfort of our families, but at the same time we could create a space of our own, an escape, a comfort zone, an oasis. Many bought pictures or rugs from the local dealers who were allowed on the base. Many bought up various comfort items from the base exchange, which offered an impressively good variety of the usual things you'd normally expect in Walmart, K-Mart, Target, etc. In the high stress environment of a combat zone, some of the most mundane things begin to take on greater significance, and procuring these items (whether they are movies, music, comfort foods, etc.) can become an obsession, a drug, a distraction to relieve the boredom, the danger, the loneliness.

Furthermore, such mundane things can connect us to memories and people back home, and those memories were very important to sustain our morale. It is only one link in a chain, a lone stone from a creek bed, but a series of such links and stones can provide the strength to hold on. Not being able to make those connections or having them taken away could result in a more momentous event—an event driven by despair. Such seemingly trivial things help people make the choice to get up every day and feel like it's worth it to go on.

Wrestling with Time and Self

As we settled into our routines and tried to determine how we would get through the rest of the year, we soon became aware that time was our enemy. A year doesn't seem to be a long time when you are living in a relatively normal life, even with the usual challenges that we all have at home, in the workplace, in the neighborhood, etc. But imagine your life suddenly interrupted by being flown into a foreign, sometimes hostile, country away from all of your emotional supports of family and friends and having all of your normal diversions, distractions, entertainments and activities. You'll find the year much more daunting. Most of us live such distracted, busy, and entertained lives of mass consumption in the comfort of our home and our familiar surroundings—without serious and life-threatening circumstances, all things under our control, and all events predictable—but a year of deprivation and danger away from the comfort, connections, familiar things and people that we cherish, and being denied the strength that we derive from all these is a very long year.

We dealt with it the best way we could, all in our own individual ways. One of the ironic ways that we coped with this tyranny of time was by tracking it with "the donut of pain" on our computers. The donut of pain was a simple tool that some anonymous person devised. It's a computer desktop application that graphically displayed your combat time served versus time left to serve in the form of donut icon. It was keyed in to the computer's time and date stamp, and all you had to do was to enter your expected redeployment (return or go back home date). The macro would then work with the Excel capabilities to set up a donut-shaped graph that would tell you how much of your deployment you have spent and how much is left. The colors of the graph were very simple and archetypal. The red represented the amount of time left. The green represented the amount of time that had passed.

I can't say that the colors were carefully chosen for their psychological value, but they certainly fit. The red on the graph seemed to aptly stand for danger and the amount of it left. The green seemed to represent the burgeoning growth of hope as we got closer to our redeployment date. It was a simple and silly thing, but when one is enduring a difficult experience, little tricks like this can produce enough sense of progress and encouragement to get you through the next day. I'm sure this is true of prisoners or POWs. Getting through a long, unpleasant experience may require certain tricks of the mind and will.

But the passage of time is a funny thing. Most of us feel we don't have enough of it, but when we are in unpleasant circumstances, time can't pass fast enough.

In spite of its importance, we don't really understand time. Most of us hold to a Newtonian idea of the passage of time as being constant and steady. But Einstein proposed that the passage of time is relative, being affected by such things as the perspective (relative position or point in time) of the person experiencing and observing. At times, it seemed to us like we were in one of Einstein's time warps while we were in Iraq.

At first, it was difficult. In the first few days, we were aware of every single tick of the clock and every minute change in the donut of pain. We preferred not to acknowledge it, so our awareness was mostly subconscious. But in such situations, the soldier begins to play tricks on himself. He ignores the obvious painful emotions which he might possibly feel by immersing himself in work and other distractions.

The initial distractions focused on exploring our environment—our home—for the next year. We learned our way around, and we made efforts to feather our nests with rugs or pictures or whatever or experience simple pleasures of certain foods or activities. In between the distractions, we would occasionally look up and realize that time was passing very slowly. But, with our distractions and increasingly busy work lives, before we realized, days turned into weeks and weeks into months. We began to feel better as we realized that an increasingly large part of our tour was over.

Our first priority in coping with the time monster was to plan mid-tour Rest and Recuperation leave or R&R. For all soldiers, R&R was a significant milestone in their tour. It gave them a short breather, an alleviation from the loneliness and stress, and it gave them a marker to focus on. To them, it was a little bit of hope that would provide strength to get through some hard days.

You tend to do that in the army—finding such markers to give you hope to continue on. When you're going through something really difficult, you learn to look past the discomfort and set up milestones, typically some kind of break, relief, or reward. It's one way of coping and is, in fact, not new to soldiering. In Tolstoy's *War and Peace*, the French soldiers, demoralized and retreating from Moscow, kept focusing on the next town, hoping for relief from that place. But the continual hope kept many of them from giving up and dying in place.

Focusing on the milestones is a constructive way of keeping you from dwelling on the unpleasant or the terrifying in a war zone. However, the bad thing is that it teaches you to delay certain emotions and issues. Stress can build up until it is almost explosive, and the explosion usually occurs back at home where it can no longer be contained and where it frequently comes out in negative or harmful ways.

Nonetheless, the army teaches you that you have to delay and ignore. You can't afford to show any weakness. You can't afford to pause or catch your breath or slow down. You can't afford to feel. You ignore the pain and drive on. You do whatever you have to do to keep going. This just makes things worse over time because there comes a point of saturation. You can't keep on indefinitely. You can't run forever on an empty tank.

The Building Stress and Introspection

None of us had reached empty yet. We were just beginning to develop routine and learn ways to divert ourselves. We were also starting to build our family here, making deeper emotional connections to the friends around us. If you looked at our daily lives, there was vibrancy and determination. We missed our families and lives in the States terribly, but we owed it to them and to our comrades to survive, so we had to go at life with equal determination. You can't halfway commit to life in a danger area. You have to be very determined and committed. Otherwise, when you get into the situation that will require a decision or instinctive reaction, you may fail. The consequence could be a body bag, a funeral, and a grief for your family.

But there are a lot of pressures in war, and the troops are always looking for a diversion to take away the edge from the constant grinding pressure. The easiest thing is to focus on any pleasure; you might over-emphasize eating or smoking or almost anything that comes with that immediate gratification, feeling, or pleasure. Each person's outlet can be multitudinous as our own personalities and backgrounds. Some might focus more on intellectual, spiritual, or emotional fulfillment. Seeking to express vitality, and maybe largely to soothe the deeper fears and loneliness, many turned to emotional connection with friends that were on the deployment with them.

But there are almost always crutches that people grasp at, and there are frequently excesses, but one absolutely cannot be partly committed to life in a war zone. You have to be committed day in and day out. This opens you up to thoughts, beliefs, and understandings that you might have never faced before. It can easily lead you to strange or new experiences.

My first taste of such new experiences was the New Year's Eve watch service supported by the gospel chapel. It was very raucous, very physical, and extremely emotional. I was somewhat unprepared for this because I came from a more conservative Protestant denomination. I was accustomed to very orderly, largely formal services. I had even attended Catholic and Jewish services during my adulthood and found them to have largely the same formal character.

Up to this time, I was unlikely to seek out or willingly take part in such emotionally focused services. However, my previous world was already beginning to seem distant and inadequate. Although I had been largely at peace during the transition from home to war zone, the pressures were mounting quickly, and I was already beginning to feel unprepared for the year ahead. I was willing to open my heart to anything that would help me make it through.

Another new and very unpleasant experience I faced was living my life totally free from the normal diversions. Up to this time in my adult life, I had always been striving toward the next accomplishment or goal as I built my career. I was also totally focused on raising my children and enjoying them. I did make some time for charity and religious work early on, but when my children started arriving, I felt that I owed them the lion's share of my time outside of work.

When I wasn't so busy with job and family, my free time was spent in traveling or pursuing projects or hobbies. I was always busy doing something. When I got to the desert, I found those diversions and distractions reduced dramatically and unexpectedly to almost nothing. More surprisingly, I found out how dependent I was on the distractions.

Without those competing activities to keep me occupied, I had a lot of time on my hands to think. As a result, I came face-to-face with myself, with some of my unresolved emotional baggage. I saw myself in some ways for the first time. In other ways, I was seeing something that I no longer wanted to see. I was seeing weaknesses in me, fractures in my world, and fissures in my psyche—some I knew about and had ignored, but some I didn't realize at all.

This new experience of myself was dredging up old pains from a painful past and troubles I had gotten into while fleeing that past. I was being pushed into a struggle for my existence—for me, something much deeper than my mere physical being. I have never feared physical harm, but I deeply feared the pain of my wounded heart and soul. In facing this struggle, I found out that a year can be a very long time to struggle under such burdens without escape or relief.

I found out in time that others struggled as well. Many probably didn't reach the depths I reached, a depth at which I frequently questioned whether or not I really wanted to live. But even though I felt so alone in my struggle, I did find out from daily reports I saw and read that, at least, a few others had similar struggles. Some resorted to suicide.

Ironically though, there was frequently no way of knowing that there were others going through the same struggle and thereby preventing the final solution, since all soldiers, despite all the briefings to ask for help, are immersed in a culture where weakness or admission of weakness is to be avoided at all costs. True, it's impossible not to experience weakness at least a few times in one's life, so our tough training did not expunge all of that from our souls. Rather, we merely learned how to hide it well. The result is that even though military leaders have told us to watch out for the signs of struggle in others, at the same time, we've been taught by our Spartan culture to hide that weakness. So, who can really know a soldier's struggle merely by looking into a face?

Religion in the Combat Zone

It is because of the intense pressures in a combat zone that many people seek higher meaning or divine help in order to cope with the stress. Although Americans are generally known as very religious people, many individuals only have an intellectual understanding of Christianity and don't regularly attend services.

But there are two pressures that pushed many into experiencing religion more personally or to seek out religion for the first time in their lives. First, we don't have the same distractions as before. Without those distractions, one tends to have more time than he or she knows what to do with. Moreover, that abundance of time tends to lead to boredom or excessive time to dwell on negative thoughts or, perhaps, fears, so that soldier is probably more open to thinking about religion or spirituality regardless of how he or she lived at home.

Second, as the old adage suggests, there are no atheists in foxholes. The violence of war or the tremendous stress can catch some soldiers by surprise, even to soldier's that have trained rigorously for this event. Despite our toughness, we are still human beings. In times of fear or anxiety, humans are inherently emotional, and the natural emotional response to confusion or anguish is to call on a higher power. Some may cast aspersion on this as a supposedly vestigial evolutionary tendency or the ignorant imaginative ramblings of primordial man. Others may see it as an inbred spiritual intuition, which encourages us to reach out to the cosmos, to a God who we instinctively know is there based on the amazing wonder, complexity, variety, and order of the universe.

Regardless of what we believe, it is hard to deny that we have an instinct to seek out a higher being. We have an instinct to believe there is something higher than ourselves. We have this natural feeling when we look at the stars that there is something greater than we know or see or can explain. If we are wise, the more we look at what we see, we realize that we are looking at greatness, at something unusual and inexplicable. How do we explain it? How did it get there? We can say, "By chance or accident." While that may satisfy the intellect of some people, I would venture to say that it is emotionally satisfying to a very few. In our heart and spirit, we sense there is much more to the story.

Some people will call upon that divine higher Spirit when in trouble. I have been a deep seeker in the past, finding my answers in the Bible I grew up with and the Jesus I had heard so much about in church. When I arrived in Iraq, I was stable in my relationship with God, but with the deterioration of my emotions, I would seemingly lose my grip on my faith. It was ironic that my own relationship with God would be unstable in this environment because I always expected that the opposite would be true in the deepest adversity of my life.

When we reach the end of our ability, our humanity, our strength, and our capability to produce answers (usually in times of extreme crisis), we have to reach higher. And when we reach higher, we have to believe that there is something greater and wiser than us. If there is such a being and we realize we need him, then we should approach very humbly.

Religion is a search for something higher. When we question, explore, and seek, we really desire truth. When we manipulate and argue, we reject truth and are really only searching for ourselves.

But in the search for a higher being, one often asks the great questions such as, "Why am I here? What is my purpose in life?" Ecclesiastes 12:13–14 (NKJV) gives us one answer:

> "Let us hear the conclusion of the whole matter:
> Fear God and keep His commandments,
> For this is man's all.
> For God will bring every work into judgment,
> Including every secret thing,
> Whether good or evil."

So we learn from this verse that, if there is a God, He would want us to honor Him and abide by certain rules for our own good.

We also might ask, if there is a God, what does He expect of us? In Isaiah 58:6–12 (NKJV), the prophet addresses this question when he confronts people over their hypocritical and morally empty religious observance of fasting. He tells them from God's viewpoint that fasting is simply a form of worship, but the highest form of worship that God wants is for them (and us) to lovingly serve the people around them, meeting whatever needs they may have:

> Is this not the fast that I have chosen:
> To loose the bonds of wickedness,

To undo the heavy burdens,
To let the oppressed go free,
And that you break every yoke?
Is it not to share your bread with the hungry,
And that you bring to your house the poor who are
    cast out;
When you see the naked, that you cover him,
And not hide yourself from your own flesh?
Then your light shall break forth like the morning,
Your healing shall spring forth speedily,
And your righteousness shall go before you;
The glory of the Lord shall be your rear guard.
Then you shall call, and the Lord will answer;
You shall cry, and He will say, "Here I am."

If you take away the yoke from your midst,
The pointing of the finger, and speaking wickedness,
If you extend your soul to the hungry
And satisfy the afflicted soul,
Then your light shall dawn in the darkness,
And your darkness shall be as the noonday.
The Lord will guide you continually,
And satisfy your soul in drought,
And strengthen your bones;
You shall be like a watered garden,
And like a spring of water, whose waters do not fail.
Those from among you
Shall build the old waste places;
You shall raise up the foundations of many generations;
And you shall be called the Repairer of the Breach,
The Restorer of Streets to Dwell In.

Moreover, when Jesus was asked about the most important commandments (Matthew 22:36–40 and Mark 12:28–31), he said that the first was to love God with all of one's heart, soul, mind, and strength. But he said there was a second commandment that was inextricably linked to it, that one should love his neighbor as himself. Also, in Matthew 25:32–46, Jesus made it clear that any expression of love or pity for the lowliest and neediest people around them was akin to loving and caring for Jesus himself.

So, a true and deep understanding of Christianity must focus on the centrality of love and service and not just a love for those whom you're expected to love (family and friends). This love must extend beyond our zone of comfort and make us sacrifice. Perhaps, because they sacrifice so much on a daily basis, soldiers can more easily identify with the concepts of sacrifice in traditional Christianity. In any case, worship services were very well attended, and religion became an inextricable part of daily life for many of us.

My wife and I at the green ramp as we awaited my departure.

My children and I at the green ramp.

Soldiers and their families from our unit awaiting departure.

On board the aircraft shortly after liftoff.

Bangor, Maine, from the window of our aircraft.

Our aircraft shortly after we had disembarked in Kuwait.

The Kuwaiti countryside from the bus
window on the way to Camp Virginia.

A hazy, dust-filled sky hangs over Camp Virginia.

My temporary home while in Camp Virginia.

On the way to Iraq in the back of an Air Force C-130.

My room at Balad Logistics Base.

The exterior of our prefab houses.

A small grove of trees on Balad Logistics
Base in front of our theater.

Waiting to board a Black Hawk en route
to Al Asad Airbase, Iraq.

The pooled water and sticky mud from the short rain season.

Sherpas awaiting our group to board for
a trip from Balad to Q West.

A reasonably comfortable ride in the back of a Sherpa.

The Tigris River and the Iraqi countryside from the window of our Sherpa.

A grassy field and our Sherpa on the
runway after our flight to Q West, Iraq.

Sunset over Balad Logistics Base, Iraq.

One mortar round that came a little too close for
comfort for soldiers in the operations cell.

Loaded for bear: HUMVEEs with turrets and
heavy guns for convoy escort missions.

An Iraqi entrepreneur trying to make a buck.

Lush palm groves on the side of the road during a convoy.

New friends: Iraqi boys who came out to investigate as we tried to repair a broken down vehicle.

Dust from the Shamal winds decreases visibility dramatically.

A typical, very hot day in Iraq at 120 degrees Fahrenheit.

PTSD and the Lonely Road Home

When Johnny comes marching home again,
Hurrah! Hurrah!
We'll give him a hearty welcome then,
Hurrah! Hurrah!
The men will cheer and the boys will shout,
The ladies they will all turn out,
And we'll all feel gay,
When Johnny comes marching home.[1]

I learned the words of this old Civil War era tune in a music class when I was in grade school during the '70s. The lyrics for this song were written by Irish-American bandleader Patrick Gilmore during our nation's Civil War and were published in 1863. He matched the lyrics to a slightly older drinking song that was also popular during the Civil War era. The song was popular in both the North and the South during the Civil War, but the sentiment on both sides was the same—that there was much reason to celebrate when that long bloody war was over and the soldiers finally came home.

Unfortunately, for many soldiers in that era and the current generation, after the initial celebrations, some very hard realities began to settle in as they tried to grapple with their wartime experiences and memories, with many of them developing post-traumatic stress disorder (PTSD). Many of these returning warriors were permanently changed by their wartime experiences. Despite the joyous homecoming, there were many soldiers from our past wars and our current wars who have faced or will face a long lonely road on their way home as they try to fully return home mentally and emotionally and make sense of and heal from their experiences.

Being numbered among those with PTSD, I have researched extensively on the subject, hoping to understand what I was up against. While trying to find healing, I have gone through countless hundreds of hours of talk therapy and thousands of hours in prayer, finally finding some measure of peace and healing after nine years of grappling with these inner demons. Moreover, having found that peace and healing, I hope to be able to provide answers to others. Knowing the magnitude of my struggle through PTSD and hearing in the media about the struggle of other returning troops (with as many as twenty-two veterans a day committing suicide by some estimates), my heart and mind (as well as so many of my prayers) constantly go out to them.

Like Odysseus in Homer's epic, *The Odyssey*, the story of a man's years-long struggle to return home from war, many of these veterans may still have had some of the battlefield within them years after the end of their service. The HBO documentary *Wartorn* (2011) opens with a quote from The Odyssey that captures this struggle of the veteran to return home: "Must you carry the bloody horror of combat in your heart forever?"[2]

But on my road home through my PTSD, I learned that PTSD is just a "normal response to an abnormal situation," to use the words of an online pamphlet published by The Post Traumatic Stress Disorder Association of Canada (PTSDassociation.com). PTSD is very common throughout any given population as I've found in my research, but it is especially prevalent among troops who have deployed to combat.

The veteran's organization Iraq and Afghanistan Veterans of America published a report, "Invisible Wounds," January 2009. In this report, they explain the pervasiveness of mental health issues among our veterans of those two wars:

In early 2008, the RAND Corporation completed a land-mark study of Iraq and Afghanistan veterans that offered the most thorough information to date about the rates of PTSD, TBI, and major depression among new veterans. According to the RAND study, 14 percent of Iraq and Afghanistan veterans screen positive for PTSD, 14 per-cent screen positive for major depression, and 19 percent of those surveyed reported a probable TBI.[3]

In the study, some of these categories overlapped, but the bottom line is that "30% of Iraq and Afghanistan Veterans Screen Positive for Probable PTSD, TBI, or Major Depression," the so-called invisible wounds (Williamson, Vanessa and Erin Mulhall). Based on information about veterans of previous wars, overtime these numbers are likely to rise significantly as veterans succumb to delayed onset PTSD or as they gradually discover that they have one of these invisible wounds that they previously attributed to other causes or conditions. Or some may simply be hiding the conditions and not reporting them, but as they worsen overtime or the symptoms become too overwhelming to hide, they will be added to the number.

PTSD Symptoms and the Portrayal of PTSD in the Media

Since PTSD is common, many Americans can probably recognize the symptoms in those veterans you encounter daily or maybe live with. You may even find depictions of characters with PTSD in the media. Some of the depictions of mental illness in media are respectful and as accurate as possible. For instance, in the 2003 western *Open Range*[4] with Kevin Costner and Robert Duvall, Costner plays a cowboy, Charlie Waite, who is obviously suffering from PTSD (which a modern audience can recognize from the symptoms that Waite exhibits during the course of the movie).

In one scene, Charley Waite is aroused from a PTSD night-mare by the kind woman, Sue Barlowe, played by Annette Bening, who is letting them rest at her house. Barlowe means well but does not know that Waite is troubled by bad memories and nightmares (symptoms of his PTSD). As she awakens him in this one scene, he does not realize where he is, does not realize that it has all been a dream and that he is now awake. Still being alarmed by the images of his nightmare, he draws his gun on Barlowe, confusing her for the man in his nightmare.

This is a common occurrence among PTSD sufferers (i.e., at the worst, waking and attacking another person thinking that the dream is still playing out in real life, or, at the least, awaking in an alarmed state, not knowing right away that the real life sur-roundings are not the imaginary surroundings of the dream). I have often awoken from sleep in the latter state, quite alarmed and alarming my poor wife, although I have, thankfully, never struck her. But I was told by one psychiatrist at the Veterans Administration when we were discussing PTSD nightmares that one of his patients came out of a PTSD nightmare and started choking his poor wife, thinking that she was the enemy soldier he saw in his nightmare.

I myself still have some of the PTSD nightmares eight years after returning from Iraq. I have also heard many stories from other veterans (or about other veterans through a secondary source who knew the veteran personally). When I rise in the morning after a supposedly good night's rest, my wife has reported to me on countless occasions my funny and sometimes not-so-funny antics during the night. She said that I would do such things as sit up, flail my arms and legs apparently in response to whatever experience I was dreaming. She's also told me that I have entire conversations or arguments, sometimes yelling and cursing at people in my dreams. Additionally, I have woken up many times with bruises and scratches on my arms or legs with no memory of how I got them.

Moreover, my experiences are not unique to me. In an article from the Indy Week web site, Dan Frosch tells one particularly harrowing incident experienced by one soldier's wife.

> The first time Kristin Peterson's husband hit her, she was asleep in their bed. She awoke that night a split second after Joshua's fist smashed into her face and ran, terrified and crying, to the bathroom to wipe the blood spurting from her nose.
>
> When she stuck her head back into the bedroom, there he was—punching at the air, muttering how she was coming after him and how he was going to kill her. Kristin started yelling but Joshua's eyes were closed. He was still asleep.
>
> The next morning Josua saw the dried blood on his wife. "Oh God," she recalls him saying. "I did that."[5]

Unfortunately, this couple's experience is not uncommon. While these violent examples are in the extreme, I have had verification from friends, from fellow veterans, and from psychiatrists and therapists discussing their patients and patients' families' experiences that physical manifestations of what's playing out in the veterans' minds during sleep, like the veteran in the Indy Week article, are quite common.

In addition to the dreams, for the PTSD victim, there are also the intrusive thoughts about the traumatic event. There's another scene in the movie *Open Range* in which Waite refers to his PTSD in layman's terms. While in a saloon trying to coerce the reluctant townspeople to stand up to the local bullies (a wealthy rancher and his political pawn, the local marshal), Waite tells one father who is reluctant to make a stand with his sons to resist the control of the marshal. "There are some things that gnaw at a man worse than death."[6]

His point is that these people all fear death when he knows by personal experience that there are some experiences that are far worse than facing the threat of death. This pretty well encapsulates the suffering of many troops who suffer the invisible wounds of PTSD, not to mention other public servants, police, firemen, paramedics, etc., or people in the general population who might have encountered a horrifying experience. Like Waite in the movie *Open Range*, the memories and the symptoms from their PTSD continue to gnaw at them day in and day out for years after their traumatic experience that precipitated the PTSD.

In another scene, Waite apologizes to Barlowe for drawing his gun on her after awakening from his PTSD nightmare. He tells her, "I want to apologize for…earlier." He pauses and then says, "Trying to put some bad times behind me, but sometimes they don't stay put."[7]

To this confession about his PTSD and his bad memories, Barlowe responds, "Always makes me feel better to let them breathe a little bit, [and then] bury 'em."[8] This is, of course, one of the keys to coming to terms with a traumatic event and reducing the control of the PTSD symptoms. It is absolutely essential to tell the story and let the bad memories breathe a little bit.

To give you another example of the commonality of mental health issues as illustrated in various media portrayals, one of my favorite sitcoms addressed mental health in one particular episode, although it's arguable as to whether it was positive or negative. The sitcom I'm referring to is from the 1990s and is entitled *Hanging with Mr. Cooper*. For those that are not familiar with the program, the storyline of the series is built around the comedy of the star of the show, Mark Curry, and the character he plays, Mark Cooper.

The show I watched was episode 3, which was entitled "On the Rebound." The main story line for the episode was about the central character, Mark Cooper, who is reunited with an old girlfriend who manipulates him. In the course of the story, the script includes several references to mental/emotional health and therapy. Unfortunately, some of the references are disparaging and reveal common negative stereotypes about mental health.

Again, I'm not sure whether the writers were posing the stereo-types to enlighten people who subscribe to those outdated ideas or whether they were making fun of people who seek mental health counseling. It's hard to tell from the script, acting, and scene composition.

During the episode in one scene, Mark's ex-girlfriend mentions that she went to three years of therapy in order to arrive at the conclusion that all her problems were reduced to the need to be reconciled with her former boyfriend.

> Geneva: "She's a crazy woman. Okay. Did you know she actually went to go see a shrink? "
>
> Vanessa: "There's nothing crazy about going to therapy."
>
> Geneva: "Yeah, right."
>
> Vanesssa: "Some very normal people use therapists."
>
> Geneva: "Really? Stop. Not you."
>
> Vanesssa: "Well, just for a little while. I had a few inter-personal conflicts to work out with my parents and some semi-obsessive behavior patterns, which I'm completely cured of. Can you see that spot?"
>
> [While speaking, Vanessa obsessively rubs at a spot on the kitchen table, indicating that she, perhaps, is not in full possession of her wits since she is imagining a spot on the table that is not really there, so, therefore, the writers are suggesting that she is not "normal" as she claims to be].
>
> Geneva: "It's a knot hole."

Geneva's comment reveals that Vanessa's sensory faculties are not connected with reality or that they are misinterpreting reality, indicating that she might be "unbalanced" leaving us to assume that the main point that we are supposed to take away from this scene in the episode's dialogue is that only "crazy" people go to see therapists. Moreover, anyone going to see a therapist is considered abnormal or unbalanced, not in control of their wits. The implication is that "normal" people do not need therapists, psychologists, or psychiatrists.

I'm sure the scriptwriters meant well, and comedy or satire has always been used throughout the centuries in various media forums in America and Great Britain (one of our main countries of cultural heritage) to introduce sensitive topics that might be harder to discuss in polite conversation. It has also been used to poke fun at societal or individual human flaws, so this dialogue in the script is not out of the ordinary. But the dialogue does reveal that there are occasionally negative stereotypes and images in our media about mental health and the people who seek help.

Apparently, many people still view therapy as an extraordinary experience and the people seeking treatment as flawed people. I would venture to guess that you will probably encounter these attitudes from time to time in our media. And it is a common viewpoint that I have encountered often among various people along my life's journey. Despite the prejudice, lack of support, and even lack of understanding, I have not been deterred by such people in my persistence to grapple with my PTSD and my bad memories and experiences that fed into my developing PTSD.

Encountering Ignorance

Suffice it to say that these perspectives, although common, are entirely erroneous. Yet, it is likely that if you are struggling with mental or emotional issues (such as PTSD) as I have, you may encounter such attitudes from the people around you who just don't understand. Most unfortunately, you may even encounter these misguided people and various stereotypes within the mental health community.

It is an unfortunate fact of life that ignorance about mental/emotional health issues and many other things in life is very common among individual members of any given population. Suffice it to say that ignorance is an all-too-human flaw. The famous English writer and playwright William Shakespeare (1564–

1616) addressed the subject of ignorance, writing, "And seeing ignorance is the curse of God; knowledge is the wing wherewith we fly to heaven" (from *Henry VI*, Part II, act IV, scene vii[9]). He was partly right. Education (our process to obtain knowledge on the road to truth) is certainly the most effectual tool in our arsenal to dispel, expose, or deconstruct ignorance.

But ignorance is not something that God inflicts upon us. We come by it naturally. Our minds are empty vessels on the day that we are delivered into the world, fresh from the wombs of our mothers. It takes a lifetime of learning to try to fill that vessel, but our learning will never end in our lifetimes. Moreover, if we take our knowledge from bad sources, then we are just as likely to be filled with inaccurate or bad knowledge as we are to be filled with good.

To quote a more modern writer on the same subject, I would turn to Thomas Sowell (American economist, social theorist, political philosopher, and author of numerous books and articles) who once wrote, "It takes considerable knowledge just to realize the extent of your own ignorance."[10] Mr. Sowell succinctly encapsulates a profound truth that many educated people (whether through formal or informal means) discover after decades of learning and living life. They discover, as Mr. Sowell did, that a lifetime of dedicated learning will still leave us woefully short of complete knowledge and just scratching the surface of what we call truth.

If you are suffering from PTSD as I am, you may encounter some ignorant attitudes or methods in the mental health community as I did. Thankfully, these people are in the minority, but their actions and words can be quite distressing if you are already troubled by your PTSD symptoms.

To give you one example, I encountered one psychiatrist who became somewhat agitated after several medications she prescribed did not seem to be working for me at all. Now that I have done extensive research on the subject of PTSD, I have found out that adrenaline is complicit in many of the PTSD symptoms. This powerful fight-or-flight chemical, depending on the severity of the veteran's PTSD, can easily override any small effect of medications within your body. Moreover, most good doctors know that each patient is unique and that what might work for one cannot always predictably work for another. Unfortunately, my psychiatrist was not very experienced and not very well versed on PTSD and the power of adrenaline in PTSD symptoms.

Regardless of the reason though, instead of being patient and continuing to try new drugs until we found something that worked, she became antagonistic at a certain point, even going so far as to blame my pessimism about the drugs for the failure of the drugs. This, of course, makes no sense. Regardless of my attitude toward the drug, it should have either worked or not worked depending on how it interacted with my body's chemical processes.

To give you another example of ignorant attitudes that I unfortunately encountered, I had one young therapist who tried something that she called dynamic counseling on me. This counseling approach consisted of me talking and her providing little or no feedback or conversational response to things I said. I felt like I was talking to a brick wall. Needless to say, I did not work with this therapist very long, as I needed that interaction, encouragement, and open dialogue to work through the problems I was facing in grappling with PTSD.

Moreover, there are some therapists or pastors from churches who counsel using a theory called nouthetic counseling. While these people may mean well, their approach to counseling can be quite disconcerting to someone who is in severe emotional distress. Basically, the theory is that all mental illness is due to sin, so if you have bad emotions or bad memories you cannot overcome, you must have some sin in your life that you need to repent of. Of course, this does not take into account people who suffer from childhood abuse, people who are traumatized by crime, etc.

The first time I encountered one of these nouthetic counselors was when I was in my mid-twenties. I was hurting deeply and had come to this man to help me, to listen to me, to show some compassion to me, to encourage me, and to help me through a very hard time. Instead, all I got from this man, whom I otherwise thought highly of, was condescension and judgment. I left his office bewildered and feeling much worse than when I had entered.

Years later, when I ran across an article about this theory of counseling, I finally understood that confusing and upsetting experience with that pastor/counselor. I also understood that his approach was not biblically sound because Jesus also encountered such a misguided belief among His disciples. In John 9:2–3 (NKJV), we read, "And His disciples asked Him, saying, 'Rabbi, who sinned, this man or his parents, that he was born blind?'

Jesus answered, 'Neither this man nor his parents sinned, but that the works of God should be revealed in him.'"

Of course, Jesus did not mean that these people had never sinned at all but rather that their sin had nothing to do with the affliction that the blind man was suffering through. So, if one truly follows biblical teaching and the lessons of our Lord Jesus, he or she will know that you cannot assume someone is suffering because they have done something wrong, nor should you assume that all people who experience blessings and wealth are better people than the rest of us.

But despite these pockets of ignorance about PTSD, we have come very far indeed in the mental or behavioral health community (psychiatrists, psychologists, therapists, nurses, and non-degree-holding workers).

Most of the change in views came from the courage and activism of our older brothers-and sisters-in-arms from the Vietnam era. That generation, in my opinion, paid a much higher cost for their service to this nation than any other era of veterans. Perhaps, they are, as one man suggested, "the greatest generation." I write this because veterans of most other wars have had general public support and, at the very least, the unanimous respect of the American citizens. The Vietnam veterans, on the other hand, seemed to only receive sporadic or lukewarm public support, or were even insulted and spat upon, which was a grievous injustice by some of our citizens during that era.

But the Vietnam War was so different from previous wars that our nation fought. These words of a Vietnam veteran in the documentary *Vietnam in HD* probably capture the difference so perfectly:

> "It didn't take us long to realize, ain't no Iwo Jimas in Vietnam. You don't get to plant our flag, claim victory..."[11]

As a consequence of this very different war, even other veterans of previous wars did not understand the tremendous courage displayed, sacrifices made, and victories won by our Vietnam troops, so tragically there were not only civilians but also veteran's organizations from prior wars that did not give these heroes the welcome that they richly deserved. One veterans' organization, the Vietnam Veterans of America, addressed this issue in their founding principle, which is posted on their web site: *"Never again will one generation of veterans abandon another."*[12]

Thankfully, largely due to the leadership of the Vietnam veterans, a new generation of Americans going off to wars like Vietnam (that are not "linear" with clean, clear objectives and well-established battle lines) has had much greater support from the American public. Moreover, this greater support is touching the Vietnam veterans as well. In fact, one of those veterans of the current generation of heroes, Staff Sgt. David Bellavia, spoke so eloquently about the Vietnam veterans at the American Legion's 95th national convention on August 28, 2013.

> Bellavia told attendees at The American Legion's 95th national convention on Aug. 28 that after his brief encounter with the Vietnam veterans, he believes the

greatest generation is those who fought for their country and never received the proper welcome home. "I think the greatest generation is an 18-year-old kid, who can't even spell the country he was drafted to serve in," Bellavia said. "I think the greatest generation is a young man who instead of being homecoming king, he was told to go fight a war overseas that he didn't ask for, he didn't vote for. The greatest generation would turn on the radio and be told that they were baby killers by popular culture. They were told by Hollywood that they were ignorant and a fool for doing what their country asked of them. In my opinion, the greatest generation was a generation that stood shoulder to shoulder and protected Iraq and Afghanistan veterans from the same unwashed ignorant classes that choose to put the soldier behind the foreign policy. The greatest generation is a generation of veterans who were treated with dishonor and shame and made sure that their sons and daughters would never be treated like they were treated."[13]

While I believe all of our veterans deserve our gratitude and respect as a country, I also think that Mr. Bellavia is correct in calling the Vietnam veterans the "greatest generation," since they served so honorably despite the poor homecoming that they received when returning from combat.

We also owe them a tremendous debt of gratitude for our knowledge of the detrimental effect of combat on the troops' psyche and to the positive change in attitudes toward those suffering from these invisible wounds such as PTSD. Soldiers with PTSD are treated with much more respect and understanding these days. The days are gone in which a misguided general (George Patton) could slap a hospitalized soldier thinking that his PTSD was a sign of cowardice.

Moreover, we've learned largely from the Vietnam veterans' experiences that combat stress or PTSD is not caused by character weakness in the troops that develop this malady. Indeed, some that develop PTSD are stronger than the average soldier, successfully hiding their emotional struggles from their peers, subordinates, and superiors, as I did. Additionally, some are more susceptible to PTSD because of events in their life that are out of their control, for example if they have been the victims of abuse in their childhood (childhood trauma makes a person, according to some studies, four times more likely to succumb to PTSD during combat).

Regardless of the reason that the individual troop develops PTSD, we can be thankful that treatment methods have become much more sophisticated now that we understand much more about PTSD.

As noted above, most of this knowledge about PTSD came out of the Vietnam generation of warriors. One particular veterans group, the Vietnam Veterans Against the War (VVAW), deserves a great deal of credit in getting PTSD recognized as an official diagnosis and getting its symptoms identified and captured in the manuals and textbooks used by mental/behavioral help professionals, specifically the Diagnostic and Statistical Manual of Mental Disorders or DSM.

The genesis of this group is explained on their web site:

> Vietnam Veterans Against the War, Inc. (VVAW) is a national veteran's organization that was founded in New York City in 1967 after six Vietnam vets marched together in a peace demonstration. It was organized to voice the growing opposition among returning servicemen and women to the still-raging war in Indochina, and grew rapidly to a membership of over 30,000 throughout the United States as well as active duty GIs stationed in Vietnam.[14]

Politics aside, VVAW was and is not only driven by opposition to war. They are and were also motivated by the desire to help veterans traumatically impacted by war. As they state on their web site:

VVAW quickly took up the struggle for the rights and needs of veterans. In 1970, we started the first rap groups to deal with traumatic after-effects of war, setting the example for readjustment counseling at Vet Centers now. We exposed the shameful neglect of many disabled vets in VA Hospitals and helped draft legislation to improved education benefits and created job programs.[15]

As a people-centric organization, VVAW is also devoted to ameliorating the traumatic consequences of war manifested in those who have participated in or who have been affected by war. As such, they have provided immeasurable services to their members and nonmember veterans, which then developed the foundation for our modern-day treatment of PTSD, beginning at a time when the mental/behavioral health community knew very little "officially" about the malady.

In an article about VVAW, Wikipedia notes:

> As VVAW gained members in the late 1960's, they realized that many veterans were having readjustment problems. As early as 1970, VVAW initiated "rap groups" in which veterans could discuss the troubling aspects of the war, their disillusionment with it, and their experiences on arriving home. They enlisted the aid of two prominent psychiatrists, Dr. Robert Jay Lifton and Dr. Chaim F. Shatan to direct and add focus to their sessions. Their continued pressure and activism caused what had been know as "Post-Vietnam Syndrome" to be recognized in 1980 as Post Traumatic Stress Disorder by the Diagnostic and Statistical Manual of Mental Disorders [the standard text and premier resource for diagnosis and treatment for the mental/behavioral health community]. The VVAW "rap group" treatment methods are the basis for treating PTSD today.[16]

The History of PTSD

However, PTSD as a disorder did not start with the Vietnam War, although much of the knowledge we have about that malady comes from that war. Now that we know what the malady is and what its symptoms are, we can recognize it in symptoms experienced by veterans of present and past wars, and even symptoms experienced by civilians who have suffered traumatic events past and present.

The *Active Living* magazine in its February 28, 2003 edition notes that the symptoms of PTSD were recognized at least as early as the Civil War ("Doing Battle with the Demons; Post Traumatic Stress Disorder," volume 11, issue 6, page 30). During that era, the affliction was believed to be in essence a heart ailment and was thus labeled "soldier's heart" or "Da Costa's Syndrome" after the physician, Dr. Jacob Mendes Da Costa, who first recognized and began speaking and writing about the affliction.

During the World War I era, PTSD was a very common malady among frontline troops and was labeled "shell shock," as it was thought to be a nervous disorder resulting in a shock to the soldier's nervous system from the explosions of the enemy's artillery in near proximity to the soldier.

There's an excellent article about PTSD that appeared in the September 2010 edition of *Smithsonian* magazine.

> "Shell shock," the term that would come to define the phenomenon, first appeared in the British medical journal *The Lancet* in February 1915, only six months after the commencement of the war. In a landmark article, Capt. Charles Myers of the Royal Army Medical Corps noted the remarkably close similarity of symptoms in three soldiers who had each been exposed to shells exploding: Case 1 had endured six or seven shells exploding around him; Case 2 had been buried under earth for 18 hours after a shell collapsed his trench; Case 3 had been blown off a pile of bricks 15 feet high. All three men exhibited symptoms

of reduced visual fields, loss of smell and taste and some loss of memory. Comment on these cases seems superfluous, Myers concluded, after documenting in detail the symptoms of each. They appear to constitute a definite class among others arising from the effects of shell-shock.

Early medical opinion took the common-sense view that the damage was 'commotional,' or related to the severe concussive motion of the shaken brain in the soldier's skull. Shell shock, then, was initially deem to be a physical injury, and the shell-shocked soldier was thus entitled to a distinguishing 'wound stripe' for his uniform, and to possible discharge and a war pension.[17]

Although they did not give the same name to the groupings of symptoms that we now call PTSD, these leaders and medical professionals were beginning to record and capture the various symptoms of the affliction. In addition to the symptoms, these leaders and professionals were beginning to recognize patterns of behavior that were replicated in soldiers who experienced overwhelming events in combat, irrespective of rank, race, nationality, etc. Additionally, they recognized this affliction as a physical phenomenon with physical features that we now can identify in all sufferers of the malady.

Moreover, they recognized back then what we are now realizing through the veterans' experiences from the Vietnam, Iraq, and Afghanistan wars: that these men and women could be suffering just as the troops with visible, more easily measurable physical wounds were and are suffering. Additionally, many with the physical wounds that are recognized by the awarding of the Purple Heart also suffer from the invisible, less easily measurable wounds on the human heart and spirit long after their physical wounds have healed.

I want to ensure that I am not misunderstood in this discussion of awards for the Purple Heart. I would not take away from the rightful and just honor that we bestow upon those who suffer what are deemed the physical wounds for their country. Many

Purple Heart recipients grapple with their wounds and handicaps years after completion of their service to the country for the duration of their lives. These people are incredibly heroic, many sacrificing for their country long after leaving the battlefield.

On the other hand, I have learned from experience, from reports and stories of veteran friends and acquaintances, from research, and from psychiatrists and therapists who have informed me about the experiences of their patients that the invisible wounds such as PTSD can also hobble and afflict veterans many decades after their service to our country has concluded. In essence, the sacrifice of these veterans for their country, like many of those with physical wounds, never ends, completely heals.

From the *Smithsonian* article, we can conclude that these internal wounds and the accompanying suffering were deemed worthy of recognition and honor, even back then in the World War I era. Given this history of awarding medals to those who are and were suffering invisible wounds for their country, it is perplexing to me why our own nation will not honor those PTSD sufferers from Vietnam or the current Iraq and Afghanistan wars with the Purple Heart, our own version of the wound stripe award. These troops have certainly suffered greatly for their country, which was the reason for the first awarding of the Purple Heart (i.e. to recognize and honor those who sacrifice and suffer for their country), and their suffering, as noted above, may in many cases last a lifetime, making the lack of recognition doubly egregious.

Moreover, as noted in the previous examples of the PTSD nightmares, it is not only the veterans with PTSD that suffer. As I have found with my own family, what affects me, especially when it invades my life so deeply as PTSD does, will affect them as well. So, these veterans' families suffer with them as the symptom manifestations and behavior patterns that constitute PTSD ripple outward with secondary and tertiary effects whether or not the veteran is aware or conscious of the effect he or she is having on others, and whether or not his or her effect on others is intentional. Even when I tried to shield my family from these effects, they were, nonetheless, impacted anyway.

Furthermore, many PTSD sufferers also experience crushing depression or they end up withdrawing from normal social interaction with family and friends when they are too depressed or anxious to be capable of living a normal life. The family, seeing their loved ones grappling with such tremendous suffering, obviously can be affected emotionally or psychologically due to their normal human empathy for those they love.

But the impact may not be merely vicarious or empathetic. The PTSD sufferer may manifest certain behaviors that are physically harmful to those around them as with the nightmares, even during their sleep as noted earlier in this chapter.

The Symptoms of PTSD and Factors for Developing PTSD

The nightmares are just one manifestation of the symptoms of PTSD. Other symptoms are outlined in an article on the US Department of Veterans Affairs (VA) web site, which describes PTSD from the newly released Diagnostic and Statistical Manual of Mental Health Disorders (DSM-5):

> PTSD (as well as Acute Stress Disorder) moved from the class of anxiety disorders into a new class of 'trauma and stressor-related disorders.'...[and] [t]he three clusters of DSM-IV symptoms are divided into four clusters in DSM-5: intrusion, avoidance, negative alterations in cognitions and mood, and alterations in arousal and reactivity.[18]

The VA article goes on to explain the four clusters of symptoms as excerpted from the DSM-5 that mental health professionals will be using to diagnose PTSD:

Intrusion is exemplified by: "Recurrent, involuntary, and intrusive memories...[or] Traumatic nightmares...[or] Dissociative reactions (e.g., flashbacks) which may occur on a continuum from brief episodes to complete loss of consciousness…[or] Intense or prolonged distress after exposure to traumatic reminders…[or] Marked physiologic reactivity after exposure to trauma-related stimuli."[19]

Avoidance is exemplified by: "Persistent effortful avoidance of distressing trauma-related stimuli after the event…[by either avoiding] Trauma-related thoughts or feelings…[or by avoiding] Trauma-related external reminders (e.g., people, places, conversations, activities, objects, or situations)."[20]

Negative alterations in cognitions and mood are exemplified by: "Inability to recall key features of the traumatic event (usually dissociative amnesia; not due to head injury, alcohol, or drugs)….Persistent (and often distorted) negative beliefs and expectations about oneself or the world (e.g., "I am bad," "The world is completely dangerous")….Persistent distorted blame of self or others for causing the traumatic event or for resulting consequences…Persistent negative trauma-related emotions (e.g., fear, horror, anger, guilt, or shame)…Markedly diminished interest in (pretraumatic) significant activities…Feeling alienated from others (e.g., detachment or estrangement)…Constricted affect: persistent inability to experience positive emotions."[21]

Lastly, the fourth major grouping of symptoms, alterations in arousal and reactivity are exemplified by: "Irritable or aggressive behavior…Self-destructive or reckless behavior…Hypervigilance…Exaggerated startle response…Problems in concentration…Sleep disturbance."[22]

Knowing what PTSD looks like and recognizing it in the people who are around us, we may ask why some people succumb to PTSD, while others don't. That is one of life's great mysteries. The factors that play into PTSD are as varied as the unique personalities and experiences of the people who enter the military service and then possibly go to combat. It has partly to do with the mental/emotional readiness or stability of the person and partly to do with the quality of important relationships in your life.

Many factors feed into who will develop PTSD. One factor is how ready they are for the experiences of combat. Another is how adept they are at coping with the unusual or extreme experiences of life, how healthy their home life was when they were growing up, and what the condition of their most important relationships (family or friends) is before, during, and after deployment. But even if you are well-prepared and well-grounded emotionally, there is no guarantee that you will not be overcome by the events that you encounter in combat.

To be traumatized to the level that you develop PTSD, to be pushed beyond the limits of your ability to cope or well beyond your level of endurance, requires a significant event or series of events. However, your ability to cope may still be affected by factors outside of your grasp such as how good your leaders are, how good the unit climate is, and how supportive the intricate web of relationships are inside of a unit (i.e. how cohesive the unit is and how much of a team they are).

Other factors affecting development of PTSD are one's experience level, the readiness for the experience. Moreover, there's the unique meaning or interpretation of the experience, how you interpret what happened based upon the collection of all your beliefs, experiences, and moral values or your worldview. Then there's the issue of how important the event was to you, how much you are emotionally invested in the people and events that you experience, and possibly the consequences coming out of the event that affect you personally.

All in all, I believe no one can accurately predict how a soldier's unique experience of life and combat will play out. As I've seen in life, people often surprise you by how well or poorly they cope with various life challenges. There are always the intangible character and personality factors that only God would be able to comprehend and calculate.

As for me, I was already very stressed out when I got to Ft. Bragg from three years of very demanding jobs for which I was, in truth, not emotionally prepared. (But on the other hand, who is ever prepared completely to face life's great challenges?) I felt that I was very close to burnout or breakdown from a series of more and more demanding tasks on the jobs I held. I had worked ever more challenging jobs for three years without enough time to decompress, working very long, exhausting hours, having to maintain physical fitness in my sometimes meager personal time with the added stress of ever-building health issues from my stressful lifestyle, sleep apnea, minor arthritis in my knees that made the required physical fitness very painful, high blood pressure, high cholesterol, and frequent pain from stomach ulcers. By the time I got to Bragg, I had even considered suicide, thinking that death was a welcome escape from my personal misery (by the grace of God, I never made any attempts, as I was reminded in my conscience of the pain I would leave behind for my traumatized family). During this period, nonetheless, I felt emotionally exhausted and sometimes very much alone.

Then, I had to go through the heart-wrenching predeployment experience of five months dreading separation from my family and feeling the weight of that separation the whole time. To that point, it was the most difficult thing I had ever gone through. I don't know how I would have gotten through without God's constant comforting and encouraging presence and without the help of medications to take the edge off of my inner emotional turmoil to make it bearable. I was prescribed Wellbutrin to deal with my depression, and later lorazepam/klonipin to help me through the anxiety spikes (this latter drug would help control the out-of-control adrenaline surges, which are a characteristic of PTSD).

Thankfully, I was able to get the help of medications without the stigma of going to a psychiatrist, although I would later have to make regular office visits with a psychiatrist shortly into my deployment as my PTSD developed and worsened.

When I started down that road of many encounters with psychiatrists, psychologists, or therapists, I sometimes found that I could not be assured of a positive experience interacting with these people. Some of them were more of an obstacle to my healing than an advantage. At times, I was not even completely sure that they understood my symptoms and the accompanying problems. Unfortunately, some mental health professionals approach patients with too much clinical and intellectual detachment when their patients are looking for compassion. A morally or emotionally wounded person needs connection, even love and assurance. Some doctors are not prepared to provide that. It's too messy, too complicated, and not scientific. Such is the world.

It was always compassion though that I was looking for first as I sought help from many mental health professionals with my mounting PTSD symptoms. But the symptoms were definitely mounting. As the weeks of relentless, pounding stress passed and the guilt from surviving when so many good men and women died continued to gnaw at my conscience, my PTSD symptoms built up ever more greatly, requiring even greater strength to remain in control and keep my peers, subordinates, and superiors from knowing what I was going through.

I did not want to let them down, did not want them to lose confidence in me, or want to add weight to their struggles from living in a combat zone, separated from their loved ones and suffering from the danger and stress just as I was. At the time, I suspected that the best thing I could do was to keep my personal turmoil a secret because so much depended on each of the team members in a combat zone, especially when the team members were key leaders in an organization engaged in combat operations throughout the country of Iraq. Moreover, as a leader, I knew that many people were looking up to me and other key leaders for strength and stability in the chaos of combat duty.

I had learned over my many years of leadership how important the example of a good, strong, dedicated, compassionate leader was, as well as how important it was for the leader to be cool, confident, and unperturbed when "the shit hits the fan." I had seen often how a nervous and visibly emotional leader could erode the confidence of subordinates very quickly, making them think that if the boss could not handle it, it must be really, really bad. Seeing those situations and the negative impact on those lower-ranking soldiers, I made a determination that I would always be that leader with the poker face and the confident, peaceful smile in the midst of chaos no matter what I might be feeling inside because I owed that to my people.

Nonetheless, no matter how strong my confidence and will-power are, I was not an automaton. There were multiple factors that fed into and exacerbated my stress, ultimately causing my PTSD. Of course, there was the ever-pounding stress of living and working in a combat zone, added to the personal trauma of grappling with the intricate details of our wounded soldiers, those killed in action, and those killed during operations not directly as a result of enemy action. Other factors that fed into my PTSD included many combat experiences to include constant indirect fire attacks on our base and a direct IED attack on the vehicle I was riding in during a convoy. Although I was not a combat arms officer and was not in a traditional war fighting unit, I, as well as those around me, was constantly confronted with combat situations.

Thankfully, I did not directly witness any casualties in the immediate aftermath of battle, but I had many constant reminders of the horror of combat by the detailed, very graphic daily casualty reports and the very physical reminder of the prop wash air blast and the ground shaking when incoming medevac helicopters brought the severely wounded, flying into our base a few hundred feet directly over our living quarters or our headquarters building on their landing approach to the airfield beside the major combat support hospital that was on our base. When I heard the regular incoming flights of medical helicopters, I knew immediately that something bad had happened, that soldiers had been injured or killed somewhere in the region.

My first such experience of the medical flights into our base was within our first two weeks on the ground in Iraq following the horrific December 2004 Mosul dining facility bombing. The helicopters were constantly ferrying wounded directly over our heads day and night, seemingly nonstop for a couple of days. I was horrified at the attack like many in our unit, but I felt powerless to do anything other than pray for those affected by the attack.

In my research, I have found that my empathetic response to these casualties, even if I did not know them personally is a common phenomena called secondary trauma, compassion fatigue, or vicarious trauma.[23] Even though I was not a caregiver to these casualties, each one, nonetheless, touched me deeply, knowing what a loss to the world their deaths were. Plus, my survivor's guilt continually gnawed at my peace of mind, making me think that those who died or had been wounded were, perhaps, better people than I was.

In addition to these factors, one of the biggest causes leading to my PTSD was probably my feelings of helplessness as a leader to control any of the chaos or danger to protect my people. I continually prayed and desired not to lose anyone, although I had a harrowing night when I thought I had lost my deputy on a convoy that was hit by a roadside bomb (or improvised explosive devise—IED). Moreover, my obligation to personally brief daily casualties to my commanding general if there were deaths (which happened all too frequently) and to include personal details about the soldier's family, career, home of origin gnawed away steadily at my conscience. This level of detail made the deaths all too real and too personal for me. It also made me feel helpless as a leader in this organization to do anything to prevent the deaths—not that I had any direct influence over combat operations, since I was not a commander, but a sense of survivor's guilt that combat soldiers often feel. And since I was a leader in this organization, somehow, I felt that I bore some responsibility for these soldiers.

Plus, life in a combat zone for almost everyone was very intense most hours of the day. There were long hours with few breaks or no significant breaks (enough to decompress and feel refreshed to handle the next onslaught of challenges, leaving you with an ever-building cauldron of percolating emotions that seemingly could not be dealt with in the combat zone, so they were continually packed away for a later time). Most of us had very early waking hours. Most mornings I was up at five o'clock to prepare for the morning briefing. Others got up early to conduct personal fitness routines at the gym or running around the base, etc. Still, others simply got up for early chow because they liked getting an early start on their daily duties.

After my morning briefing, I was usually at my desk steadily grinding away on briefings, e-mail communication, coordination with other staff sections, the normal daily grind of maintenance actions to keep all operations going and to keep my team motivated, and the regular, unexpected emergencies that would pop up with hair-on-fire urgency practically every day. I was usually unable to get away from my desk for very long and working most days ten to twelve hours with many days going to sixteen and eighteen hours. Most nights, I did, however, get away to take in the dinner meal for an hour or two, but I would usually be right back to work at my office to tie off a few more loose ends. With such long stressful days ending work late at night, I was still wound up tight when I got to bed.

Even if I had had free time during the day to break away, there were simply very few places where you could go to take your mind completely off of the combat environment, to completely forget where you were, to really escape. Except for our fifteen days of Rest and Recuperation (R&R), we had no significant breaks, no vacations, no weekends. Moreover, in Iraq on our base, there were no nice parks, no shopping malls, no bowling alleys, no sports bars, no upscale restaurants, and no golf courses. In short, there are very few of the normal distractions you would have to relieve stress back at home station, although we did have some creature comforts in the post exchange (our shopping center or our version of Walmart) in the recreational building with games and movies, one hard facility movie theater, and a couple of movie tents. Moreover, some soldiers displayed their seemingly endless ingenuity by making some interesting oases or social gathering areas within their communal living areas with creative use of camouflage netting, Christmas lighting, lawn chairs, etc. So, suffice it to say that conditions could have been worse, but life in a combat zone was not a day at the beach.

Sleep becomes one of the most important coping mechanisms in a high-pressure environment, but personal sleep times are constantly being interrupted. If you could wind down sufficiently from the stressful grind of the day and get off to a pleasant and deep sleep, there were the constant noises that broke into your sleep, including air raid sirens periodically, vehicles traversing the gravel parking lots beside the sleeping quarters, the high whine of the ubiquitous generators, and the incoming helicopters that sometimes came in the middle of the night shaking the ground with their prop wash. Noise and intensity were everywhere around the base. There's no chance to get away—it's all in your face, and it stays that way the entire year.

Of course, this is what we signed up for, and we willingly took on these sacrifices knowing the importance of our commitment to the well-being of our country and the protection of our way of life; however, all troops, in the end, have their limits. No matter how tough the troop is, everyone has his or her breaking point.

In trying to cope with all the pressures, I turned first to my faith, my trust in God, and my relationship with Him. When I first arrived in Iraq, I prayed a great deal. I prayed constantly that we would not experience many deaths, or even avoid any deaths at all. I know that it was a presumptuous prayer, but I hoped that

God would bless our unit with miraculous coverage, keeping our casualty rates low. Given the level of attacks, I would certainly say that God answered in keeping the casualties to a minimum, but we did not escape any harm to our troops. During our year-long tour of duty starting at the end of 2004 and lasting throughout most of 2005, the US military in Iraq was entering one of the bloodiest periods of the Iraqi insurgency. The insurgents were getting organized and coordinating their attacks for greater violent efficiency, and they were receiving help from outside Islamic terrorist organizations as well as the government and military officials from the country of Iran.

So, it was only a couple of weeks when we experienced our first hostile and nonhostile deaths, not to mention the numerous casualties from enemy action. There was the young sergeant who died in a traffic accident early on, and there were many living injuries that still stick with me. There was one particular soldier with a wife and two children waiting for him back in the States who had sustained a severe head injury. I'm not sure if he ever lived, but if he did, it would have taken some miracles for him to overcome his injuries. After he was medevaced to our base hospital, he was not expected to leave our base, Balad, alive.

I prayed so hard for him, that he would, at least, be able to make it to Germany or the States so his wife could say good-bye to him (I can't imagine how hard even that would have been to say good-bye to a spouse in such trying circumstances). Thankfully, he did make it back to Germany. His wife did get to see him there at the military hospital in Landstuhl, Germany, and he eventually made it back to the States. I'm not sure how he fared after that, but, at least, he was still alive to return to his loved ones, so I know God answered my prayers (and surely the prayers of others) for him. Whenever I think of him though, it still cuts to the depth of my heart to know what suffering this man and his family went through.

Although this was an essential part of my job (i.e. tracking these casualties, the extent of their injuries, their progress through treatment, their progress through the medevac system, their personal details, family situation, etc.), it was an aspect of my job that was the most challenging. They all still bother me very deeply today. Knowing who they were, or feeling that I knew, made the knowledge of their deaths and injuries that much more personal and painful. Somehow too I felt responsible being a high-ranking leader, and I felt guilt at not being able to do anything about their situations.

In addition to these stressors, I wanted my team's operations to go well so that we conducted our human resource services to all of our soldiers as well as possible (I knew how critical many of our functions were to the morale of the troops, so I did not want to add to the burden of our troops by providing substandard services). I no longer believed in perfection but rather desired that my team would do all that we could to the best of our abilities.

And finally, in addition to my concerns about my duties and about the casualties, I was also constantly worried about the safety of my own team with regular indirect fire attacks on our base. It was very disconcerting to realize that I didn't have enough power to ensure their safety, or even sometimes that they were treated fairly.

In time with all of the pressures, I gradually became more pessimistic and then disillusioned, leading to a fracturing and eventual shattering of my worldview (our patchwork of beliefs and experiences that allow us to make sense of the world). I was disillusioned about the military being a place that was generally honorable, as I thought I saw, in my growing negativity and the pressure of a combat zone, that not everyone would do the right thing. I became disillusioned by leaders in our organization and other organizations that seemed, from my limited perspective, to be more concerned with what was legal than what was right and good. I became disillusioned by seeing leaders who seemed to not take their responsibilities to their people as seriously as I did for mine (but again, looking back from the perspective of several years, I can also see how many of my judgments were decidedly pessimistic and, perhaps, not accurate).

It wasn't just my professional environment that caused me to become disillusioned though. I also became disillusioned by some in the religious groups on base when I saw that they did not live up to their values in their daily life. But then overtime, God increasingly showed me the measure of myself, and I realized that I was flawed as well. Moreover, in time, I learned how foolish it was for me to look for my hope in other people rather than in God. In time, God would teach me to look to Him for my hope and encouragement rather than to inherently flawed people, especially since I myself was also inherently flawed, and, if I had the eyes to see clearly with spiritual truth, I would probably find out that I had let people down as well. But at the time, my faith and my spiritual insight were not as mature as they would become in time (largely through the trials of my PTSD that sifted the error out of my character).

Perhaps, worst of all, I became disillusioned about God. In my spiritual ignorance, I thought at the time that he had not answered my prayers and was not with me in the way that I expected Him to be. Of course, looking back with the wisdom of several more years in walking closely with Him, I can see that the error was not in God but rather in my perception, my expectations and understanding of God, my understanding of what my responsibilities were to him and to the people around me, and even my overly negative interpretation of events. Thankfully, God is patient and kind, so He gently taught me bit by bit, lesson by lesson, about my ignorance and my misunderstanding or misinterpretation of situations.

Moreover, I know that the many thousands of hours that I spent in prayer with him in secluded places, which I would go to to be alone after work over the years, were critical to my healing.

Feeling safe and secure in these secluded places, I felt that I could let out the worst of my emotions and lay them at His feet, and I know that He, in turn, placed more and more of His spirit within me, displacing the pain, the grief, and the guilt.

Furthermore, I know that He has made me wiser, either by teaching me directly or by leading me to sources of knowledge and wisdom, so that I had the tools for healing. He has dispelled much of my ignorance about PTSD and helped me to see through ignorance that I have encountered. For instance, contrary to how PTSD was previously viewed and sometimes still is, the person who contracts PTSD is not at fault, nor is he weaker or more flawed.

Moreover, almost anyone can be affected. In a study of security professionals (police, fire, rescue and disaster, military, and emergency medical), it was discovered that there are two sources of the type of stress that can ultimately lead to PTSD. There is the cumulative stress (the daily grind of stressors over a long period of time)[24] and post-traumatic (also spelled "posttraumatic") stress (your mind, emotions, and body reacting to one or more traumatic events).

It is important to remember that, contrary to some of the peer-review literature or studies, PTSD can simply come from daily grinding stressors that eventually push a person to the breaking point over time. Many who have PTSD may have a hard time pinning down one particular event that caused their PTSD, but the only common denominator is that the person somehow experienced something that they interpreted as traumatic.

It was previously thought that this traumatic event had to necessarily include a threat to life. But studies have found that virtually any traumatic event can cause PTSD, such as being a victim of a crime, especially a violent crime, having a family member be a victim of such a crime, childhood abuse (physical or emotional), or observing a traumatic event happen to someone else, even though you may not have been harmed physically at all or threatened with harm; you were merely an observer, but observing the trauma or tragic event was enough to overwhelm you.

Another source of trauma and PTSD is dealing with the aftermath or effects of trauma, such as the soldiers whose job it is to process the remains of other soldiers during war (sometimes called mortuary affairs). This is an example of the secondary trauma, compassion fatigue, or vicarious trauma mentioned earlier. These mortuary affairs troops have been known to have a high rate of PTSD because they are traumatized by seeing what war can do to a human being, a fellow soldier, sailor, airman, or marine.

I was first made aware of PTSD among these troops even before I deployed to Iraq. From 2002 to 2004, while I was stationed overseas in Germany with my family, I worked a human resource management job, managing the careers and assignments of most of the enlisted army troops stationed in US Army Europe (USAREUR) units. In this job, I was the army enlisted career and assignments manager of all enlisted soldiers in the European theater of operations where we had approximately one hundred thousand troops of all services and ranks stationed at the time in various countries, mostly a result of our World War II occupations.

While in this job, I was visited one day by a sergeant major from the mortuary affairs unit that was processing the remains of troops coming out of Iraq and Afghanistan. As you can imagine, this was a very important but grim job for these young troops. During his visit, the sergeant major explained to me the heavy emotional toll that his soldiers endured from this difficult job, many of them succumbing to PTSD. This visit with this man was one of many events that educated me about PTSD.

And along my path of learning, one of the things that have stuck with me is that you cannot blame the PTSD victim for succumbing to this malady, although human nature sometimes makes certain people blame the victim. But the human psyche has limits, and war is abnormal albeit very common. It's hard to predict which soldiers will fall prey; many times, it even surprises us. But sometimes too the damage that they sustain emotionally and psychologically far outweighs and outstrips physical injury in terms of impact to their lives and the lives of those around them. This is not to downplay physical injury, however, because there are certainly debilitated veterans who will endure their physical injuries for the rest of their lives. Moreover, many who have physical wounds will also have the invisible wounds of PTSD as well.

Life in the Military

During the research for this book, I came across a surprising statement about the returning combat soldier not having marketable skills, not learning anything in the military that would be useful in the civilian work world. I suppose that this is a common misunderstanding among people who know little about soldiers and the military life. But suffice it to say that nothing could be further from the truth. There are a plethora of skills that young men and women learn during military service.

This may not be an exhaustive list, but I researched several web sites and compiled a composite list of many other lists and then added some of my own thoughts. The following are skills that, I believe, all of our military men and women develop or are encouraged to develop during their time in uniform.

Personal discipline is, perhaps, the main area where people develop personally while in the military. Laozi (or Lao Tzu), a fifth century B.C. Chinese philosopher, once wrote, "Mastering others is strength. Mastering yourself is true power."[1] Sometimes, the hardest things to control are yourself, your habits, emotions, etc. The military services develop this personal discipline by: toughening you up and demanding that you act more responsibly, always taking into account the repercussions that your actions have on others; teaching you to remain calm under pressure and to appear confident no matter how you may feel inside; teaching you to control your emotions, even in the most trying of circumstances; teaching you to subordinate personal desires and urges to a higher purpose; teaching you to follow orders, sometimes without question (but not always; you learn not to be an automaton but rather an empowered moral actor who chooses to follow others for a higher purpose); teaching you good habits of personal discipline in training challenges, deployment challenges, physical fitness, and hygiene; learning how to build professional skills and further professional or academic education (troops are always encouraged to improve themselves and their lives); keeping ego in check; and learning to critique self to catch many errors before others find them.

People skills or social skills are probably the second biggest area where people develop personally while in uniform. The military teaches you: communication skills or how to give and receive orders for very complex tasks in a way that people with a variety of perspectives and experience levels will understand and how to organize and present information in briefings on complex subjects; how to live, work, and get along with people of very different personalities, of different cultures, and of different perspectives; how to work as a member of a team for a common goal and how to subordinate your own urges and desires to the team and mission requirements; self-sacrifice and an orientation toward other; and etiquette or manners and respect of civilians, peers, subordinates, and superiors (taught through military traditions, customs, and courtesies such as parades, saluting, customs for terms of address of superior-ranking troops, even formal dining skills, etc.).

Another area where the military develops you personally is in teaching you tenacity or perseverance as you: learn to exercise willpower, getting in the habit of never giving up and having bulldog determination, even in the face of seemingly insurmountable odds or obstacles; learn to work well under stress; learn creative problem-solving in the face of multiple obstacles; learn adaptability to any situation; learn creativity in the use of resources or tools at hand; learn to foresee and prepare for or adapt to unforeseen problems and in the face of problems; learn to adapt the mission plan in order to still accomplish the overall mission or the commander's/leader's intent.

Certainly, one area where the military develops people personally is in leadership. The military services teach leadership skills even down to the lowest-ranking troop since, in the event of disaster or the chaos of combat, higher-ranking leaders may be incapacitated, or even may be removed for greater needs elsewhere in the unit, necessitating the lower-ranking soldier to step up and "take charge." They teach personal initiative and desire to lead, since you may recognize an exigency in the course of your duties when there is no one else to step up and do something or when you realize that there is no one else willing or able to do so. They teach you how to define goals for overall mission accomplishment, break down the overall mission into individual tasks, and assign tasks to various team members based upon their strengths and weaknesses (which itself requires another ability that must be cultivated, i.e. how to assess people and recognize their good and bad points). And they teach you how to motivate others, to praise them when they do well, and to counsel or correct them when they get offtrack.

Lastly, the military teaches a variety of general skills that can make you into a better person and make you more valuable to others such as: working with confidence in high-risk, multicultural environments during military (weapons or equipment) training and deployments (to the seas or to foreign countries); problem-solving and organizational skills at a variety of tasks; time management and prioritization of tasks according to importance; learning to juggle a tight schedule with many tasks in a high-pressure environment and to get everything done or, at least, discern what the critical tasks are and get them done; critical observation and attention to detail; and a highly developed sense of ethics/morality (commitment to duty, honor, and country), learning to do the harder right over the easier wrong.

This is not, of course, an exhaustive list, but this will give you an idea of the many ways that the military develops men and women who serve. Any time served in the military, regardless of what occupation you have in the military, leaves a young man or woman with many usable skills that will make you more valuable in whatever endeavor you enter after military life. Moreover, they develop these skills because we demand a lot from our troops (whether lower enlisted, warrant officer, noncommissioned officer, or simply officer), so, at the end of their career or tour of duty, if they do not complete a full career of twenty years (sometimes fifteen years in times of severe force cuts), they are, nonetheless, highly skilled in many professional skills that employers and companies tend to value greatly.

As to what it is like to serve on active duty, or even short tours of active duty (for reservists or national guard troops), it is not just working an occupation such as you would expect in a civilian job, although there are jobs that come close to operating like their civilian counterparts, such as law enforcement, logistics, medical, culinary occupations, etc. Even if your daily tasks are similar to a civilian occupation, there are still an entire litany of tasks that you might have to accomplish in addition to your daily work duty. And with these additional demands, any military occupation becomes much more challenging than most civilian lines of work.

For instance, most units have daily physical fitness training, which must start before most civilians even get out of bed in the morning, and all services have regular fitness tests a couple of times a year in order to ensure that the troops maintain a high level of personal fitness so that they will be in peak shape to accomplish wartime or peacetime requirements. Also, most military units are subject to periodic ceremonies or parades that require much practice and much time standing absolutely still at attention or parade rest without any movement, regardless of how hot it is, how many gnats are buzzing about your head, how much wind, how much rain, etc.

Moreover, most military units are subject to multiple inspections during the year. They can expect inspections of their uniforms, their quarters, their work areas, their military equipment, their weapons, their military vehicles, etc. And preparations for these inspections require extensive amounts of time.

Furthermore, troops are subject to various professional test requirements themselves to test their job proficiency, their readiness for advancement, and their fitness for military service or deployment and to test them for illegal substances like drugs or steroids.

And as if this were not enough, beyond the daily requirements of their jobs, there are often detail tasks, periodical tasking that is assigned regularly and often tracked on rosters to ensure that everyone in the organization or post participates equally. Examples are cleanup details for various buildings or outdoor areas around buildings, head count and meal fee collection at the local dining facility, guard duty or watch, officer or noncommissioned officer on duty (to handle whatever emergencies or problems arise after normal work hours at a headquarters unit), charge of quarters (an officer or noncommissioned officer who is on watch in a building where troops are housed), or a cornucopia of similar taskings, whatever a unit, base, or sea vessel might need done on a regular basis and which cannot be pinned on any one particular person or section.

With all of these taskings and requirements on top of the regular job requirements, the military troop's life is one of regular and constant sacrifice: sacrifice of personal time, sacrifice of free time on weekends and holidays, sacrifice of family time during deployments and various military training exercises and events, sacrifice of body and personal comfort during training exercises and military operations (including combat operations), and, if need be, sacrifice of life.

But despite all these challenges and sacrifices, I have always enjoyed or have been deeply satisfied with my military duties, although I gave up many holidays for duty, worked many weekends, worked late hours into the evening many times, sacrificed family time for training, temporary duty away from home (TDY), and a combat deployment. Moreover, I had to endure some very hard and demanding bosses, most of whom challenged me to ever higher standards and making me into a better person, even if I did not like the job conditions or the men or women in charge of me at the time. Looking back from the perspective of a few more decades of adulthood and a complete military career while I realize that those hard bosses could have been a little more encouraging, I am still thankful to have worked for them and thankful for the ways in which they helped mold me into the man of character, great strength, and morals that I am now.

However, there was one particular boss who was purely abusive, the worst boss by far that I have ever had and the worst military leader. He berated me many times in front of other troops, which is an egregious violation for a leader in the military, and he never had anything good to say about my performance, no matter how well I did. I am and was willing to endure any measure of demand and bear any burden, any stress, but I have never been able to withstand leaders who publicly humiliate their subordinates like this bad leader did. To make matters worse, this boss came early in my career at a time when I really needed positive leadership to convince me that the hardships of military life were worth the sacrifice. Thankfully, most of my leaders after that point were much better leaders, which helped me keep my commitment to the military until I completed over twenty years.

Of course, I know that sometimes leaders need to be tough or strict in order to get the best out of their troops, to push them through critical missions, or to pull out of them great deeds that the subordinates may not know or believe they are capable of. Furthermore, I have even been strict on many of my soldiers, pushing them to do things that I knew they could do but which they did not want to do or did not believe they could do.

While I was in company command (1995–1997), my first sergeant and I (as a young captain, O3) put a lot of effort into one particular soldier who was acting out like Klinger from the well-known television show *M*A*S*H* (1972–1983). This soldier did anything and everything he could do to get kicked out of the military, but we met him at every point and forced his hand, refusing to give in to his desire to leave the service. I knew that it was just normal lack of self-confidence, some character weakness from not being sufficiently trained at home possibly, but, above all, an inability to see his own potential, an inability to see the big picture, and an inability to see how he fit into that picture, how he could impact the world with his life. Not being able to see these things, he subsequently couldn't understand why it was so important for him to fulfill his military obligations that he had committed to as an adult in his enlistment contract and why we were being so insistent on his living up to those obligations.

Thanks to my persistence and that of my first sergeant, this young soldier finally gave up on his efforts to leave the service and redirected his energy instead to completing his initial military training, going on to be a fine and capable soldier. I was proud to learn that he had ultimately fulfilled his training obligations and had done well, but I was so surprised when he brought his father with him one day after he completed all his initial training, wanting to simply shake my hand and tell me, "Thank you for not giving up on me." Although he may have thought that my first sergeant and I were the meanest people on earth, forcing him to do something that he did not want to do in every fiber of his being and detested with all of his heart, he finally came around and realized what a gift we had given him by refusing to give up on him and doing the harder right of persisting in corrective action so that he could grow into a man that he, his family, and his friends could be proud of.

However, some bad leaders cross a line from merely being authoritarian or tough for good reasons to simply being bullies to put it bluntly. I've learned to spot this bad leadership and will stand up to them without hesitation because I know it's not just me for which they are making life miserable. But hard bosses and bullies are thankfully not the norm in military life. I have learned to live with the worst that they can throw at me and not let them control my life.

Such people are part of what can be a hard experience in the military, but life is often what you make of it. I got in the habit of always being up for new adventures, new experiences, seeing new places, trying new foods, exploring the treasures of the region around me while stationed in Germany, and even traveling into the furthest corners of Europe while on leave, getting in the habit of courage, knowing that God was always with me and that he wanted me to live my life to the fullest.

Courage is an essential character trait for a soldier, and courage, like all worthy character traits, must be exercised to make it bigger and stronger. Since troops away from home and living in danger often turn to their religion for courage and comfort, prayers and Bible passages were a common part of many soldiers' daily routines.

One particular biblical passage that addresses courage, Psalm 91 (NKJV), was constantly popping up ubiquitously among units and individuals going to Iraq and among worship groups in Iraq. One enterprising chaplain had even ordered from somewhere bandannas with that Bible passage printed on them, one of which I still possess today.

> He who dwells in the secret place of the Most High
> Shall abide under the shadow of the Almighty.
> I will say of the Lord, "He is my refuge and my fortress;
> My God, in Him I will trust."
> Surely He shall deliver you from the snare of the fowler-
> And from the perilous pestilence.
> He shall cover you with His feathers,
> And under His wings you shall take refuge;

His truth shall be your shield and buckler.
You shall not be afraid of the terror by night,
Nor of the arrow that flies by day,
Nor of the pestilence that walks in darkness,
Nor of the destruction that lays waste at noonday.

A thousand may fall at your side,
And ten thousand at your right hand;
But it shall not come near you.
Only with your eyes shall you look,
And see the reward of the wicked.

Because you have made the Lord, who is my refuge,
Even the Most High, your dwelling place,
No evil shall befall you,
Nor shall any plague come near your dwelling;
For He shall give His angels charge over you,
To keep you in all your ways.

The promises in that Psalm gave tremendous courage to countless soldiers, knowing that they went into battle with the Lord on their side. Religious faith was a big part of life for many people in the combat zone, and I know for a fact that many units, platoons, or squads would gather together for prayer as a collective group before commencing a mission.

And we certainly needed encouragement as all our troops do during deployment because of the dangers, hardships, and separation from loved ones. Moreover, although all services are contributing to the war effort, sharing in the sacrifices, some may be surprised to find out that it is the army that has borne the bigger share of the deployment load.

The Hardships Borne by Our Troops

The army has borne the brunt of these wars, unlike past conflicts in which military and civilian political leaders of the military tried to more evenly spread out the workload among the major military services. A RAND Corporation study in 2013 authored by Dave Baiocchi used numbers provided by the Defense Department to measure the troop years invested by each of the military services up to that point. Baiocci determined that the army had borne 54 percent of the workload of fighting the Iraq and Afghanistan wars, while the navy contributed 17 percent, the Air Force 15 percent, and the marines 14 percent.[2]

Of course, there are many other factors that should be considered when trying to get a measure of the true impact of the wars on the troops. The RAND Corporation figures merely measure the workload distribution of all the troop deployments, which were necessary to fight the wars, but they don't show the percentage of each service that deployed to the wars, which would show how hard the war hit each service within their ranks. Such a factor, in addition to the troop years measurement, would be essential to get an understanding of how hard these wars have been on the troops.

To get at that percentage of each service deployed, one would have to take into account the size of each branch of service (the pool or the raw material from which they drew their human resources). The bigger the pool, the greater the ability of the service will be to ameliorate the impact of the rigors of combat and the resulting psychological injuries.

The army, according to an article in *The New York Times* "took on the brunt of the fighting and the casualties in Afghanistan and Iraq" and drew from a pool of "a post-9/11 peak of 570,000."[3] Unfortunately, at the beginning of our War on Terror, the US Army had only about 480,000 men and women, having been reduced from the previous Gulf War, Desert Storm, as a peace dividend to bankroll various social programs. The end result of the drastic reduction was that when we embarked on the wars in Iraq and Afghanistan, we did not have nearly enough men and women in uniform to fight those wars effectively and efficiently without burning out most of our troops.

The previously mentioned RAND Corporation report authored by Baiocchi, measuring the services in numbers during the decade of 2001 to 2011, showed that the army, with a force of 554,000 at the time, had deployed 72.7 percent of their force; the remaining 27.3 percent were primarily "recent recruits that are still in training or are in their first unit of assignment and [are] preparing for deployment."[4] For comparison of sizes and percentage of population having deployed to fight the Iraq and Afghanistan wars, in the Rand study, the navy had 318,124 personnel in uniform and had deployed 66 percent of their force; the Air Force had 327,937 and had deployed 59.1 percent of their force; and the Marine Corps had 199,947 and had deployed 61.4 percent of their force.[5]

To get a complete picture, it is also important to point out that the army deployments ranged from twelve to fifteen months during this time period, and by the time of the 2011 RAND report, 95,000 Army soldiers (17 percent) had completed two or more of these twelve to fifteen-month deployments.[6]

When I deployed to Iraq (November 2004 to October 2005), all of the other services had much shorter deployment times. The Air Force deployment was only three months long, although it was extended to four months at one point.[7] The Marine deployments were running about seven months, as were the navy deployments, since the two services are linked together in many ways to include many personnel policies.[8]

The bottom line is that the army troops were taking a bigger hit in the sacrifices and difficulties of combat deployments. I write this merely to state a fact, not to denigrate the value of the service of the other branches. I truly believe in the quote from the Vietnam era: "All gave some; some gave all." The sacrifice and value of each and every man or woman for their country, regardless of the service, the length of service, or the conditions of service, is something to which we should all give honor and respect. This is why, even though I am a veteran myself, I always praise the contributions of other veterans, regardless of the era they served or the branch under which they served (you will see many of them wearing the baseball-style caps with embroidery proclaiming which unit, ship, war, etc. they served in, or you might see them wearing patches on jackets or vests, which show the units, ships, wars, etc., the places where they laid their sacrifice on the altar of their country to preserve our freedoms and our American way of life).

Nonetheless, it is true that the personal cost for military service is variable. This has always been true throughout our nation's history and wars. The variability of experience, capabilities, skills, conditions, orders, missions, willingness, etc., make it impossible to calculate the value of each veteran's service or to compare it to other experiences of veterans for purposes of rank-ordering the magnitude of suffering. Nonetheless, I believe the Vietnam veterans paid a much higher price than any other era or group of veterans throughout our nation's military history.

Heavy Toll on Reserves and National Guard

I know there will be some who say of the Reservists and National Guardsmen that "they knew when they signed up for military service that deployment would always be a possibility." But we have used these forces so sparingly throughout our national history. Plus, in the last few decades, we have taken many shortcuts with these forces by not completely filling out their units with the required manpower by law and regulations, by not affording them the full training opportunities that their active duty counterparts were getting, and by giving them the worn-out, cast-off equipment that the active duty forces no longer wanted rather than the top-of-the-line, cutting-edge equipment that the active duty was getting. Of course, this did not happen in all cases, but from what we discovered from their deployments in 2003 and 2004 to

Iraq and Afghanistan, they were just as likely to have substandard equipment as they were to have good equipment.

This was one of the egregiously unfair issues that instigated the famous mutiny of the 343rd Quartermaster Company on October 13, 2004.[9] They were being sent out on dangerous roads with inadequately armored vehicles, making them sitting ducks for the roadside bombs (or improvised explosive devices or IEDs). Plus, some of the vehicles they drove were old and inadequately maintained, making them prone to breakdown, increasing the danger. These facts came out in numerous articles, and because the problems became widely known after the soldiers refused what was essentially a suicide mission, it is not surprising that leaders decided not to pursue court martial.

Nonetheless, there existed an understood agreement that reservists such as these would be used sparingly, an agreement that was repeated in countless commercials for many years. In Stacy Bannerman's book about the unique challenges facing reservists, *When the War Came Home*, she gives us a first-person view of all the problems that her husband's reserve unit faced before, during, and after deployment. In speaking of the general agreement that reservists would rarely be used, she writes, "For more than half a century, unless you were an officer, being a member of the Army National Guard was just what the television ad promised: 'One weekend a month, two weeks a year. Earn money for college and protect your local community.' That's what the citizen-soldiers thought they were signing up for when they registered, and little in the last sixty-plus years has indicated otherwise, even after the draft ended on June 30, 1973."[10]

However, she points out that the seeds were sown for this extensive use of reservists starting way back in the Nixon administration when our military transitioned from the draft to an all volunteer force. She writes, "Shortly after the military became an all-volunteer force, the Nixon administration adopted the Total Force concept, which mandated the National Guard and

Reserves as the primary source for augmentation of active duty troops. The new policy was strongly supported by the Pentagon, primarily because it significantly lowered the costs associated with recruiting, training, equipping, and maintaining a large standing military. The other rationale presented by the Pentagon was that it would ensure a greater cross-section of America would be invested in overseas military operations."[11]

While everyone understood that there could possibly come a day when these forces would have to be leaned on very heavily, no one really believed that it would actually happen. It was sort of like writing a large check and dating it far in the future, then living as if you would never have to pay the cost. We did gradually start using them more and more for short humanitarian tours of duty or volunteers in such places as Bosnia, Somalia, Haiti, etc., but this was usually to plug the holes in active duty units, and the activations of such reserve and guard soldiers was still usually on a volunteer basis and for a very limited duration.

But extensive use of these forces or large-scale deployment of many of their units was not expected to happen, unless we faced a dire national emergency, an all-out war such as World War II. But all this changed during the Wars on Terror after 9/11. At first, it was in smaller numbers, but eventually, because of the heavy toll on repeatedly deploying active duty units and soldiers, we got deeper and deeper into this quicksand until these reserve and National Guard forces became indispensible.

Some might argue that we were in an all-out war with a horrific attack on our own soil, the first time such infamy has occurred since Pearl Harbor. But these were the first significant, long and sacrificial wars to be conducted with the new volunteer military. In previous all-out wars, there was a much bigger military force: 12 million in World War II as opposed to approximately 1.5 million currently. Moreover, during large military commitments, Vietnam and earlier conscription, the draft, was used, thereby spreading out the burden of the war fairly across the entirety of America, making the war reach into every segment and class of society (although certainly, the rich and powerful sometimes shirked this duty).

With these first big significant wars, the most significant since Vietnam, in which we sustained large numbers of casualties, the military has tried to recruit a multicultural force so that the services are representative of the American population. But even with this attempt to field a multicultural force, given that the force is comprised of volunteers, there is still a much smaller portion of the population affected or personally invested in the wars, with sons, daughters, mothers, fathers, sisters, and brothers deployed.

The use of the reserve forces reaches into a broader segment of society, further spreading the burden of fighting the war. But while that may be a welcome social indicator to some, this unexpectedly extensive use of the reserves (comprised of the various branch reserve components and the state National Guard branches) during the War on Terror, although seemingly necessary and completely legal, was, in the minds of many, a breach of promise by our national leaders. Essentially, these part-time citizen-soldiers were activated in the unprecedented numbers and for the unprecedentedly long durations because the national leaders did not want to do the hard, perhaps unpopular, but necessary work of building up the active duty forces, nor were they willing to make the hard decisions to build the active duty forces, which might result in a sacrifice of their various cherished pork projects or social programs. It was much easier to quietly let the burden slip to the reservists, growing ever greater over time.

Additionally, in many ways, these reserve and National Guard forces bear a heavier burden for their active duty service. In spite of the laws on the books protecting those who serve from such things as losing their jobs, there are, nonetheless, many who still end up losing their jobs when they deploy. Also, many of these people take a big hit financially in spite of the extra pays that are given to the troops in combat zones. For instance, they may hold a job with much higher pay, but when they deploy, they may do so as a lower-ranking troop whose pay is not very high and certainly not nearly as high as their civilian jobs. All in all, there are, arguably, just many more hardships that these reserve and National Guard troops endure for their deployments than do the active duty troops.

The hardships of their deployment are a little known fact. Also, the excessive use of the reserve and National Guard forces instead of building up the active duty forces like they should is another dirty little secret, which doesn't get much attention because the reservists don't have the strong military and political connections to fight back against this unfairly extensive use of their ranks or to make any kind of a media stink over the issue. But most of them have anted up without complaint and done their duty, even when they were forced into it without a choice, and even when their extensive overuse were sometimes violated egregiously through arbitrary policy changes in the Pentagon and the Army Human Resources Command.

Of course, it is true that they did sign contracts with the understanding that deployments were a possibility, but as with all troops—active and reserve—we always hope and expect that our leaders will do the right thing and honor commitments made when the time comes. Why? Because moral values are an intrinsic part of military life as exemplified in their inclusion in countless training sessions, ceremonies, conversations, posters in military units and buildings, various monuments or displays on military posts, etc.

Military Values and Leadership

I spent my thirty-year career (twenty-three of it on active duty) in the army. In every single unit that I have been a member of or have visited and on every single military post that I have been on, I can always find within a few minutes prominently displayed posters, placards, and other such displays that proclaim our army values (loyalty, duty, respect, selfless service, honor, integrity, and personal courage). We know these values because they are drilled into us constantly from basic training until the very end of our careers, and we remember them using the mnemonic *leadership* (LDRSHIP—the initials of each of the values).

In addition to this constant reminder of the army values, we are continuously reminded of our constitutional origin, function, and duty: "I (state your full name), do solemnly swear (or affirm) that I will support and defend the Constitution against all enemies foreign and domestic."[12] We speak these words in all of our ceremonial oaths upon entering the service, upon joining various organizations within the military, and upon reenlisting or being promoted. Moreover, since soldiers are always at such ceremonies either as the central honorees or simply as observers, the end result is that we hear these words incessantly. I would venture to say that hardly a day passes in the life of a soldier that he or she does not hear or see these two sets of values.

While I cannot speak from personal experience about the other major military branches (navy, marines, Air Force, and Coast Guard), I would not be surprised to find that all their troops also are constantly trained on moral values for their nation and their service branch. This is as it should be. The military is one of the few institutions that are mentioned by name in the US Constitution. The military possesses a potentially dangerous power to destroy and kill, and it is charged with a critical constitutional mission—that is, to uphold and defend that constitution. In meeting this mission, the military must, by logical extension, preserve our American freedoms and way of life as stated in the Preamble to the Constitution: "We the People of the United States, in Order to form a more perfect Union, establish Justice, insure domestic Tranquility, provide for the common defence, promote the general Welfare, and secure the Blessings of Liberty to ourselves and our Posterity, do ordain and establish this Constitution for the United States of America."[13]

Since the military is such a quintessentially moral organization, then their officer and noncommissioned officer leaders must uphold and are expected to uphold the highest moral values. They should be exemplars of their service's and their nation's values. When they fail to be such paragons of moral virtue, looking to self-interest instead of national service or instead of the best interests of their subordinates, the impact on the troops is deep, excruciating, and enduring.

As previously mentioned in this book, H.R. McMaster's book *Dereliction of Duty* exposes that abdication of moral leadership during the Vietnam War by the civilian leaders and by many of the officers, and even higher-ranking non-commissioned officers.[14]

There were physical consequences to this failure of leadership, although it would be impossible to calculate the extent of the harm, but another result of the abdication of leadership responsibilities during the Vietnam War was the long-lasting emotional and psychological consequences on individual troops that Dr. Jonathan Shay covered in his book, *Achilles in Vietnam*. Shay writes, "Combat trauma destroys the capacity for social trust, accounting for the paranoid state of being that blights the lives of the most severely traumatized combat veterans. This is not a selective mistrust directed at a specific individual or institution that has betrayed its charge, but a comprehensive destruction of social trust. Lies and euphemisms by the soldier's own military superiors and civilian leaders of course undermine social trust by destroying confidence in language."[15]

Perhaps, the most egregious failure of leadership was the unwillingness of many of these leaders during the Vietnam War to share in the risk of their men. Shay writes in the first chapter of his book, "Soldiers grow most doubtful about the fair distribution of risk when they see that their commanders shelter themselves from it."[16] Shay quotes well-respected military historian Edward

Luttwak: "In Vietnam, the mere fact that officers above the most junior rank were so abundant and mostly found in well-protected bases suggested a very unequal sharing of the risk."[17]

Moreover, as Shay and many others have pointed out, the higher-ranking officers leading the war in Vietnam as well as controlling it from the Pentagon created a dangerous system of careerism that too often placed unprepared and incompetent officers in charge of combat units to the danger and detriment of the troops. These higher-ranking officers "(1) designed a system of officer rotation that rotated officers (above second lieutenant in and out of combat assignments every six months [while their men served 12-month tours with few breaks]. (2) were responsible for training, evaluating, and assigning officers to combat command [with career considerations as the driving factor rather than combat efficiency], and (3) placed institutional and career considerations above the lives of the soldiers under their responsibility."[18]

To top it all off, according to Dr. Shay, these corrupt leaders subjected their men to unnecessary risks and deprivation by forcing lower-ranking officers to make dangerous shortcuts in battlefield tactics designed to keep the men safe[19] by forcing on the troops dangerously ineffective equipment such as the infamous fielding of the (at the time) new M-16 and by subjecting them to shortages of "food, water, ammunition, clothing, shelter from the elements, medical care," etc., not because of unavoidable contingencies, but all too often because of "indifference or disrespect."[20]

All of these things and the central and essential role of leaders in military units (especially during combat) were one of the main reasons for the high rate of PTSD among Vietnam veterans. And leadership failure is often complicit in PTSD cases of veterans in other eras and other wars because it is a central factor in the breakdown of the veteran's worldview (his tapestry or lens of values, experiences, beliefs, etc. through which all people experience and interpret the world).

Whether it be a breach of contract or a breach of promise, the emotional, psychological, and even spiritual impact to the individual is the same. There can be a breakdown in unit morale, or soldiers can simply pack it all away in their subconscious such as the troops did in Vietnam until they returned back to the States.

To be fair, not all leaders in Vietnam were bad. There are many stories of good leaders that have made into the media in books, and even movies, such as the 1992 book *We Were Soldiers Once...And Young*,[21] followed by the movie *We Were Soldiers Once* in 2002.[22] Some of these books have become required reading for young officers in training such as James R. McDonough's auto-biographical *Platoon Leader*.[23] In the narrative of the book, we find the young McDonough as the model of the selfless, self-sacrificing, strong, confident, servant-leader who puts the interests and welfare of his men ahead of his own and places the mission ahead of personal momentary discomfort.

And I'm sure that McDonough was not alone. When I entered the military service in 1979, I encountered many good officer and noncommissioned officer leaders from the Vietnam War still in service, and many of these good leaders remained in the services for many years afterward, rebuilding the hollow military of the mid to late '70s into a formidable, professional force in the mid-eighties and later.

True, honorable, and patriotic military leadership feels a deep sense of responsibility for those entrusted to his or her care. I always felt like a father to my troops and tried to conduct myself as a father, treating them with the love and respect that I would my own children, looking out for their best interests by promoting their success above my own, even assisting them in various ways with their dreams and ambitions beyond the military, tutoring sometimes, writing letters of recommendation sometimes, serving as a reference to jobs, assisting with resumes, etc. I have even gone so far as to help with resumes of my soldiers' wives, successfully helping them to get jobs in the government and private sector, thereby promoting the overall interests of my troops and their families. In a word, this is simply love. When you truly love your troops, you care about what they care about and you want (like a good father or mother) to see them succeed, to see them do their best, to see them grow and challenge themselves, and to see them learn to function in this world as caring individuals who give back to people and to the world around them.

Moreover, part of the caring leader's work is doing the hard work of enforcing justly and compassionately the tough but necessary standards of military discipline, regulations, and mission and task requirements as well as reinforcing the good moral values of our nation and of our military branch. It does our troops no good to overlook or dismiss substandard performance without correction because doing so robs them of the chance to improve themselves and to learn. Furthermore, it sends a message to all those around that see someone get away with violating rules or standards. It tells all around that the rules, standards, or morals are not important or that they are situational and can be subordinated to any individual's personal morality.

To enforce such rules, standards, and morality, one must know what real morality is. One source for those values, since our nation has been predominantly Christian throughout its history, is in the sound, tried, and true principles of the Christian religion as found in the Bible with the sure foundation of God's love and with the purpose of spreading and enacting that love in all human endeavors.

Regardless of your source though, real morality, which is indispensable in the military, should be grounded in sound principles that do not change. It promotes the general welfare of people, which leads them to higher, nobler, more compassionate and self-sacrificial lives of service to others. Also, good rules must be built upon those moral principles. This principle in itself is absolutely necessary to understand and enforce the rules and standards to be able to articulate just reward and punishment in the gray areas or

the Solomon-like conundrums and to avoid the dangers of legal-
ism (rules that are torn away from their moral foundation and go
to logically and morally absurd places).

The Psychology and
Science of PTSD

There is so much misunderstanding, disbelief, and confusion about PTSD. PTSD has probably existed as long as mankind has been around as some people's response to overwhelming and abnormal circumstances. What we call PTSD is best defined as psychological injury, but when we talk about it or treat people, the primary focus is on the body's response to that initial shock or injury.

As to how someone develops PTSD, there will probably be some precipitating event or multiple events centered on a trauma. For the troops, that trauma is the horror of war—the danger and harsh environment, the incredible physical demands, the deaths, the injuries, and the horrific aftermath or after-effects on people, whether you know them or not. War is not normal, but we know sometimes it is a necessary evil in order to oppose greater evil in the world (such as the fight against Nazi Germany and Imperial Japan during World War II). Nonetheless, even in a war with a just cause, the violence is still not a normal experience for those involved. In war, there are so many violations of "what's right," to borrow a phrase from Dr. Jonathan Shay's 1995 bestselling book, *Achilles in Vietnam*,[1] about his decades of work with Vietnam veterans and PTSD.

As Dr. Shay noted, there's no escaping the moral implications of war. When the human heart encounters the horror, it cannot but be injured in some way. Moreover, Colonel John Bradley, M.D., chief of Psychiatry at Walter Reed, commented on the totality of war's effect on our troops during the filming of HBO's *Wartorn* (2011), a documentary about PTSD among combat veterans. He said, "I would say that nobody is really unscathed unless you have no compassion for human life, you have a total disregard. Maybe the only thing you feel is recoil. Everybody else carries something with them."[2]

Regardless of whether they were participants or witnesses, most people recognize the moral violation of war, and no matter how hard they may resist or how well they may be prepared or how sound they may be prior to war, they can still be psychologically wounded and can still develop PTSD. The HBO documentary *Wartorn* even opens with the poignant story of one Union soldier during the Civil War, Angelo Crapsey. The story is told through his letters during the course of the war. In the beginning, he sounds very dedicated to the cause and is high in spirits, but through the course of the succeeding two years, his letters reveal his increasing mental distress at the bloody violence until he is discharged from the service as being mentally unfit for service after only two years. Upon returning home, he is completely broken and eventually commits suicide.[3]

Although not all will develop PTSD, based on Dr. Bradley's expertise in dealing with soldiers, it is likely that few returned from war completely unscathed. Why? Because we are all human, and we are all subsequently bound by empathy. A normal human heart cannot encounter the suffering of another without being affected, so it is not just the infantrymen in war that are affected by PTSD but also doctors, nurses, medics, military police, graves registration or mortuary affairs soldiers, and others.

Anyone who encounters the horror of war and suffers personally or vicariously can develop PTSD. I was a staff officer who reported the deaths and injuries of our unit's soldiers to my superiors. For injuries, I had to read the medevac reports with the doctors' cold precision of tragic detail. For deaths, I had to research their lives—who they were, their family, their hometown, etc. My leaders being dedicated patriots and decent people didn't want to ever treat any death casually, but the cost for me in this knowledge was to personalize the death of another and to know that a real family somewhere would suffer, inviting gnawing and ever-growing guilt and emotional pain because I was still alive.

There were many other events that contributed to my psychological injury, including one incident when I thought I had lost a friend in a combat incident. Within a few months of my deployment, I would develop crushing anxiety and depression that were barely controlled by medication and my own willpower. During all this time, I lived on the edge, getting very little sleep and living from meal to meal with no real joy or relief. The temporary respites that were supposed to serve as relief never really helped, whether it was a movie or a game or some other diversion. It became increasingly difficult to enjoy anything anyway.

The dark cloud of my depression and anxiety never left me at any time. I was always aware of it. In all this, we were always working long days, never really thinking or feeling and hoping to remain in that numb state, and hoping at the end of it that you would just feel exhausted enough to climb into bed without thinking and escape it all into the hopeful bliss of sleep. But it didn't take long until all this pressure even invaded the few hours of sleep that I got each night and started giving me the nightmares beginning with the faces of those whose deaths I reported, until I started waking fighting back tears when the sleep drained away enough to for me to realize that I was still in this living nightmare.

I encountered a moral violation, and my worldview or belief in the inherent goodness and rightness of things was shattered. This moral breach was the major part of what those Vietnam vets cited in Dr. Shay's books, and it haunted them for decades after.

The moral violation may come in one event or a series of events, or it can be the culmination point or breaking point after attrition from a series of moral violations and the gradual wearing down of the body and mind from the harsh working and living environment. Regardless, this is the input that causes the shock, which develops into the PTSD symptoms. The main discussion of PTSD literature focuses on the symptoms or the body's response.

As discussed in chapter 6 in the DSM-5, there are four clusters of symptoms, which are used to identify PTSD in a patient. First, there are the intrusive memories or thoughts.[4] Second, there's the avoidance or withdrawal.[5] Third, there are the negative alterations in cognitions and mood, which includes episodic or amnesic memory about the trauma; persistent negative beliefs and expectations about self or the world; persistent distorted blame of self or others for causing the traumatic event or its consequences; persistent negative trauma-related emotions; significantly diminished interest in normal life activities; feelings of alienation, detachment, or estrangement from others; and constricted affect or persistent inability to experience positive emotions.[6] Fourth, there are alterations in arousal and reactivity such as irritable or aggressive behavior, risky, reckless, or self-destructive behavior, hypervigilance (always feeling like you're on the edge, not being able to relax, or feeling like you can't let your guard down since you constantly feel unsafe), exaggerated startle response, problems concentrating, and sleep disturbance (interrupted sleep, inability to sleep, or even erratic sleep from the PTSD nightmares, which are common).[7]

Someone with PTSD may not feel all of the symptoms listed. Everyone is unique. As for me, the hyper-arousal or hypervigilance that is connected to adrenaline has been the most prominent symptom of my PTSD. This has been the most persistent symptom, with the adrenaline storm being triggered by a smell, a sound, a feel, a sight, or a situation that reminds me of Iraq. Or it can simply be triggered by too much stress, too much social interaction (such as being in crowded places), or simply too much coming at me at one time. In the early years, these triggers resulted in days of being on edge, not able to settle down or sleep or relax, much like an anxiety attack on steroids way out of proportion to the original stimulus and seemingly out of my control. Thankfully, the symptoms have decreased in severity as enough time has passed and God has healed me enough that the symptoms no longer consume my life.

For several years, I also experienced the avoidance, withdrawal (from relationships and the normal closeness that one experiences in relationships), numbing (feeling emotionally numb or empty), or amnesic symptoms (inability to remember certain events that have been walled off in my subconscious mind). These symptoms are a defense mechanism to protect you against the overwhelming shock of your trauma, giving you space to rest or regroup, adjust, and make meaning of the trauma. But such strong emotions cannot be permanently restrained or walled off in the recesses of your subconscious. At some point, these emotions and the experiences that caused them will have to be addressed, talked about, or let out. However, it is this self-defense mechanism that helps all people to encounter bad events and still survive, and I believe it is a gift from our merciful God who allows us to endure the harshness of life and hold off the pain until we are stronger or more experienced and thus able to understand or grapple with the hard memories and powerful emotions.

But even with this defense mechanism, I discovered that even the worst of my memories and emotions could not stay buried forever. If your experience was like mine, your mind may release the pressure in sometimes random ways. Your memory of events may jump around and seem erratic when you try to recall certain events that have been walled off. It can be confusing trying to construct memories that are fragmented between these compartments, but there are processes of the brain that allow even these deeply buried memories to surface.

Nonetheless, sooner or later, your brain, like mine, will try to reengage those thoughts because they have to be processed. They cannot be buried without reconciliation forever. This leads to the intrusive thoughts. The mind tries to acknowledge, engage, and ameliorate by reviving the thoughts or memories and somehow making sense of them. These thoughts and memories (and associated feelings) are sometimes triggered by feelings, thoughts, or circumstances you encounter during the day. Or they may simply come floating into your conscious during the day. However, you will probably more likely experience them in the bad dreams at night, or even full flashbacks during the day, a sort of daydream on steroids that may put you momentarily right back into the horrific event or events as if they were happening right now.

If these emotions and memories surface during sleep, most commonly this will happen during our deep sleep in the dreams of our rapid eye movement (REM) cycle, the deepest part of our sleep. It is in the crazy dreams that the brain tries to consolidate and make sense of the day's events, perhaps, interspersed with bits of the random and walled-off memories and emotions, because there may be threads that connect your current experience back to that painful memory that you can't even consciously acknowledge.

Other than the above-listed symptoms, I also experienced at times deeply crushing depression, a continual death wish or sense of doom, a feeling of isolation or detachment from life, a feeling of disconnection from life, a loss of interest in many activities that I enjoyed prior to my deployment, and, if not paranoia, at least, a very unhealthy pessimism about the motives of others.

In addition to the emotional symptoms, if you have PTSD, you may also experience many secondary psychosomatic symptoms as I did. Most people probably know about the impact that our emotions can have on our bodies, but I doubt that very many know how powerful an effect that strong emotions can have.

The Psychosomatic Impact of PTSD

In an article entitled "Can You Die of a Broken Heart?" Stephen Evans, a BBC News reporter, tells the story of attending the funeral of a married couple who "died within a week of each other."[8] In his article, he goes on to cite a few other cases of couples who, after one spouse passed on, the other followed within a very short period of time.[9]

In another article, "You Really Can Die of a Broken Heart," in the British newspaper *Daily Mail*, medical correspondent Jenny Hope reveals the stories of still more people who died the same way. A photo in the article bears a caption with the story of just one such couple: "Doctor Who actress Mary Tamm died in July 2012, and her husband, Marcus Ringrose, died the day after her funeral of Sudden Adult Death Syndrome."[10]

These tragic stories make it clear that a grieving heart can have a tremendous, and even deadly, psychosomatic impact on the body of the person in grief, as the body responds to the powerful emotions in a very real way. The worst impact from these strong emotions, sudden death, can be caused by cardiac arrest in a phenomenon called "takotsubo cardiomyopathy." In layman's terms, the heart's normal pumping mechanism is interrupted as a result of the release of stress chemicals (the fight-or-flight chemicals) in the aftermath of an overwhelming emotional event, leading to the grieving person's death.

Moreover, it is likely that psychosomatic reactions within the body to the initiating trauma or stress can disrupt many other bodily processes, causing serious health problems up to and including death. It is important to grasp this scientific phenomenon because it is too easy to dismiss the private suffering of the trauma victim or the person who develops PTSD as invisible wounds. Due to the body's reactive processes and chemicals following a tragic event, people who are affected by the tragic event may experience deep emotional pain, but this pain can also lead to many health problems as the invisible becomes very visible, tangible, and real.

The symptoms of PTSD become manifested in numerous body systems and processes after the emotional wound to the psyche. Of course, the body is designed to take various stresses and usually is capable of returning to homeostasis or a normal state afterward, but in extreme circumstances where a tragic event is experienced or overwhelming events lead to an emotional breakdown, these bodily processes do not return to normal but rather become a new normal with the fight-or-flight processes and chemicals becoming stuck in the "on" position.

Dr. John J Medina explains the process in an article in the January 2008 edition of *Psychiatric Times*. He writes:

> Whether the stress becomes damaging is the result of a complex interaction between the outside world and our physiological capacity to manage it. The body's reaction to stress is partly a matter of what stress it encounters, partly the duration of the stress, and partly the somatic substrates (many of which are genetic) that the person brings to the experience. [Bruce] McEwen has even given a name to the point at which stress becomes toxic – the allostatic load. You could call the allostatic load a 'system breach.' PTSD also can be thought of as a system breach. Because people will have different allostatic load thresholds, their response to the stressors they encounter will also be different.[11]

Dr. Medina uses the term "system breach"[12] to explain how the body manifests the emotions into very real health problems, which are in response to an overwhelming event or situation— a breakdown, so to speak. And when PTSD causes this bodily system breakdown, it can also lead to permanent conditions and permanent damage to the body and brain. It's also important to understand how individualistic the experience is, completely unique to the individual with some factors being genetic and some being environmental, "nature versus nurture." But the interpretation of the event as traumatic is, in many ways, subjective to the individual: their experiences, their value systems, their personality, their level of involvement or commitment to the event, and their unique interpretation of the event based upon their unique life experience, their unique point of view.

In another article addressing the flood of fight-or-flight chemicals into the body during stress, we learn of the impact when this process continues nonstop in the body of the PTSD sufferer. Normally, these fight-or-flight chemicals in our body are beneficial, but in the body of the PTSD sufferer, they can be very destructive. In an article about trauma victims' stress on the web site of the United Kingdom's National Workplace Bullying Advice Line, BullyOnLine.com, we learn:

> The body becomes awash with cortisol which in high prolonged doses is toxic to brain cells. Cortisol kills off neuroreceptors in the hippocampus, an area of the brain linked with learning and memory. The hippocampus is also the control centre for the fight or flight response, thus the ability to control the fight or flight mechanism itself becomes impaired.[13]

Suffice it to say that these physical, psychosomatic manifestations of PTSD can result in a myriad of health problems with some of the effects possibly becoming permanent. This allostatic load or overload to your body's systems as a result of powerful emotions can lead to numerous very real and very physical problems.

In an article in *The Washington Times* entitled "Stress Damages Brain," Gabriella Boston explains "that when we have chronic stress, the brain gets flooded with an enzyme that effectively breaks down part of the structure (the dendritic spines) of the neurons in the prefrontal cortex…"[14] This stress response is normally an event which the body later ameliorates, bringing all chemical systems back into balance after the stressful event has passed but with "underlying conditions such as bipolar disorder [dramatic manic-depressive mood swings], post-traumatic stress disorder, or chronic depression and anxiety" the body does not return to its normal state, and "the brain doesn't get a break to recover."[15]

Moreover, in ScienCentralNews, a June 24, 2003 article reports: "after studying nerve cells in a banana-shaped area of the brain called the hippocampus, a hub for learning and memory, neuroscientists say chronic stress can have devastating effects on our brains." The article goes on to explain that the brain's dendrites ("places where other never cells make connections and transmit chemical signals") become damaged by stress as the "branches become shorter and less branched, as a result of repeated stress. That means there are fewer synaptic connections, and it means these cells are not receiving as much information as they normally do."[16]

Furthermore, the article reports that the hippocampus ("a hub for learning and memory") can become damaged from this assault on the dendrites, causing in this brain structure "shrinkage after repeated stress."[17] Moreover, the article reports that chronic stress, as experienced by PTSD sufferers, can lead to change in another key structure of the brain, the amygdala, which is "the part of the brain that regulates fear and emotion..." The article reports, "With a chronic stress, neurons in the amygdala grow, they become larger says [professor and head of the endocrinology laboratory at Rockefeller University, Bruce] McEwen. And there's evidence that in depressive illness the amygdala may even become larger, and it certainly becomes more active."[18]

The end result of the changes to the hippocampus and amygdala are further explained: "If the cells in your hippocampus are shrinking, and the cells in your amygdala are growing, 'you may have all sorts of anxieties and anger and fear and yet you don't have the hippocampus to help you connect it to where you were and what you were doing to make it specific. So you may have generalized anxieties as a result of this."[19]

I myself have experienced this phenomenon many times with my own PTSD as generalized anxiety many days with no memory of any event that relates to the anxiety and no other specific connective events in my life or my daily activities that can be identified as causation. Furthermore, I also still experience many anniversary memories, days every year on which I have terrible emotional feelings, depression, and overwhelming anxiety, and without any specific memory of why I am feeling this way, no memory of what exactly happened on this day in my past or during my combat deployment to cause the intense emotions. Of course, this experience is not unique to me. I have read and have heard of other PTSD sufferers report these same experiences of anxiety or depression without an associative memory, without context.

Additionally, these vague feelings without the associated memory become permanent and are stored in the short-term memory, causing them to bring constant anguish to the PTSD sufferer. In an online article, "Three Ways Trauma Affects Your Brain," reporter Michele Rosenthal explains this process: "Adjacent to the amygdala the hippocampus is responsible for the formation, organization, storage and retrieval of memories. Technically, it converts them from short-term to long-term, sending them to the appropriate parts of your outer brain for storage. Trauma, however, hijacks this process: the hippocampus is prevented from transforming the memories and so those memories remain in an activated, short-term status. This stops the memories from being properly integrated so that their effects diminish."[20]

Moreover, Ms. Rosenthal explains other changes to an important part of the brain for memory recall and emotional regulation, the prefrontal cortex: "Lastly, the prefrontal cortex (located in the front, outer most layer of your brain) contributes two important elements of recall: Your left frontal lobe specializes in storing memories of individual events; your right frontal lobe specializes in extracting a theme or main point from a series of events.

After trauma a few things can occur: your lower brain processes responsible for instinct and emotion override the inhibitory strength of the cortex so that the cortex cannot properly stop inappropriate reactions or refocus your attention. [B]lood flow to the left prefrontal lobe can decrease, so you have less ability for language, memory and other left lobe functions. [B]lood flow to your right prefrontal lobe can increase, so you experience more sorrow, sadness and anger."[21]

This process of change to the prefrontal cortex can explain unusual or high-risk behavior in PTSD sufferers as well as the increase in negative emotions. But, perhaps most important, Ms. Rosenthal goes on to explain how these changes become permanent, so the PTSD sufferer is incapable of moving beyond the trauma: "There are many reasons why we know PTSD is not 'all in your head,' and why you can't 'just get over it.'"[22]

However, the damage from PTSD is not confined to the brain alone. It can cause a number of physical ailments throughout the body. An article, "Post-Traumatic Stress Disorder In-Depth Report," from *The New York Times* explains numerous health problems that can result from PTSD. Among the problems that the article lists are: "Heart Disease. Anxiety has been associated with several heart risk factors, including unhealthy cholesterol levels, thicker blood vessels, and high blood pressure. Both anxiety and depression [both of which most PTSD sufferers experience] have been associated with a poorer response to treatment in heart patients, including a worse outcome after heart surgery."[23]

The article lists other major areas where psychosomatic symptoms can be experienced: "Gastrointestinal disorders. Anxiety frequently accompanies gastrointestinal conditions. Of note, half the cases of irritable bowel syndrome are associated with anxiety... Headache. Both tension and migraine headaches are associated with anxiety disorders...Respiratory Problems. Studies report an association between anxiety in patients with obstructive lung conditions (such as asthma, emphysema, and chronic bronchitis) and more frequent relapses…Allergic Conditions. Anxiety disorders are associated with numerous allergic conditions including hay fever, eczema, hives, food allergies, and conjunctivitis."[24]

In numerous other articles from my research, PTSD has been implicated in: arthritis, a variety of heart-related problems and disease, respiratory system-related problems and disease, reproductive system-related problems, diabetes, fibromyalgia, irritable bowel syndrome—just to name a few. This is not an exhaustive list, so PTSD and the chemical changes that it initiates in the body can cause or exacerbate a whole host of other problems throughout the body, to say the least. To reiterate, although PTSD is frequently referred to as an invisible wound, its symptoms and psychosomatic impacts are far from invisible.

I myself have developed a number of conditions that are most likely the result of the pounding stress from the PTSD upon my body's various systems, organs, and processes. I had problems with sleep for many years due to my inability to completely relax and turn off the adrenaline. My blood pressure has gotten much worse until I developed a heart condition, suffering a minor heart attack. Moreover, I have contracted adult-onset diabetes, which requires insulin to control it.

Risky Behavior and PTSD

In addition to the psychosomatic problems, many of those with PTSD engage in risky behavior. I had a few brushes with the law in the early years after Iraq. By the grace of God, I escaped any serious trouble. Looking back, I sometimes can't believe some of the things I did or the risks I took, but with the overwhelming depression, anxiety, and other PTSD symptoms, I simply was not in my right mind. Things that made sense to me then do not make sense to me now.

There have been reports in the media about the soaring rate of soldier misconduct in the services. A February 17, 2014, Associated Press article, "Misconduct Forces More Soldiers

Out," by Lolita C. Baldor explained the magnitude of the problem. She wrote, "Data obtained by the Associated Press shows that the number of officers who left the Army due to misconduct more than tripled in the past three years. The number of enlisted soldiers forced out for drugs, alcohol, crimes and other misconduct shot up from about 5,600 in 2007, as the Iraq war peaked, to more than 11,000 last year."[25]

Some military leaders who have commented on this phenomenon attributed the spike to a lack of focus on character in the military services during the last thirteen years, claiming that the focus on combat efficiency caused the services to lose sight of character issues.[26] I believe they are completely wrong. For one thing, character issues are not mutually exclusive to combat. Being effective in combat requires many of the character traits that the services hold dear (such as the army values: loyalty, duty, respect, selfless service, honor, integrity, and personal courage).

Having served twenty-three years on active duty and seven years in the military during these two long wars in Iraq and Afghanistan as well as being deployed one year to Iraq, I can say that I never saw a lapse in the emphasis on character and values in any of the units I served in or the units that I was not in but worked with. Moreover, having served on unit inspection teams as well as conducting investigations a few times, I know that a spike in disciplinary problems usually is evidence of a morale problem: a poor command climate that is legalistic and focuses on the wrong things, which drags morale down and is a tyrannical climate in which the commander is using excessive force to instill discipline instead of positive leadership methods such as reward, praise, encouragement, and trust); or simply erratic leadership that doesn't apply sound moral principles equally to all in the unit. It is possible for a group of people to have a lot of "bad apples," but it's not likely that you will find so many bad people grouped together in one single place. So, one should never automatically assume that a rise in disciplinary issues is a sign of bad people, but rather one should first consider whether it is a problem in morale and/or leadership.

Additionally, since PTSD and a few other mental health problems are known to increase risky behavior in those who are afflicted, I believe it is likely that PTSD and other psychological problems among our troops is to blame for this rise in misconduct. Unlike past wars, a historically very high percentage of army troops deployed to combat, so there are much greater pressures on the troops serving currently. Marital problems have risen dramatically in the army during this period of high deployments. Moreover, one "task force investigating the high rate of Army suicides released a report in July [2010] concluding that more soldiers died as a result of high-risk behavior last year [2009] than they did in combat."[27] This was just one snapshot in time, but the suicide rate has been consistently high throughout these ten-plus years our military has been at war (with as many as twenty-two soldiers or veterans a day committing suicide), so it is likely that the high-risk behavior has also been consistently high during this period of time.

Bureaucracy in the Flag Officer Ranks

Furthermore, this "blame the troops" mentality is highly problematic at best. The same leaders who are now attributing the rise in misconduct to lack of character among the troops are the very people who were leading the troops during combat. Perhaps, they don't realize it, but in attributing the misconduct to lax standards, they are, in essence, questioning their own leadership, which apparently allowed this to happen.

I would not be the first person to criticize some high-ranking leaders. We all know about the General David Petraeus scandal (affair with Paula Broadwell) and the General Stanley McChrystal scandal (as posted in the June 22, 2010 *Rolling Stone* interview).[28] Moreover, a few writers in various media outlets, for example the late David Hackworth (1930–2005), have exposed this misbehavior among the flag officers, suggesting that this is unfortunately a widespread phenomenon. Perhaps, a good reason for the misbehavior of these high-ranking flag officers (admirals and generals) is because they sit atop a bloated bureaucracy that is far too big and they are not accountable to anyone. In fact, this bureaucracy is—possibly bigger by some accounts—than the one which fought and won World War II. In an article on the G2mil. com web site, Carlton Meyer reports:

> Does the U.S. military need 919 active duty flag officers serving the equivalent role of corporate vice presidents? That's one flag officer for every 1,536 servicemen. Since the 9–11 terror attack, the Pentagon has added 4 additional four-star flag officers, 23 extra three-stars, 5 extra two-stars, and 12 extra one-stars. We have as many flag officers commanding the 1.4 million GIs today as we had during World War II when 12 million were in uniform![29]

In another article from the Project on Government Oversight (POGO.org), the organization posted the text from their testimony before the Senate Armed Services Committee. They explained that this boom in the flag officer ranks has resulted "in today's unprecedented top-heavy force structure." Additionally, they noted:

> During the drawdown in the decade following the end of the Cold War, lower ranks were cut much more than higher ranks. In the decade since the war in Afghanistan began, higher ranks have grown at a much faster rate than lower ranks…The top officer ranks, general and flag officers, have grown faster than lower officer ranks, and three- and four-star positions have increased faster than all other components of the DoD's [Department of Defense] force structure—a phenomenon we call star creep…The Army and Marines, which bear the greatest burden in the war on terror, have added far fewer top brass than the Navy and Air Force. In fact, the Navy and Air Force have each added

more top brass than the Army and Marines combined. Furthermore, the Air Force has a historically low number of planes per general and the Navy is close to having more admirals than ships for them to command.[30]

With these additional high-ranking flag officer positions comes a huge bureaucracy, since all of them need staffs and small kingdoms to command. Unfortunately, these added organizations are often redundant, with multiple organizations led by flag officers doing duplicate work that is covered by other organizations led by them. Moreover, these bloated bureaucratic organizations take up valuable resources, which are not used on the lower ranks for better equipment, training, housing, etc. This is not to dismiss the importance of high-ranking officers. They have an important place in the US military, just as the lower-ranking troops have an important place. However, when bureaucracies become so entrenched, bloated, redundant, and unaccountable, they tend to become "self-licking ice cream cones," existing for no good purpose other than to simply exist.

Also, aside from the problems of bloated bureaucracy at the top of the military, military discipline is still an important issue. It should always be important in every situation, not just emphasized erratically from time to time. The good leaders in our military will recognize this and will consistently encourage and enforce moral standards at all times and all places using both the "carrot and the stick" (positive and negative motivation) as necessary, avoiding tyranny or harsh leadership techniques.

But as I discovered during my career, there are periodically bad leaders at all levels who resort to negative or tyrannical leadership. And these bad leaders tend to impose or enforce military discipline erratically, avoiding the harder work of sound leadership, the careful mentoring and shaping, the emotional connection, and the stair-step, incremental disciplinary measures meant to save and not to automatically throw the soldier away at the first few signs of trouble. It is clear, however, that some leaders, such as Odierno, now prefer to blame the troops and to get rid of their "trash" rather than help these broken men and women. And most likely, if this approach is used by some leaders, then this is probably affecting more than just disciplinary issues. It probably impacts medical issues and psychological issues as well.

Don't get me wrong. There are still many good leaders in the military. You can tell them from the others because they look you in the eye with concern, truly listen, and give genuine respect and compassion that the others try to fake. They fight for the troops and don't have to raise their voice, belittle, curse, and bully to get a response from their troops. They are true leaders who understand what real leadership entails and will not accept or assume the testosterone fueled bravado, which is a cheap imitation. The troops recognize the genuine love of these leaders and would follow them to the gates of hell.

Such leaders take leadership seriously as a sacred trust and as a service to their people and not as a stepping stone to some other benefit, rank, or achievement. They often put the welfare of their people above their own welfare. They recognize that God will require much of those to whom much has been given (Luke 12:48). Moreover, they are focused on helping all troops, not just some abstract troop out there somewhere epitomized in their various programs or in the occasional drug deal they make for their buddies' friends or staff or some quid pro quo trades disingenuously portrayed as "helping." And these good leaders do the deeper work of mentoring their staffs and others close around them rather than heaping abuse on them, which is the trait that quickly exposes most hypocritical leaders.

Also, most good leaders will remember that there is no shame in seeking help, and they will not automatically assume that there is some flaw in the troop that has problems. It is essential that leaders have compassion when they come into contact with soldiers who have been in combat and are currently struggling just to keep up with military requirements when they had not had such troubles before combat. When a troop goes bad that quickly, you can bet that there is an underlying reason, and hopefully military leaders are looking for those reasons and trying to help their troops to get help rather than just kicking them to the curb or giving them the "Patton slap" of tyrannical discipline without compassion.

For those troops that develop PTSD, they will need that compassion, and they will need leaders who remember how much they have already sacrificed for their country. Moreover, hopefully these leaders will realize how much more these troops with PTSD are suffering for and sacrificing for their country, since this is a dark, difficult, and perilous path.

It is because of these sacrifices and hardships our troops endure that, I believe, God has a special place in his heart for those serving in the military because they, of all people, best understand what sacrifice means. Sacrifice is the highest act of love, nobility, and courage. The US troops sacrifice daily on the altar of their country for their fellow American citizens across our great land, for their comrades-in-arms serving beside them and for their families. And Jesus taught us about the importance of sacrifice in John 15:13 (NKJV): "Greater love has no one than this, than to lay down one's life for his friends."

But the good leaders will always remember the tremendous sacrifices that soldiers make every day and will remember that they are entrusted by the American people to treat their sons and daughters, brothers and sisters, and mothers and fathers in uniform with the due respect and honor that they deserve.

Epilogue

I read somewhere that PTSD is like adult-onset ADHD (attention deficit hyperactive disorder) . This is a very helpful simile, since I have found in my own life that, at times, I feel hyper-anxious with excessive energy from the adrenaline storms which, in turn, are triggered by too much stimulus, for example crowded public events or intense social situations. Moreover, at other times, my emotional reservoir of energy for social interaction or for various tasks in life can be very limited, more so than it was prior to my development of PTSD. The late David Hackworth described this feeling of having your "cup full," or over-stimulation beyond your ability to cope, which is similar to the ADHD sufferer's problem with too much stimuli being encountered. Likewise, the PTSD sufferer may feel overwhelmed by events or social interaction which triggers the PTSD symptoms, forcing him or her to withdraw from people and retire to a quiet, safe place to calm down.

In addition to the ADHD simile, maybe the best way to put it is that the PTSD sufferer only has so much emotional currency to spend. Each day is different. They may have less currency from one day to the next depending on the positive or negative events that happen in their lives and the accompanying anxiety or depression that they may be feeling from these events or from PTSD memories. I can tell you from my own experience that I can feel when my cup is getting full, when my emotional currency is about spent. I just have a vague but palpable sense that something bad is about to happen just under the surface of my consciousness. I can feel when it is growing or when it is subsiding, and I've learned that when I have too much intense social interaction or too many emotionally challenging experiences, my cup fills very quickly.

Furthermore, I know that if I do not get to a "safe, quiet place" when my cup gets full, I will experience an emotional meltdown. This meltdown process is entirely out of my control. I have tried to control it before to no avail. And this whole process has happened so many times that I can tell the early warning signs, giving me the opportunity to disengage from whatever situation I'm in so that my peers or family don't have to see the spectacle of me sobbing uncontrollably, which could be disconcerting at the least for some people.

It's 2014 now, over nine years since I returned from Iraq, and many of my symptoms are still with me. There are days when the nightmares are very strong, forcing me to sleep apart from my wife to avoid disturbing or harming her. And, there are days when the depression seems overwhelming and my anxiety level rises beyond my control. Moreover, I am still very limited in how much social interaction I can take, depending on a number of factors.

My main symptoms, which I grappled with in the early years after Iraq, were deep depression, nightmares, hypervigilance (feeling on edge, unsafe, or being easily agitated), and the days-long anxiety attacks. These symptoms were, I believe, driven by the adrenaline storms that kept me feeling on edge for days at a time and forced me to withdraw from many of my normal pleasures in life and from the deeper relationships that are necessary for most people to feel satisfied with their life. After my PTSD episodes ended, I needed enough time to convince myself that I was safe and that my body could process the excess adrenaline out of my system.

During these times, it was a constant battle to get through the day at work trying to maintain enough control in order to function in my various jobs in the military (which included two years in uniform teaching at West Point and an additional two years working for the Army as a civilian in military human resources). Then I would escape in the evening after work, opening the relief valve to keep my emotions from exploding, something that I feared constantly. I was afraid that these powerful emotions might prove too great, even for my strong self-control honed through years of military training, martial arts, and work.

My life through all that time was a struggle for survival against my constant death wish. As I stumbled blindly through the darkness of my PTSD, I found myself asking over and over whether or not it was worth it to go on, to suffer for another day. And if it was worth it, then why was it worth it? What reason could I give myself to endure? The answer to that was always my family. I loved them and wanted to fight for them, to struggle through this so that we could make a better life at some point in the future. Moreover, due to many painful experiences in my childhood, I never wanted to be the kind of person who caused pain to others. And it was because of my strong emotions about this that I could never take my life, since I knew that would leave behind pain.

If I found enough peace that evening wrestling with my bad memories and emotions, it was easier to embrace life, but if the week had been especially bad, I found it harder to dismiss the unhealthy thoughts of death, or even suicide. Somehow though, I had to have some peace or enough relief from my pain before I went home at night. When I walked through that front door, the last thing I wanted was to bring my pain with me. As I entered this last pure bastion of goodness in my life where I still found comfort and truth in the simple interactions, affections, and conversations that are common in daily family life, I did not want to bring any of that poison with me.

I couldn't even talk to my family about my struggles in the early years, and it was even hard many times for me to talk to a therapist, psychiatrist, or psychologist. At the time, I simply did not know how to express in words what I was going through.

Moreover, talking about it would relive it, bringing the rush of chaotic and uncontrollable memories, emotions, and pain to the surface and inviting trouble into my home. In any case, I felt that I had to protect my family—the only thing that kept me holding onto life and the one thing that still seemed untainted. Despite the immensity of my pain, the one thing I couldn't get past was my love for them and my unwillingness to bring on them the painful aftermath of a suicide no matter how great my grief was. Yet, there were so many nights when love for my family and the fear of the aftermath of a suicide seemed, at the time, like such a thin tenuous thread connecting me to the world of the living. In time, I would find out, however, that something, or someone, much stronger—God—had been with me and giving me the strength to fight through my PTSD.

Time is important for healing, and, given enough time, most wounds will heal. It can level the greatest of pains, but that's not a comforting thought when you are in the middle of the storm, especially when you don't know how large the storm is or how long it will last.

For me, the storm sometimes dwindles to almost nothing only to roar back in a short space over seemingly benign matters. The tripwire is the emotions, but the fuel that keeps it going is the accompanying adrenaline storm. Even if you are no longer feeling the same fears or worries connected to combat, any strong emotions can set off the storm of adrenaline. And once it is set off, it may be days before you come back down. That means days of little to no sleep, days of living like you're on the edge of a blade, purely focused on survival and just getting through the day or maybe just getting through the next moment. Some will find my words hard to believe, but to those who suffer from PTSD, you know exactly what I'm writing about. And your family around you knows just like my family knows.

But despite the symptoms I'm still experiencing, I know that there were many more worse days in the early years immediately after my return from Iraq. Furthermore, many more of those days were strung together contiguously with my PTSD overwhelming me for longer periods of time and keeping me from interacting with my family very much. I still struggle, but it seems that the struggle is not as hard as it was back then. The symptoms do not seem to be nearly as severe and overwhelming.

As to how I lived through the hardest times, my strength to get through each day came from God, but I had to live life one day at a time (and sometimes one moment at a time), focusing on getting through this day (or this moment) and not worrying about tomorrow because of the powerful emotions, memories, and psychosomatic effects from PTSD that had me in their grip. It's easy to become overwhelmed and to be paralyzed, unable to act if you don't stay ahead of the emotions. As I grappled with each new day's challenges, the main part of my emotional energy (your life force, your motivation to get out of bed in the morning and your motivation to engage your daily activities) was spent, first, on whatever responsibilities, duties, and stressors that I encountered at work.

I also had to spend a significant amount of emotional energy on keeping the lid on the powder keg of emotions so that they didn't control me during my responsibilities to others or interfere with my family life (although there were days in which all of my emotional energy was spent on keeping the lid on the powder keg).

Most importantly, my family was my primary motive for fighting through the challenges of work and PTSD. I never gave up because I loved them and had to be there for them.

But, thankfully, there was healing that took place over time. My most essential tool in grappling with my PTSD was the sanctuary of my thinking places. After my daytime duties concluded each evening, I would usually drive off for a few hours to a quiet, secluded spot to grapple with the ongoing feelings from Iraq and the anxieties that may have built up during the day until

I felt at peace enough that I could go home to my family and interact with them as normally as possible, trying not to drag my emotional struggles into their lives (although I would find out in time that it was futile to try to protect them from being influenced by my PTSD because they loved me and would necessarily feel vicariously some of what I felt).

But the peace of my thinking places was essential in helping me to feel safe enough to confront my demons. In these places, alone and without the pressure of social interaction and with the safety and serenity of the forest, I was able to wrestle with my memories safely, letting some steam, some pressure, out of the boiler or simmering cauldron of emotions that I always knew was just below the surface. Sometimes I just sat quietly in my truck with the windows rolled down so that I could hear the calming sounds of the woods around me, soaking in the peace, which lifted my spirits. Sometimes, I merely sat and thought quietly through the day's events or through bad memories that had been pushed up from my subconscious during the day. Sometimes I listened to music on my vehicle's radio. Sometimes I wrote in my journal to relieve my emotional pressures. After the first few years though, I was increasingly spending more and more time in prayer, taking my burdens to the Creator of the universe who invited me to do just that.

Jesus's invitation to bring all our troubles to him is found in Matthew 11:28–30 (NKJV): "Come to Me, all *you* who labor and are heavy laden, and I will give you rest. Take My yoke upon you and learn from Me, for I am gentle and lowly in heart, and you will find rest for your souls. For My yoke *is* easy and My burden is light."

Over time, my prayer time alone with God in the serenity of the forest grew until it consumed all of my time alone. Moreover, it became a critical part of my healing, as He did not only allow me to lay my burdens at God's feet but He also supernaturally changed me, bit by bit, as He built up His spirit within me even more greatly over time. The prayer was my conduit of communication with God, but it was also His opportunity to reach into my heart and soul, to heal those gaping moral wounds, and to leave a little more of His spirit in me each time we had fellowship.

Moreover, there is something that God has put into nature that brings healing, especially when you are alone out in the fields or the forests. The English romantic writers (writing during the turn of the nineteenth century), such as William Wordsworth, sensed this healing property of nature and wrote many poems about it. To them, being in nature was critical to the health and wellness of the human psyche.

A Wikipedia article about this era of English literature explains Romanticism and nature's place within our lives.

> Romanticism (also the Romantic era or the Romantic period) was an artistic, literary, and intellectual movement that originated in Europe toward the end of the 18th century and in most areas was at its peak in the approximate period from 1800 to 1850. Partly a reaction to the Industrial Revolution,[1] it was also a revolt against the aristocratic social and political norms of the Age of Enlightenment and a reaction against the scientific rationalization of nature. It was embodied most strongly in the visual arts, music, and literature, but had a major impact on historiography, education and the natural sciences. Its effect on politics was considerable and complex; while for much of the peak Romantic period it was associated with liberalism and radicalism, its long-term effect on the growth of nationalism was probably more significant. The intellectual historian Isaiah Berlin has referred to Romanticism as "the last great 'transvaluation of values' in modern history. The movement validated intense emotion as an authentic source of aesthetic experience, placing new emphasis on such emotions as apprehension, horror and terror, and awe—especially that which is experienced in

confronting the sublimity of untamed nature and its pic-
turesque qualities: both new aesthetic categories.[1]

Perhaps this was why I was so attracted to the romantic writers as an undergraduate, having spent many hours of my boyhood
out in nature alone. I could truly understand the eloquent words
in their poems that described the beauty and sublimity of nature.
And that time during my youth alone in the forest was just as
important and influential on my peace of mind as it was for those
writers. Moreover, that time alone in nature would, again, brings
me much comfort and healing from my PTSD symptoms, many
years after I grew from a boy into a man.

I am not alone in discovering and experiencing this healing
power of nature. In a March 29, 2013, article in *The Atlantic* entitled "How Nature Resets Our Minds and Bodies," writer Adam
Alter delves into nature's healing power. In the article, he cites a
study of the recovery times of hospital patients in a Pennsylvania
town. The researcher in the study found out that patients recov-
ered much more quickly when the view from their hospital rooms
faced natural settings (trees, grass, etc.) versus a man-made setting (a brick wall).[2]

Moreover, one blog writer from the non-profit organization
CaringBridge.org explained so perfectly the healing power that
is accessible to all PTSD sufferers. In an October 30, 2014, post-
ing, Stacy Bare wrote about living with PTSD: "When I returned
from Iraq seven years ago, I felt isolated, thinking that few others,
if anyone, other than those I served with, would understand what
I had been through or how I was feeling. This isolation later manifested itself in anger, addiction, and alcoholism and a split life of
putting on the best public face I could, while struggling privately."

Bare goes on to explain how nature provided healing: "I've
learned that nature has the power to heal anyone and that at some
level we all need healing. I co-founded Veterans Expeditions so I
could share this healing with other veterans. There's a mystery out
there in nature that restores us all. It's hard at times to put your

fingers on it and I don't think we have to explain everything in our lives, sometimes it's just good to know something that is, well good. However, it isn't just those of us who wander in the woods who are speaking about why time in trees matters. A growing body of research and science is pointing towards the ways, whys, and how nature works on our body and minds."[3]

Additionally, my story of healing directly from God through prayer may seem incredible to some readers. For those not walking in faith with a daily fellowship with God, the claims of countless Christians such as me about miracles and healing in our lives must seem too inconceivable. That is the way many experiences in life appear when you are looking from the outside and have no personal experience to understand, no intellectual or emotional framework to grasp. For example, I know that many people who have not been parents themselves do not fully comprehend what the experience of being a parent is like.

I say this because over the years I have often heard erroneous advice about parenting from well-meaning but imprudent people who had not been through the experience of parenting themselves. This is not to judge them. They simply did not understand because they had not been through that experience and had no frame of reference in their previous experiences by which to comprehend what it means to be a parent, although a lack of understanding won't stop some people from commenting anyway.

This is the same with a true Christian walk when we cross over from being simply legalistic participants in a very limited religious experience to being fully engaged in a relationship, in fellowship, with our God. Once we cross over that line, there are things we experience and understand that those who have not crossed over that line of faith simply do not understand.

Moreover, my experience with God and His very real power for healing in my life is not unique. Many others have experienced this healing and power when turning to God for the help that no one else could give. Christian writer Josh McDowell, in his book *More Than a Carpenter*, first published in 1977, wrote about the evidence for the Christian faith, and one of his most important points in the book was about how so many people's lives have been changed dramatically down through the centuries. When they met Jesus and accepted His gift of salvation or rebirth, He would enter their lives where He would continue to work for the remainder of their days.

While I am far from being completely healed, I know that I am better off than I was eight or nine years ago when I was just beginning to grapple with my PTSD. And I can truly see that so many situations in my life have improved. Moreover, I can see that it was God's spiritual power manifested in my life that was the biggest factor in my healing whether He intervened directly or whether He worked through people that He brought into my life. Furthermore, as He took over more and more areas in my life, He also directed me to activities that would help in my healing. I used writing and even music, learning to play the guitar, two things which seemed to alleviate my anxiety. I have heard of a plethora of other tools being used to help veterans and others suffering from PTSD such as the use of service animals. These programs put veterans into contact with or working with dogs and horses, for example. The time with the animals seems to bring peace and calm to these people who go this route of therapy. Plus, the dogs help physically with the some of the symptoms of PTSD. For instance, a nurse who was very knowledgeable on PTSD told me about one of these programs to help veterans in which one dog was trained to lick the soles of the feet of his owner when the dog saw his owner thrashing in bed from PTSD nightmares. The licking of the feet apparently woke the veteran from his nightmare, helping to break the cycle of bad dreams.

After God, the second most important influence in my life was my precious family—my beautiful, patient, and wise wife and my wonderful, talented, and intelligent children—who brought so many blessings into my life when I interacted with them, lifting my spirits and even making me laugh. Much of the literature that I have read on PTSD cites the importance of family support structures in the healing process. This would only make sense because at a certain point in everyone's lives, they usually realize that their efforts and endeavors are only meaningful when done for someone else and when shared with someone else. Moreover, life's work, experiences, and achievements simply don't bring as much of the deep satisfaction we seek, unless these things are done for someone else or for a higher purpose. And my family did bring me that deep satisfaction, knowing that I had their love and that they had mine. Their love and support were essential for encouragement to struggle through my PTSD, giving me something to fight for.

I also found much encouragement in the many friendships I formed during my military service and my short stint as a government employee with the US Army. I met so many amazing, talented, and dedicated people in many of the jobs I held down through the years. Sometimes the simple things in life, like a short, encouraging conversation or a laugh with a friend, can go a long way.

Equally as important are the many friendships that I had over the years with people at the various churches I've attended. Working in Christian services to others, visitation, and even jail ministry, I developed many profound friendships that were very encouraging and influential in my life. Moreover, sharing with other believers my deepest thoughts or feelings during Sunday school or church worship drew me closer to these people than I would have ever thought possible.

Another thing in my life that helped me find healing was my penchant for writing and research (I had a stint as a West Point English professor, one tour a few years prior to my combat deployment and one tour immediately following, which encouraged me to research and write as I taught writing and research for writing to hundreds of students). The writing and research helped me understand and grapple with the most severe aspects of my memories and PTSD. It was important to understand what I was experiencing, which I found out through the research, and it was important to relieve the intense pressure of the boiling cauldron of emotions in my subconscious, which I was able to do through my journaling, through prayer, and through talk therapy (by telling the story I relieved the emotional pressure bit by bit).

Telling the story, talk therapy, was a very important process on my road to healing, so I have gone through one-on-one therapy countless times through mental health professionals in the years after Iraq. Talking has most definitely helped. The psychiatrists were a crap shoot, a gamble. Some helped, some merely made my symptoms worse. Medication has most definitely helped, although I cannot say that the medication was a primary cause of my healing.

But in grappling with PTSD, I had some very powerful weapons in my arsenal, such as the presence, encouragement, assistance, power, and wisdom of God who was continually with me, comforting me, teaching me, and guiding me, even when I sometimes, in my ignorance, did not ask for Him to be there or did not perceive His work and His presence. And God, in His infinite wisdom, guided me to sources of knowledge that gave me power over my affliction.

As they say, "Knowledge is power," and knowledge truly can provide power to someone suffering through a malady which seems insurmountable. Knowledge can help you to see the challenge in front of you as it truly is and not as you have worked it up to be in your imagination, and knowledge can help you to know the steps to surmount the seemingly insurmountable. Add to that the tremendous spiritual power of our God, and you become "more than conquerors" (Romans 8:37, NKJV).

Notes

Preface

1. Powell, Colin. Govleaders.org. Accessed December 12, 2014. <http://www.govleaders.org/powell.htm>

Introduction

1. Kipling, Rudyard. "Tommy." The Norton Anthology of Poetry. Shorter 5th. Ed. Margaret Ferguson, Mary Jo Salter, and Jon Stallworthy. New York: Norton, 2005. 765.
2. Bechard, Raymond. "Why Vietnam Vets are America's Greatest Heroes." Good Men Project Website. January 22, 2012. Accessed March 3, 2014. <http://goodmenproject.com/ethics-values/why-vietnam-vets-are-americas-greatest-heroes/>
3. Shay, Jonathan. Odysseus in America: Combat Trauma and the Trials of Homecoming. New York: Scribner, 2002. 109.
4. Cole, William. "The Forgotten." Star Advertiser. November 11, 2010. Accessed October 7, 2014. <http://www.staradvertiser.com/news/20101111_The_Forgotten.html?id=107183253>
5. "Mental Health Issues Rise Among US Troops." Associated Press article printed in the Boston Globe. May 20, 2011. Accessed October 8, 2014. <http://www.boston.com/news/nation/washington/articles/2011/05/20/mental_health_issues_rise_among_us_troops>

6. Kemp, Janet, and Robert Bossarte. "Suicide Data Report, 2012." Department of Veterans Affairs, Mental Health Services , Suicide Prevention Program. Accessed October 7, 2014. <http://www.va.gov/opa/docs/suicide-data-report-2012-final.pdf>

7. Bradford, John. "There, but for the grace of God, goes John Bradford." <http://www.thisdayinquotes.com/2011/07/there-but-for-grace-of-god-goes-john.html>

Preparation and Departure

1. Milton, John. "When I Consider How My Light Is Spent." The Norton Anthology of English Literature. Ed. M.H. Abrams. 5th ed. New York: Norton and Company, 1986. 1443.

2. "Operation Market Garden." Wikipedia. December 7, 2014. Accessed December 13, 2014. < http://en.wikipedia.org/wiki/Operation_Market_Garden>

3. McMaster, H.R. Dereliction of Duty. New York: HarperPerennial, a division of HarperCollins, 1997.

4. Shay, Jonathan. Achilles in Vietnam: Combat Trauma and the Undoing of Character. New York: Scribner, 1994.

5. Shay, Jonathan. Achilles in Vietnam: Combat Trauma and the Undoing of Character. New York: Scribner, 1994.

6. Shay, Jonathan. Achilles in Vietnam: Combat Trauma and the Undoing of Character. New York: Scribner, 1994.

7. Cooper, Tom, and Brig. Gen. Ahmad Sadik. "Iraq Invasion of Kuwait: 1990." 16 Sep. 2003. Air Combat Information Group (ACIG.org). Accessed 10 Oct. 2013. <http://www.acig.org/artman/publish/article_213.shtml>.

8. Gregory, Derek. The Colonial Present: Afghanistan, Palestine, Iraq. Malden, MA: Blackwell Publishing, 2004.

9. Shay, Jonathan. Achilles in Vietnam: Combat Trauma and the Undoing of Character. New York: Scribner, 1994.

10.   Frost, Robert. "Stopping By Woods On a Snowy Evening." Anthology of American Literature II: Realism to the Present. Ed. George McMichael. 3rd ed. New York: Macmillan, 1985. 1006.

The Journey Begins

1.   Hinckley, David. New York Daily News. "History Channel's 'Vietnam in HD' Delivers a Clearer Picture Than Ever of Terrible Conflict." November 7, 2011. Accessed August 21, 2014. <http://www.nydailynews.com/entertainment/tv-movies/history-channel-vietnam-hd-delivers-clearer-picture-terrible-conflict-article-1.972307#ixzz3B1dss240>

2.   Frost, Robert. "Stopping By Woods On a Snowy Evening." Anthology of American Literature II: Realism to the Present. Ed. George McMichael. 3rd ed. New York: Macmillan, 1985.

The Purgatory of Kuwait

1.   Hastings, Michael. "The Runaway General." Rolling Stone. June 22, 2010. Accessed October 7, 2014. <http://www.rollingstone.com/politics/news/the-runaway-general-20100622>

The Iraq War, Our Mission,
and the Telling of History

1.   Ricks, Thomas E. Fiasco. New York: Penguin, 2006.
2.   "Ba'ath Party." Encyclopaedia Britannica Online. Encyclopaedia Britannica. October 7, 2014. <http://www.britannica.com/EBchecked/topic/55912/Bath-Party>.
3.   "Ba'ath Party." Encyclopaedia Britannica Online. Encyclopaedia Britannica. October 7, 2014. <http://www.britannica.com/EBchecked/topic/55912/Bath-Party>.

4.   "Joint Base Balad." Wikipedia. September 14, 2014. Accessed October 7, 2014. <http://en.wikipedia.org/wiki/Joint_Base_Balad>

5.   "Balad." Wikipedia. June 17, 2014. Accessed October 7, 2014. <http://en.wikipedia.org/wiki/Balad,_Iraq>

6.   "Counter Rocket, Artillery, and Mortar." Wikipedia. November 26, 2014. Accessed December 13, 2014. <http://en.wikipedia.org/wiki/Counter_Rocket,_Artillery,_and_Mortar>

7.   "15th Reconnaissance Squadron." May 12, 2014. Wikipedia. Accessed October 7, 2014. <http://en.wikipedia.org/wiki/15th_Reconnaissance_Squadron>

8.   Operations in Iraq. August 12, 2005. C-Span. Accessed October 7, 2014. <http://www.c-span.org/video/?188458-1/operations-iraq>

9.   Operations in Iraq. August 12, 2005. C-Span. Accessed October 7, 2014. <http://www.c-span.org/video/?188458-1/operations-iraq>

10.   Operations in Iraq. August 12, 2005. C-Span. Accessed October 7, 2014. <http://www.c-span.org/video/?188458-1/operations-iraq>

11.   Fontaine, Yves J. and Donald K. Wols "Sustaining the momentum: the 1st Corps Support Command in Iraq." Army Logistician. March 1, 2006. Accessed December 13, 2014. Army Combined Arms Support Command, Department of the Army. Fort Lee, Virginia. <http://www.alu.army.mil/alog/issues/MarApr06/sustain_momentum.html>

12.   Fontaine, Yves J. and Donald K. Wols "Sustaining the momentum: the 1st Corps Support Command in Iraq." Army Logistician. March 1, 2006. Accessed December 13, 2014. Army Combined Arms Support Command, Department of the Army. Fort Lee, Virginia. <http://

www.alu.army.mil/alog/issues/MarApr06/sustain_momentum.html>

13. "The Red Ball Express, 1944." U.S. Army Transportation Museum. Accessed October 7, 2014. <http://www.transchool.lee.army.mil/museum/transportation%20museum/redballintro.htm >.

14. "The Red Ball Express, 1944." U.S. Army Transportation Museum. Accessed October 7, 2014. <http://www.transchool.lee.army.mil/museum/transportation%20museum/redballintro.htm >.

15. Fontaine, Yves J. and Donald K. Wols "Sustaining the momentum: the 1st Corps Support Command in Iraq." Army Logistician. March 1, 2006. Army Combined Arms Support Command, Department of the Army. Fort Lee, Virginia.

16. Tolstoy, Lev Nikolayevich. War and Peace. Trans. Constance Garnett. 1904. New York: Random House, 2002.

Life in "The Box"

1. Bunnell, Dewey. America. "A Horse with No Name." 1972. New York: Warner Brothers. Lyrics cited from Access Backstage website. Accessed October 14, 2014. <http://www.accessbackstage.com/america/song/song005.htm>

2. Bishop, Jerome. August 28, 2005. "How Much Is That Jackal in The Window." Anaconda Times, page 7. Published at Balad Air Base, Iraq. Accessed December 13, 2014. <http://www.dvidshub.net/publication/issues/0288>

3. Bishop, Jerome. August 28, 2005. "How Much Is That Jackal in The Window." Anaconda Times, page 7. Published at Balad Air Base, Iraq. Accessed December 13, 2014. <http://www.dvidshub.net/publication/issues/0288>

PTSD and the Lonely Road Home

1. "When Johnny Comes Marching Home." Wikipedia. November 14, 2014. Accessed December 13, 2014. <http://en.wikipedia.org/wiki/When_Johnny_Comes_Marching_Home>
2. Wartorn: 1861-2010. Dir. Jon Alpert and Ellen Goosenberg Kent. Home Box Office, 2011.
3. Williamson, Vanessa and Erin Mulhall. "Invisible Wounds: Psychological and Neurological Injuries Confront a New Generation of Veterans." Iraq and Afghanistan Veterans of America. Issue report, January 2009. Accessed October 7, 2014. <http://iava.org/files/IAVA_invisible_wounds_0.pdf>
4. Open Range. Dir. Kevin Costner. Touchstone, 2003.
5. Frosch, Dan. "Soldier's heart: Thousands of Iraq war veterans will come home to face serious psychological problems— and a system that's not ready to help them." Indy Week. Accessed August 15, 2014. <http://www.indyweek.com/indyweek/soldiers-heart/Content?oid=1193810>
6. Open Range. Dir. Kevin Costner. Touchstone, 2003.
7. Open Range. Dir. Kevin Costner. Touchstone, 2003.
8. Open Range. Dir. Kevin Costner. Touchstone, 2003.
9. Shakespeare, William. Henry VI, Part II, act IV, scene vii. The Globe Illustrated Shakespeare. Ed. Howard Staunton. New York: Greenwich, 1983.
10. Sowell, Thomas. "A Childish Letter." Jewish World Review. August 17, 1998. Accessed October 7, 2014. <http://www.jewishworldreview.com/cols/sowell081798.html>
11. Vietnam in HD. Dir. Sammy Jackson. Prod. Scott L. Reda and Lou Reda. History Channel. New Video, 2011.

12.   "Who We Are." Vietnam Veterans of America website. Accessed December 13, 2014. <http://www.vva.org/who. html>

13.   Richardson, Cameran. "The greatest generation: Vietnam veterans." The American Legion website. August 28, 2013. Accessed August 29, 2014. <http://www.legion.org/convention/217038/ greatest-generation-vietnam-veterans>.

14.   "VVAW: Were We Came From, Who We Are." Vietnam Veterans Against the War website. Accessed August 13, 2014. <http://www.vvaw.org/about/>

15.   "VVAW: Were We Came From, Who We Are." Vietnam Veterans Against the War website. Accessed August 13, 2014. <http://www.vvaw.org/about/>

16.   "Vietnam Veterans against War." Wikipedia. June 16, 2014. Accessed October 7, 2014. <http://en.wikipedia. org/wiki/Vietnam_Veterans_Against_the_War>

17.   Alexander, Caroline. "The Shock of War." Smithsonian Magazine. September 2010. Accessed October 7, 2014.   <http://www.smithsonianmag.com/history/ the-shock-of-war-55376701/?page=1&no-ist>

18.   "DSM-5 Diagnostic Criteria for PTSD Released." PTSD: National Center for PTSD. U.S. Department of Veterans Affairs. January 3, 2014. Accessed October 7, 2014. <http://www.ptsd.va.gov/professional/PTSD-overview/diagnostic_criteria_dsm-5.asp>

19.   "DSM-5 Diagnostic Criteria for PTSD Released." PTSD: National Center for PTSD. U.S. Department of Veterans Affairs. January 3, 2014. Accessed October 7, 2014. <http://www.ptsd. va.gov/professional/PTSD-overview/diagnostic_criteria_dsm-5.asp>

20.   "DSM-5 Diagnostic Criteria for PTSD Released." PTSD: National Center for PTSD. U.S. Department of Veterans Affairs. January 3, 2014. Accessed October

7, 2014. <http://www.ptsd.va.gov/professional/PTSD-overview/diagnostic_criteria_dsm-5.asp>

21. "DSM-5 Diagnostic Criteria for PTSD Released." PTSD: National Center for PTSD. U.S. Department of Veterans Affairs. January 3, 2014. Accessed October 7, 2014. <http://www.ptsd.va.gov/professional/PTSD-overview/diagnostic_criteria_dsm-5.asp>

22. "DSM-5 Diagnostic Criteria for PTSD Released." PTSD: National Center for PTSD. U.S. Department of Veterans Affairs. January 3, 2014. Accessed October 7, 2014. < http://www.ptsd.va.gov/professional/PTSD-overview/diagnostic_criteria_dsm-5.asp>

23. Boscarino, Joseph A., Richard E. Adams, and Charles R. Figley. "Secondary Trauma Issues for Psychiatrists." Psychiatric Times. November 17, 2010. Accessed October 7, 2014. <http://www.psychiatrictimes.com/secondary-trauma-issues-psychiatrists>

24. Finley, Joseph. "On Guard against PTSD." Security Info Watch.com. Cygnus Business Media. January 28, 2013. Accessed October 7, 2014. <http://www.securityinfowatch.com/article/10859999/stress-reduction-techniques-for-your-guard-force>

Life in the Military

1. Tzu, Lao. Brainy Quote website. Accessed December 13, 2014. <http://www.brainyquote.com/quotes/quotes/l/laotzu130742.html>

2. Baiocchi, Dave. "Measuring Army Deployments to Iraq and Afghanistan." Rand Corporation. Accessed 7 October, 2014. <http://www.rand.org/content/dam/rand/pubs/research_reports/RR100/RR145/RAND_RR145.pdf>

3. Shanker, Thom, and Helene Cooper. "Pentagon Plans to Shrink Army to Pre-World War II Level." New York

Times. February 23, 2014. Accessed October 7, 2014. <http://www.nytimes.com/2014/02/24/us/politics/pentagon-plans-to-shrink-army-to-pre-world-war-ii-level.html?_r=0>

4. Baiocchi, Dave. "Measuring Army Deployments to Iraq and Afghanistan." Rand Corporation. Accessed 7 October, 2014. <http://www.rand.org/content/dam/rand/pubs/research_reports/RR100/RR145/RAND_RR145.pdf>

5. Baiocchi, Dave. "Measuring Army Deployments to Iraq and Afghanistan." Rand Corporation. Accessed 7 October, 2014. <http://www.rand.org/content/dam/rand/pubs/research_reports/RR100/RR145/RAND_RR145.pdf>

6. Baiocchi, Dave. "Measuring Army Deployments to Iraq and Afghanistan." Rand Corporation. Accessed 7 October, 2014. <http://www.rand.org/content/dam/rand/pubs/research_reports/RR100/RR145/RAND_RR145.pdf>

7. Powers, Rod. "Joint Chiefs Continue to Examine Deployment Lengths." About.com. April 14, 2007. Accessed October 7, 2014. <http://usmilitary.about.com/od/terrorism/a/deploylength.htm>

8. Powers, Rod. "Joint Chiefs Continue to Examine Deployment Lengths." About.com. April 14, 2007. Accessed October 7, 2014. <http://usmilitary.about.com/od/terrorism/a/deploylength.htm>

9. "GIs Who Refused Fuel Won't Face Court-Martial." CNN. December 5, 2004. Accessed October 7, 2014. <http://www.cnn.com/2004/WORLD/meast/12/05/iraq.reservists/index.html?iref=newssearch>

10. Bannerman, Stacy. When the War Came Home: The Inside Story of Reservists and the Families They Leave Behind. New York: Bloomsbury, 2006. 19.

11. Bannerman, Stacy. When the War Came Home: The Inside Story of Reservists and the Families They Leave Behind. New York: Bloomsbury, 2006. 18.

12. "Oaths of Enlistment and Oaths of Office." U.S. Army Center of Military History website. Accessed December 12, 2014. <http://www.history.army.mil/html/faq/oaths.html>

13. Constitution of the United States. Ratified June 21, 1788. National Archives website. Accessed October 7, 2014. <http://www.archives.gov/exhibits/charters/constitution_transcript.html>

14. Shay, Jonathan. Achilles in Vietnam: Combat Trauma and the Undoing of Character. New York: Scribner, 1994. 34-35.

15. Shay, Jonathan. Achilles in Vietnam: Combat Trauma and the Undoing of Character. New York: Scribner, 1994. 34.

16. Shay, Jonathan. Achilles in Vietnam: Combat Trauma and the Undoing of Character. New York: Scribner, 1994. 12.

17. Luttwak, Edward. The Pentagon and the Art of War. New York: Simon and Schuster, 1985. As quoted in Jonathan Shay, Achilles in Vietnam. New York: Scribner, 1994.

18. Shay, Jonathan. Achilles in Vietnam: Combat Trauma and the Undoing of Character.. New York: Scribner, 1994. 16.

19. Shay, Jonathan. Achilles in Vietnam: Combat Trauma and the Undoing of Character. New York: Scribner, 1994. 16.

20. Shay, Jonathan. Achilles in Vietnam: Combat Trauma and the Undoing of Character. New York: Scribner, 1994. 19.

21. Moore, Harold G. We Were Soldiers Once…And Young. New York: Random, 1992.

22.   We Were Soldiers Once. Dir. Randall Wallace. Paramount, 2002.

23.   McDonough, James R. Platoon Leader: Memoir of Command in Combat. New York: Random, 1985.

The Psychology and Science of PTSD

1.   Shay, Jonathan. Achilles in Vietnam: Combat Trauma and the Undoing of Character. New York: Scribner, 1994.

2.   Wartorn: 1861-2010. Dir. Jon Alpert and Ellen Goosenberg Kent. Home Box Office, 2011.

3.   Ibid.

4.   "DSM-5 Diagnostic Criteria for PTSD Released." PTSD: National Center for PTSD. U.S. Department of Veterans Affairs. January 3, 2014. Accessed October 7, 2014. <http://www.ptsd.va.gov/professional/PTSD-overview/diagnostic_criteria_dsm-5.asp>

5.   "DSM-5 Diagnostic Criteria for PTSD Released." PTSD: National Center for PTSD. U.S. Department of Veterans Affairs. January 3, 2014. Accessed October 7, 2014. <http://www.ptsd.va.gov/professional/PTSD-overview/diagnostic_criteria_dsm-5.asp>

6.   "DSM-5 Diagnostic Criteria for PTSD Released." PTSD: National Center for PTSD. U.S. Department of Veterans Affairs. January 3, 2014. Accessed October 7, 2014. <http://www.ptsd.va.gov/professional/PTSD-overview/diagnostic_criteria_dsm-5.asp>

7.   "DSM-5 Diagnostic Criteria for PTSD Released." PTSD: National Center for PTSD. U.S. Department of Veterans Affairs. January 3, 2014. Accessed October 7, 2014. <http://www.ptsd.va.gov/professional/PTSD-overview/diagnostic_criteria_dsm-5.asp>

8.   Evans, Stephen. "Can You Die from A Broken Heart." BBC News Magazine. August 13, 2014. Accessed October 7, 2014. <http://www.bbc.com/news/magazine-28756374>

9. Evans, Stephen. "Can You Die from A Broken Heart." BBC News Magazine. August 13, 2014. Accessed October 7, 2014. <http://www.bbc.com/news/magazine-28756374>

10. Hope, Jenny. "You Really Can Die of a Broken Heart: Losing a Loved One Doubles the Risk of Heart Failure or Stroke." Daily Mail Online. February 24, 2014. Accessed October 8, 2014. <http://www.dailymail.co.uk/health/article-2566854/Grief-broken-heart-doubles-risk-heart-attack-stroke.html>

11. Medina, John J. "Neurobiology of PTSD: Part 1." Psychiatric Times. January 2008: 25: 29-34.

12. Medina, John J. "Neurobiology of PTSD: Part 1." Psychiatric Times. January 2008: 25: 29-34.

13. Scaer, Robert C. "Symptoms of Post Traumatic Stress Disorder (PTSD)." Bully Online. December 4, 2005. Accessed October 7, 2014. < http://www.bullyonline.org/stress/ptsd.htm>

14. Boston, Gabriella. "Long Term Stress Damages Brain." Washington Times. December 2, 2009. Accessed October 7, 2014. <http://www.washingtontimes.com/news/2009/dec/02/stress-damages-brain/?page=all>

15. Boston, Gabriella. "Long Term Stress Damages Brain." Washington Times. December 2, 2009. Accessed October 7, 2014. <http://www.washingtontimes.com/news/2009/dec/02/stress-damages-brain/?page=all>

16. Lurie, Karen. "Stress Changes Your Brain." ScienCentral.com. June 24, 2003. Accessed October 7, 2014. <http://staff.sciencentral.com/articles/view.php3?language=english&type=&article_id=218391988>

17. Lurie, Karen. "Stress Changes Your Brain." ScienCentral.com. June 24, 2003. Accessed October 7, 2014. <http://staff.sciencentral.com/articles/view.php3?language=english&type=&article_id=218391988>

18. Lurie, Karen. "Stress Changes Your Brain." ScienCentral. com. June 24, 2003. Accessed October 7, 2014. <http://staff.sciencentral.com/articles/view.php3?language=english&type=&article_id=218391988>

19. Lurie, Karen. "Stress Changes Your Brain." ScienCentral. com. June 24, 2003. Accessed October 7, 2014. <http://staff.sciencentral.com/articles/view.php3?language=english&type=&article_id=218391988>

20. Rosenthal, Michele. "Three Ways Trauma Affects Your Brain." HealthyPlace.com. November 27, 2013. Accessed October 7, 2014. <http://www.healthyplace.com/blogs/traumaptsdblog/2013/11/27/three-ways-trauma-affects-your-brain/>

21. Rosenthal, Michele. "Three Ways Trauma Affects Your Brain." HealthyPlace.com. November 27, 2013. Accessed October 7, 2014. <http://www.healthyplace.com/blogs/traumaptsdblog/2013/11/27/three-ways-trauma-affects-your-brain/>

22. Rosenthal, Michele. "Three Ways Trauma Affects Your Brain." HealthyPlace.com. November 27, 2013. Accessed October 7, 2014. <http://www.healthyplace.com/blogs/traumaptsdblog/2013/11/27/three-ways-trauma-affects-your-brain/>

23. "Post-Traumatic Stress Disorder In-Depth Report." New York Times. Accessed October 7, 2014. <http://www.nytimes.com/health/guides/disease/post-traumatic-stress-disorder/print.html>

24. "Post-Traumatic Stress Disorder In-Depth Report." New York Times. Accessed October 7, 2014. <http://www.nytimes.com/health/guides/disease/post-traumatic-stress-disorder/print.html>

25. Baldor, Lolita C. "Misconduct Forces More Soldiers Out." Associated Press. Posted on Yahoo News. February 17, 2014. Accessed October 7, 2014. <http://news.

yahoo.com/ap-exclusive-misconduct-forces-more-soldiers-145434065.html>

26.   "Odierno: Army Losing Focus on Character." WILX. com. February 15, 2014. Accessed October 7, 2014. <http://www.wilx.com/news/headlines/Odierno-Army-Losing-Focus-on-Character-245709521.html>

27.   Barnes, Greg. "Many Troops Turning to Drugs, Crime." Fayetteville Observer. September 26, 2010. Accessed October 7, 2014. <http://www.fayobserver.com/news/local/many-troops-turning-to-drugs-crime/article_d0a5c8ea-2ab7-5da3-a702-4a7782747434.html>

28.   Hastings, Michael. "The Runaway General." Rolling Stone. June 22, 2010. Accessed October 7, 2014. <http://www.rollingstone.com/politics/news/the-runaway-general-20100622>

29.   Meyer, Carlton. "Tenure Flag Officers." G2mil.com. February 28, 2009. Accessed October 7, 2014. <http://www.g2mil.com/tenured.htm>

30.   Freeman, Ben. "POGO's (Project on Government Oversight) Ben Freeman's Testimony Before the Senate Armed Services Committee Subcommittee on Personnel on 'General and Flag Officer Requirements.'" September 14, 2011. Accessed October 14, 2014. <http://www.pogo.org/our-work/testimony/2011/ns-wds-20110914.html>

Epilogue

1.   "Romanticism." Wikipedia online. December 5, 2014. Accessed December 14, 2014. < http://en.wikipedia.org/wiki/Romanticism>

2.   Alter, Adam. "How Nature Resets Our Minds and Bodies." The Atlantic. March 29, 2013. Accessed December 19, 2014.   <http://www.theatlantic.com/archive/2013/03/how-nature-resets-our-minds-and-bodies/274455/>

3.   Bare, Stacy. "Exploring Together Changes Lives." CaringBridge.org. October 30, 2014. Accessed December 21, 2014. <http://caringbridge.org/healing-power-of-nature/>

CPSIA information can be obtained at www.ICGtesting.com
Printed in the USA
LVOW04s1338170815

450434LV00033B/1042/P